# VISIONS
## OF THE
## FUTURE

**ART, TECHNOLOGY AND COMPUTING
IN THE TWENTY-FIRST CENTURY**

# VISIONS OF THE FUTURE

## ART, TECHNOLOGY AND COMPUTING
## IN THE TWENTY-FIRST CENTURY

Edited by

## CLIFFORD A. PICKOVER

ST. MARTIN'S PRESS
NEW YORK

All rights reserved. For information, write:
Scholary and Reference Division,
St. Martin's Press, Inc, 175 Fifth Avenue, New York, NY 10010

First published in the United States of America in 1992.

Printed by Whitstable Litho Ltd, Whitstable, Kent

ISBN 0–312–08481–1

**Library of Congress Cataloging-in-Publication Data**

Visions of the future : art, technology, and computing in the twenty-
first century / edited by Clifford A. Pickover.
     p.   cm.
   ISBN 0–312–08481–1
    1. Computers and civilization,    2. Technology–Social aspects,
3. Computer art.    I. Pickover, Clifford A.
QA76.9.C66V57   1992
004–dc20                     92–35648
                                        CIP

# Table of Contents

# Preface

*"Vision is the art of seeing things invisible."* – Jonathan Swift

This book will suggest how 21st century computers and computer art will provide humankind with an unlimited landscape for exploration, and unparalleled aid for the imagination. From traffic control, to sculpture, to weather prediction, to golf, the eclectic mix of topics in this book all indicate the fantastic potential for computers in our lives.

Since their rapid growth following the Second World War, computers have changed the way we perform scientific research, conduct business, create art, and spend our leisure time. Today, we rely on computers more heavily than we may realize. According to scientists I recently surveyed, the sudden 24-hour failure of all microprocessors on earth would result in a loss of several million lives and 100 billion dollars – even if all systems returned to normal after the 24-hour period. (See *Computers and the Imagination* for more on this study.) The average predicted international money loss was 520 billion dollars. Operations hit hardest would be finance, banking, communications, transport, emergency dispatching, and weather forecasting. Other "victims" of the 24-hour microprocessor failure would include: factories, airplanes, submarines, automobiles, telephones, clocks and watches, household appliances, television and radio stations, organizations with a computer-based working environment, railways, air traffic control, stock markets, satellite and space equipment, elevators, military equipment, and environmental control systems. It is not surprising that respondents indicated the countries most affected would be the USA and Japan.

Some of you may not be aware of the futuristic technology available even today. For example, in the 1990s, researchers working with computer models of buildings, molecules, and mountains can "take a walk" through their 3-D structures using special goggles that receive infrared signals from a computer monitor. With today's devices the viewer gets a realistic impression of depth from a 2-D computer screen. Viewers can stand on an imaginary Martian mountain or dive into an infinite red sea! Also in the 1990s, orthopaedic implants can be custom-made, using 3-D CAD and numeric control to manufacture parts. In the future, more and more body parts will be replaceable by artificial parts.

Why should sophisticated future computers be difficult to use? Most computers of the future will be responsive to human modes of communication including touch, gestures, speech, and eye movements. High-precision exoskeletons, such as *Series 2 Dextrous Hand Master* shown in Figure 1, already permit one to manipulate computer-generated images in artificial reality environments, control robotic hands, and measure hand strain. Within the next few years, musicians, dancers, artists, film-makers, sports enthusiasts, surgeons, and masseuses will have access to these devices. Applications of exoskeletons are limitless.

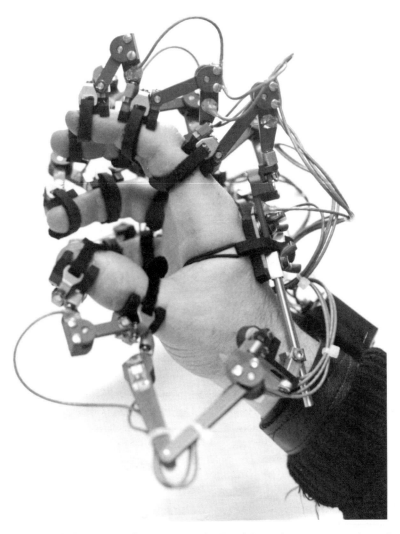

**Figure 1** *Exoskeletons may be worn on the hand in order to communicate hand movements to personal computers at rapid rates.* Figure used with permission of Exos Inc., 8 Blanchard Rd., Burlington, Massachusetts 01803, USA.

Both science-fiction and non-fiction writers have written much on the subject of futuristic technology. One of my favorite non-fiction books written on the future of computing and communications is *Technology 2001* by Derek Leebaert (see References), and you are urged to explore this interesting book for the technical information presented by American scientists and strategic planners. However, the present book,

*Visions of the Future,* is notable for the sheer range of unusual topics in both art and science. As you will find when reading this book, the line between art and science often becomes indistinct.

Bob Berger in the October 1990 issue of *OMNI* magazine posed an interesting question: "If Leonardo da Vinci were alive today, would he forsake canvas and brush for a computer terminal?" I think Leonardo would be quite interested in computer graphics. Even if Leonardo could not obtain funding from the National Science Foundation or the National Endowment for the Arts, he could – with just a personal computer – create, manipulate, and store fairly sophisticated art works. Colors could be mixed and chosen from a palette of millions of different hues. Screen resolution could emulate the grit of the canvas. His colleagues from around the world could receive his images over their phone lines for their comment and collaboration. Probably Leonardo would spend a large amount of his time inventing entirely new computer input devices to substitute for today's standard mouse. These devices would allow him to precisely emulate his own masterful brush strokes, the viscosity and drip of wet paint, or a chisel chipping away at an imaginary chunk of shiny marble. Within the next decade, personal computers will feature hands-on manipulation of computer-generated images along with tactile sensations and force feedback. If Leonardo were alive in the next decade he would work within an artificial reality, where computer sensors measure the position of the head, and track eye and hand movements. Voice recognition programs will allow Leonardo to make voice requests, and special goggles will allow him to peer into colorful new worlds limited only by computers, and the imagination.

Let's conclude this introduction with some thoughts about the future of publishing and communication. According to the *Vision 2020* report of the American Physical Society (discussed in the March 1, 1991 issue of *Science*), rapidly evolving computer technology will soon transform the nature of publishing, of libraries, and of scientific communication. Compact disks can already store hundreds of thousands of digitized scientific journal pages on a platter less than 12 centimeters across. Gregg Keizer in the June 1991 issue of *OMNI* notes that by the year 2020 we will be custom building our newspapers and magazines by viewing only the sections we want through our home personal computer. We'll also be printing out books written by the world's best writers. You and I will become both the printer and publisher. Will bookstores be obsolete?

There are diverse views on this subject of publishing and "paperless" offices of the future. Computer technology once promised offices without paper, but paper use increased six times in the decade following the introduction of the personal computer. Pete Turner in *OMNI* magazine recently noted, "Office technology promised more leisure time, but in the years following the advent of computers, mobile phones, and fax machines, work hours spread over another six hours." Will the computer in the 21st Century make our lives so complex as to create a mass revolt against technology in industrialized countries?

Arthur C. Clarke has noted that "developments in the field of computers have been so swift that yesterday's miracle is today's obsolete junk." In just a few years slide rules and mathematical tables became obsolete, and the equivalent of several million vacuum tubes sits on our office desks. Clarke and many others believe that soon computers will be in the palm of everyone's hand, and a little later they may be floating around in our bloodstreams. Computers shape the way we think, imagine, and remember. They expand our imagination, allow us to create amazing new art forms, and to dream of scientific problems not possible before the computer age. However, it's a sobering thought to consider our growing reliance on computers, and the catastrophic results of even a temporary failure.

The cover of this book is a computer graphics representation of a mathemetical mapping exhibiting fractal behaviour. Fractals are intricate shapes which will continue to provide raw material for computer art in the 21st century. I computed this image of a "Glynn mapping" ($z \rightarrow z^{1.5} - 0.2$ for complex values of $z$) using an IBM 3090 mainframe computer. Other chapters in this book discuss the use of fractals in art and science.

**Clifford A. Pickover**
*Yorktown Heights, New York*

## Reading List

The following reading list should stimulate your interest in the future of art and technology.

1   Leebaert, D. 1991. *Technology 2001: The Future of Computing and Communications.* MIT Press, Massachusetts.
2   Platt, C. 1989. *When You Can Live Twice as Long, What Will You Do?* William Morrow, New York.
3   Turner, P. 1991. Techno-wizards and couch potatoes. *OMNI.* August **13**(13), 82.
4   Staudhammer, J. 1991. *Computer graphics – toward the next millennium.* January, 21–22.
5   Keizer, G. 1991. Home office: 2020. *OMNI.* June **13**(9), 10.
6   *Speculations in Science and Technology.* A journal filled with interesting speculative papers in the physical, mathematical, biological, medical and engineering sciences. Science and Technology Letters, PO Box 81, Northwood, Middlesex HA6 3DN, England.
7   *21st Century Science and Technology.* A journal dedicated to providing information on advanced technologies and science policies. 21st Century Science, 60 Sycolin Road, Suite 203, Leesburg, VA 22075.
8   Feingold, S. 1989. *Futuristic Exercises: A Workbook for Emerging Lifestyles and Careers in the 21st Century and Beyond.* Garrey Park Press, Maryland.
9   Mel, B., Omohundro, S., Robinson, A., Skiena, S., Thearling, K., Robinson, A., Young, L. and Wolfram, S. 1988. Tablet: A personal computer in the year 2000. *Communications of the ACM.* **31**(6), 639–646.
10  Luke, T., Thearling, K., Skiena, S., Robinson, A., Omohundro, S., Mel, B. and Wolfram, S. 1988. Academic computing in the year 2000. *Academic Computing.* May/June **1–13,** 8.
11  Dereska, S. 1990. DARPA's advances provide basis for rapid progression. *SIGNAL,* the Official Publication of the Armed Forces Communication and Electronic Association. February Issue, pp.29–33.
12  Hsu, F., Anantharaman, T., Campbell, M. and Nowatzyk, A. 1990. A grandmaster chess machine. *Scientific American,* October **263**(4), 44–54.
13  Cohen, I. 1985. *Revolution in Science.* Harvard University Press, Massachusetts.

14  Hart, M. 1978. *The 100: A Ranking of the Most Influential Persons in History.* Hart Publishing, New York.

15  Pickover, C. 1992. *Mazes for the Mind.* St Martin's Press, New York.

16  Pickover, C. 1991. *Computers and the Imagination.* St. Martin's Press, New York.

## Appendix

Over the last few years, I have conducted a number of "non-traditional surveys" regarding technology and science. Often the surveys deal with future scenarios. Here is a current list:

1  Pickover, C. 1991 What if scientists had found a computer in 1900? *IEEE Computer.* May **24**(5), 120.

2  Pickover, C. 1991. An informal survey on the scientific and social impact of a soda can-sized super-super computer. *Computers in Physics,* May/June **5**(3), 290–301.

3  Pickover, C. 1990. Who are the ten most influential scientists in history? *The History and Social Science Teacher,* **25**(3), 158–161.

4  Pickover, C. 1991. What if all computers failed tomorrow? *IEEE Computer,* September, **24**(9), 152.

5  Pickover, C. 1991. What if all scientists had a wallet-sized graphics supercomputer? *Computer Graphics World,* November, **14**(11), 59–64.

# The Virtual Science Center: "A Museum of Everything That Could be Imagined"

**Dawn Friedman**

*Department of Chemistry, Harvard University, 12 Oxford Street, Cambridge, MA 02174, USA*

*In the last few decades, science museum exhibits have been transformed from glass cases displaying artifacts to interactive devices that engage the visitor physically and intellectually. Advances in computer technology will only accelerate this development. In the science center of the future, a combination of computational power and virtual reality techniques will allow visitors to view, touch, and explore simulated worlds – and create their own.*

## Introduction: Science Museums and Interactive Learning

A museum is a place where objects or ideas of interest are gathered together, a distillation of the fascinating aspects of the world at large. Visitors to art museums expect a concentrated dose of aesthetic appreciation, to be provided by a rich collection of beautiful or thought-provoking creations. Similarly, visitors to science museums wish in some way to appreciate science. But in the last several decades, science museums have come to recognize that collections of scientific artifacts do not provide the engaging experience of science that visitors seek. Most people who visit science museums want and expect to learn.[1] It is reasonable to assume that they see science much as scientists do: as a realm of ideas, not objects, in which the essential experience is not viewing but discovering and understanding (Figure 1).

The science museums of the present concentrate on ideas rather than objects, discovery rather than display.[2] Their collections of artifacts may be diminished to the point that they have no curators, and the term "science center" is considered more accurate than "museum" with its connotation of dusty cases disturbed only by specialists. In place of collections, they create embodiments of scientific concepts in the form of exhibits, and these exhibits tend increasingly to be interactive. The visitor is invited to play with a device that illustrates a scientific law, to make a change in a model of some subset of the world and learn from the result. In this museum of embodied ideas and model worlds, computer simulation is only beginning to fulfil its enormous promise; in an environment where user interaction is the goal, the technology that allows

**Figure 1**    *An interactive exhibit attracts children and adults at The Computer Museum, Boston, MA.* Photograph by Linda Holecamp/The Computer Museum, courtesy of The Computer Museum.

users to reach into artificial realities is still beyond the reach of most facilities. But as computational power increases and hardware and software solutions are invented, it will become possible to use them to create an ambitious, comprehensive science center – a virtual science museum whose exhibits exist in the interface between the computer and the human mind.

## Computer Simulation and Virtual Reality

Whenever a scientist uses a set of equations to describe a system, builds a physical model, or runs a numerical simulation of a natural process, he or she is creating a miniature universe, a kind of artificial reality. The artificial universe will be many orders of magnitude simpler than the real system it is meant to resemble; it may consist of a few pieces of wood or a single equation. It is a tool for isolating a piece of the universe, a subset that can be understood. Operations on this small world produce effects which can be extrapolated to the system being modeled to yield scientific insight – provided, of course, that the model is sufficiently accurate. When a museum exhibit is designed to function in the same way as a scientist's model, it might also be described as a form of artificial reality.

The use of computers has led to a tremendous increase in the complexity of scientific models. With the power to solve thousands of iterated feedback equations or millions of integral matrix elements, scientists can produce enormous quantities of numerical data from computer simulations. The usefulness of this method, however, is limited not only by the simulation's accuracy but by the scientist's ability to assimilate the data. A simple model, the kind that scientists jot down on a handy scrap of paper, usually has the virtue of producing simple results which can be taken in at a glance. This is not so for most computer models. Some scientists appear to have solved this dilemma by developing an ability to perceive physical reality in columns of eight-digit numbers. Others, however, are finding solutions that use computer graphics techniques to improve the perception of scientific information within computer-generated data. These scientific visualization techniques are, for scientists, the natural extension of manually created figures and plots.[3] But they can also provide a bridge between the simulated world within the computer and any person, scientist or not, who wants to learn from it. Without these and similar graphic techniques, a museum exhibit based on computer simulation would be inaccessible to the great majority of visitors. With them, computer simulation exhibits can display compelling artificial worlds.

The term "virtual reality" describes a further step in making simulated worlds accessible to the user. Virtual reality refers to the goal of allowing the user to experience computer simulations, not as columns of numbers or even graphical displays, but as environments. By wearing interface devices like specially designed goggles and gloves, users can feel as if they are seeing and touching real three-dimensional worlds (Figure 2). To a scientist, this can mean walking through a world that exists only as a hypothetical solution to a set of equations. It can mean "picking up" a drug molecule that has never been synthesized and fitting it into a receptor site, guided by molecular forces the scientist can actually feel (Figure 3). To the designer of science exhibits, it will mean revolutionary possibilities.

Exhibits based on virtual reality technology will be able to explore the scientific concepts and fields which are inaccessible to standard museum techniques. Using this technology, designers can create exhibits that would be impossible to set up in physical reality. Pure thought experiments can be carried out before the visitor's own eyes and ears. Demonstrations too dangerous to be casually performed in a laboratory, much less a museum, can be recreated safely. Perhaps still more important will be the power to improve existing types of exhibits, enhancing their effectiveness so that their message is clearer, more universal, and more memorable.

While artifacts, text panels, "real" demonstrations, and physical hands-on exhibits will dominate science museums for some time, there may come a point where virtual reality exhibits are actually more economical to produce and update than traditional ones. In the future, some science centers may be essentially collections of virtual reality exhibits – virtual museums, where in a few rooms a universe can be explored.

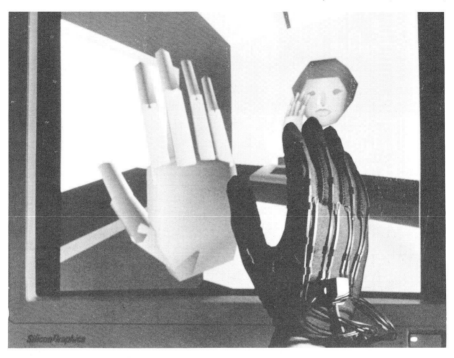

**Figure 2**   *Virtual reality: a special sensor-equipped glove permits manipulation of simulated objects in a computer-generated "world" on the screen.* Courtesy of VPL.

## Rules of Speculation

Scientists have had varying success in describing the science museum of the future.[4] In 1675, Leibnitz proposed the establishment of a public museum of scientific instruments and marvels, at a time when all such collections were private. Though his scheme was not acted upon at the time, some of his proposed exhibits are remarkably like those to be found in present-day museums of science. For example, his idea for "a representation of the heavens and stars and of comets" remains a crowd-pleaser today. "Optical wonders" are displayed in hundreds of museums, as are "exhibits of the muscles, nerves, bones," ballistic machines, and "new experiments on water, air, vacuum." Most modern of all, perhaps, is an exhibit bordering on the interactive: a demonstration "to show how a child can raise a heavy weight with a thread", similar to a participatory pulley device at the Museum of Science in Boston. Leibnitz promised that a museum like the one he proposed would "open people's eyes, stimulate inventions, present beautiful sights, instruct people with an endless number of useful or ingenious novelties.... It would be a general clearinghouse for all inventions, and would become a museum of everything that could be imagined.[5]"

How can a present-day scientist hope to speculate as daringly as Leibnitz, at a time when this dream museum is almost a reality? The imagination has not nearly so far to

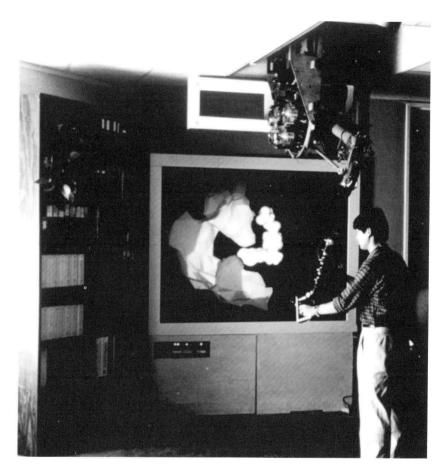

**Figure 3** *A scientist studies enzyme-substrate interactions using virtual reality. Goggles display a three-dimensional image of the two molecules. By moving the robot arm, the user manipulates the substrate molecule. Motors in the arm provide force feedback, so that the scientist experiences the forces between substrate and enzyme, and can use these forces to find an optimum molecular configuration.* Courtesy of Project GROPE.

leap. However, some limitations still exist on what computer hardware and software can accomplish; the speculator can assume these limitations to be temporary.

For example, in this article, nearly infinite computational power and I/O speed will be assumed to be available, even to such financially limited people as museum directors and exhibit designers. (To assume ample funds for any museum would be irresponsible speculation.) Remarkably, much of what would seem to require immense resources is already being attempted. Ingenious stratagems may allow the creation of exhibits like those described here much sooner than predictions based on the use of "brute force" methods would suggest.

In terms of input-output devices and software, most computer graphics and virtual reality researchers acknowledge that "parts of the frontier are hard to move",[6] particularly in the area of three-dimensional user interfaces. Furthermore, current virtual reality interfaces tend to be cumbersome and klutzy – bulky feedback gloves with motors at each joint, joysticks attached to heavy motors, headsets bigger than space helmets. The virtual reality devices in the museum of the future will be assumed to be utterly unobtrusive. They will also be flexible enough to run an exhibit simultaneously in several different configurations: private experience by a single visitor, display to non-participating passers-by, or interaction by multiple users with the exhibit and with each other.

Again, current research is moving faster than anyone but a specialist in the field is likely to suspect. For example, several research groups are working on direct transmission of signals to and from the nervous system, starting with experiments on rats in which nerves are encouraged to grow through implanted semiconductor chips.[7] Their goals involve transmission of real-world data – for example, creating a bridge over damaged nerves in the wrist to allow sensory information from the fingertips to reach the brain. But it is a short step from transmitting information about the real world to creating and transmitting sensory information about a simulated world. While museum exhibits may not be the first application of this technology, someday it will be a commonplace.

By ignoring current practical limitations in this way, speculation may hope to keep ahead of reality – but just barely. We are close indeed to the "museum of everything that could be imagined."


## The Virtues of Virtual Exhibits

A discussion of the value of computer simulation and virtual reality techniques in science museum exhibits might be expected to proceed along scientific lines. For example, it should begin by citing studies on the qualities which make an exhibit useful or effective. Unfortunately, there is little hard data on this subject.[8] While it may be accepted that a good exhibit allows the visitor to learn, the kind of learning that takes place in a science museum has not been intensively studied. The design of exhibits is still an art rather than a science.[1,8] Given the lack of a rigorous definition, Victor J. Danilov suggests that an effective exhibit for a science center is one for which the answers to the following questions are yes: Does it stimulate and hold interest? Does it involve viewers physically or intellectually? Does it interpret ideas or concepts in an understandable manner? Does it result in a pleasurable experience? Does it communicate the message?[9]

Computer simulation and virtual reality technology could enhance the effectiveness of an exhibit for every one of Danilov's suggestions. Below are examples.

## Interest

The power of virtual reality to stimulate and hold interest is enormous, even when the participants are unaware that they are experiencing its effects. Users of vehicle simulators like Atari's Hard Drivin' video arcade game, in which turning forces and road feel are transmitted through the steering wheel, may not be explicitly conscious of those forces until they are turned off.[7] What they do experience is increased enjoyment and interest.

## Involvement

Any attempt to teach science in a museum exhibit demands intellectual involvement from the visitor. An example would be the multi-panel or multi-stage exhibit in which the visitor is asked to predict the outcome of an event: "What do you think will happen when the feather drops in a vacuum?" Physical involvement can be simple: just by asking the visitor to push a button to set off some event, the exhibit designer has improved the chance that the visitor will be paying attention to it.

More ambitious exhibits attempt to combine both kinds of involvement: for example, by having the visitor physically carry out an experiment. In an exhibit at the Museum of Science in Boston, visitors place weights on pendulum swings and observe their motion. In doing so, they are guided by interactive computer text that enables them to form a hypothesis and design an experiment to test it, within a very small world consisting of three swings and a set of weights.[10] This combination of physical and intellectual involvement is effective but demands a good deal of the visitor's time; the process of switching back and forth between computer screen and physical experiment can be tedious or distracting. Furthermore, the physical apparatus limits the number of possible experiments.

A simulation-virtual reality system could integrate the physical and intellectual elements of this pendulum problem into a single, absorbing exhibit. It would allow the visitor to select "physical" setups of increasing complexity as his understanding grew, permitting him to test more interesting hypotheses. Instead of being limited to changing weights, the visitor would be able to alter the pendulums' length, rigidity, even their equations of motion. The physical aspects of the exhibit could also be enhanced. Using a force feedback seat analogous to the feedback gloves or arms that already exist, young museum-goers could safely "ride" a pendulum through space, experiencing its acceleration first-hand. They would be able to compare a ride on a rigid pendulum to a ride on a playground swing – and find out whether the big kids really get a better ride.

## Interpretation and Communication

In the past, the need to keep the message understandable has sometimes limited the realism or accuracy of the exhibit - in order to get heuristic understanding, you had to start with a heuristic model. The synergy of advanced virtual reality systems with sophisticated simulation will make this unnecessary. The message to be understood by the visitor must remain comprehensible; the concept behind the exhibit should be simple, and the results of the visitor's actions clear. But the accuracy of the model used to generate those results can be far higher. Advanced levels of calculation can be performed "behind the scenes"; because the results can be transformed into compelling sensory experience, they need not overwhelm the museum visitor. What seem to be meaningless digits in raw output will metamorphose into dazzling clarity in a visual display or convincing detail in the feel of a simulation. Instead of losing the visitor's attention through numerical overkill, an exhibit based on an accurate, complex model will have the compelling power of realism.

*Pleasure*

Virtual reality excels at the task of making an exhibit an enjoyable experience. Not only is virtual reality a powerful aesthetic experience in itself, but it removes many constraints on the design of exhibits. Considerations of safety and maintenance limit the amount of hands-on, climb-over participation that can be allowed in a physical exhibit; but virtual objects cannot be damaged by handling, nor can children be hurt in a fall from a virtual building. Most of all, perhaps, the dimension of pleasure is increased through the visitor's power of choice. With increased computational power an exhibit need no longer represent a single choice of design, color, and feel, imposed by the designer or artist on every visitor. Each visitor can customize the exhibit environment – and designers can learn from visitor's choices.

Using these criteria, it is possible to develop – as yet, in the mind alone – exhibits in every field. From these, a modest science center of the future, a virtual museum, can be designed.

## The Virtual Museum: General Principles and Organization

In the 1940s, when it was proposed that the new Museum of Science in Boston be a museum not only of natural history but of all the sciences, Karl T. Compton, then president of the Massachusetts Institute of Technology, warned that "you've got to be brutally selective" to remain within the realm of physical possibility.[11] Perhaps the virtual museum of science will be more expandable, since it may be possible for exhibits based on software to share physical space and hardware; a large collection of these exhibits could be displayed in rotation simply by changing access defaults. Whatever the limits of the virtual museum itself, however, any discussion must remain selective. This description will include exhibits in a number of fields of pure science. Exhibits in fields not covered are left as an exercise in speculation for the reader.

Most principles in the general design of science museums will also apply to the virtual museum. For example, people should be able to move freely through spaces of comfortable size. Visitors should have a way of locating exhibits which is efficient enough to prevent frustration but leaves room for serendipitous discovery. If finances permit, a building created expressly for the museum, with its exhibits and their organization in mind, is ideal.[12]

One principle which will require special attention in the virtual museum is the need for each exhibit to "advertise" to passers-by. Studies by Judy Diamond and by John Falk have shown that visitors tend to examine a large number of exhibits in a brief period of time, spending less than a minute at each one, while devoting five to thirty minutes each to a select few.[1] In other words, they browse through many exhibits and choose the ones they want to investigate more thoroughly.

At more traditional museums of science, the outward appearance of an exhibit suggests the experience it offers. The sight of a moving pulley or a mist tornado has some immediate meaning to the visitor. Computer software, including the most dramatic simulation or virtual reality, is invisible until it is activated. At The Computer Museum in Boston, many of the most interesting exhibits, particularly in the computer graphics section, are software-based. The problem of advertising their content is dealt with ingeniously, using colorful wall posters, illuminated panels, and animated screen displays. Nevertheless, from a distance, the computer graphics area is less glamorous than the rest of the museum. Until the visitor approaches one of the exhibits and becomes involved, the arrays of workstations almost suggest a classroom. The designer of virtual exhibits will have to devote attention to two kinds of visitors: the visitor who has already chosen to devote time to the exhibit, and the one who is just passing through. Without a public display that does at least partial justice to the wonders within, the virtual exhibit will never be experienced at all.

Existing science centers organize their exhibits according to various schemes. It is possible to group exhibits in large galleries devoted to the traditional academic fields; as elements of broad interdisciplinary displays; or in clusters whose themes are specific concepts or groups of concepts. In the virtual museum, to counteract the isolating quality of workstation-based exhibits, it may be helpful to organize exhibits so that public displays that are visible together illustrate related concepts. A single flow of ideas, elaborated but not interrupted by diversions and eddies, could be made to convey visitors through the entire museum.

This is the plan that will be followed in the virtual museum to be discussed here – a rather traditional one, to offset the futuristic elements of the individual exhibits. Visitors will pass through six large galleries devoted to the fields of mathematics, physics, chemistry, biology and medicine, earth sciences, and astronomy: the Hall of Numbers, the Hall of Forces, the Hall of Molecules, the Hall of Life, the Hall of the Earth, and the Hall of the Universe (Figure 4).

As visitors walk through the Halls, they will pass partitioned areas or alcoves, each one containing a group of related exhibits. At each alcove, a set of displays would be projected to passers-by: some of them the real-time visual output of exhibits currently in use, others images selected from particularly striking previous runs, others still announcing the concepts to be explored within. Because several alcove displays will be visible at a time, each one will be limited to a few images to avoid overwhelming visitors with information.

Visitors who are interested by one of the displays will turn out of the general traffic stream and approach that alcove. As they do so, the displays of other alcoves will to

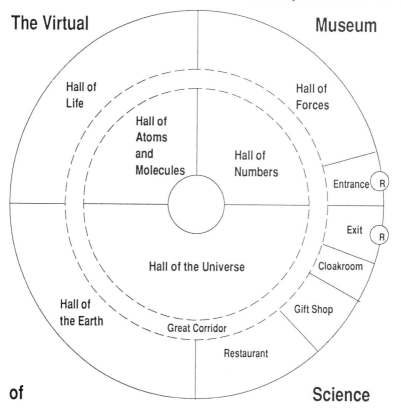

**Figure 4**  *Design for a virtual science museum. Visitors walk along the Grand Corridor and pass the Halls and their displays in turn. There is no physical divider between the Corridor and the Halls, though there should be some visual demarcation. Similarly, the Halls are separated from each other by visual clues, not by solid walls. All exhibits within sight are easily accessible.*

longer be visible to them; that visual space will instead be filled with further information about their chosen alcove – the technology needed to make images visible only from certain positions and angles is already well on the way. Visitors will wander around within the alcove, browsing among exhibits. When anyone comes within a certain distance of a given exhibit, it will run a quick advertisement for itself, no more than fifteen to thirty seconds. Exhibits in use will project selected components of their output: probably anything more than visual and auditory display would be distracting rather than appealing to other visitors.

In a few minutes, a visitor will be able to learn about the many exhibits on that alcove's topic, eventually either choosing one or returning to the flow of traffic to view displays on other topics, from other alcoves. When she chooses a particular exhibit, perhaps by sitting down at a workstation or pressing a button, the learning interaction will begin.

What would that interaction be like? Here are sample exhibits from each of the Halls of the Virtual Museum. Many are based on existing exhibits; others cannot be conceived without advanced simulation and virtual reality technology.

## *The Hall of Numbers*

The abstraction of mathematics might seem to lend itself to pure, intangible reason, but in fact the senses are excellent avenues to mathematical understanding.[13] Perhaps because numbers are the native realm of the computer, computer exhibits on mathematics are already to be seen. The arguments used in designing exhibits for the Hall of Numbers, based on the successful aspects of present exhibits, are outlined below. Other exhibits in the Virtual Museum will be developed using similar principles.

At the Museum of Science in Boston, IBM's Mathematica gallery features a computer exhibit called "A Mathematical Journey", including five separate sections, one of which teaches analytic geometry. In one lesson, a monitor displays cartesian coordinates and a straight line, with the equation $y = ax + b$. The visitor is instructed by a recorded voice to choose values for $a$ and $b$. As he changes $a$ and $b$, the line is redrawn to match the new equation.

Even this level of control over the exhibit gives a pleasing sense of discovery. Although the screen display might be identical to a textbook figure, the ability to create the figure for oneself is empowering. The visitor is asking a question about the world of straight lines: "What does a line with $a = 2$ and $b = 5$ look like?" and receiving an immediate, graphic answer.

If this exhibit has a flaw, it is a technological one: the graphics are unspectacular, and responses are slow. However, visitors were able to overcome similar difficulties when using another program within the exhibit, called "Orbits". Children and adults were enthusiastic about choosing the speed with which their hypothetical spacecraft would circle a planet of a given mass. Selecting speeds and planetary masses by touching the screen was slow and somewhat awkward; the ship's orbit was shown as a single line, rather sluggishly described around the simply-drawn planet; but the inherent interest of seeing whether a ship would orbit, crash, or escape into space was enough to hold visitors' attention. It may be that an exhibit based only on mathematical concepts, without a fictional storyline or application, requires more convincing aesthetics. At The Computer Museum, the beautiful visual displays of exhibits on fractal geometry drew attention even when no real-world or fictional applications were cited.

If two successful elements of a mathematical exhibit are fictional challenges to the user, along with arresting visuals, what sort of virtual exhibit might use both these tactics? An exhibit on analytic geometry can be constructed around a role-playing adventure. In the "Geometrical Dungeon" and "Analytical Space" exhibits, understanding a mathematical concept will allow the visitor to use it as a tool in the quest or a defense against simulated perils. For example, to search for treasure hidden in a dark corner of the display, the visitor must correctly choose the variables in the line equation to define the path he wants his lantern, flashlight, or laser beam to shine along. This is already feasible. Using more elaborate 3D projections and perhaps other kinds of sensory output, a user who provides the correct equations will be instantly encircled by a visible, ellipsoidal field of protection, or armed with a hyperbolic shield. For this and many other exhibits, visitors will want hard-copy graphics of favorite scenes to take home.

On a more earthly plane, people tend to be interested in exhibits that give insight into familiar objects or provide new understanding of overlooked commonplaces. They may be more comfortable with mathematics as the servant of reality, not its supervisor. Equations can be presented, not as representations of an ideal or standard that real objects fail to attain, but as descriptions of those objects in simplified terms. Virtual reality input will make possible a group of exhibits that work from reality to mathematical description, translating the motion of a visitor's hand through the air into a vector, or giving the equations for the changing slope of her cheek as she traces it with a finger. In the "Make it So" exhibit, simplified versions of real objects will be created on screen from the tracing motions of the visitor's hands, with realism increasing as she adds details, approaching reality as nearly as she cares to.

A more adventurous alcove of virtual exhibits will explore the strange world of topology. Just as it is now possible to seem to "fly" around the image of a protein molecule, peering into its nooks and crannies or even exploring them by touch,[3] it will be possible to fly through the arches and holes of a topological curiosity, or use a virtual knife to discover how many cuts are required to separate it into two pieces and determine its order. Figures and virtual objects created by specifying an equation can be altered by changing that equation – or by "physical" manipulation with a feedback glove. The rules of topological transformation allow stretching and compressing a hypothetical object, but not tearing or cutting; the "Topostuff" exhibit will provide a virtual substance that could be molded but never torn, so that a visitor can mold a doughnut into its topological equivalent, a coffee cup, or invert an inner tube through its air valve.

## *The Hall of Forces*

The use of virtual reality techniques for teaching physics is already being explored. Margaret Minsky of the Massachusetts Institute of Technology believes that a simulated construction set of virtual springs and pulleys could give children a literal grasp of physical forces. She has created a demonstration system at the MIT Media Lab.

On the screen of her demonstration setup, a dot connected to two squares represents the user's hand dragging two cubes across a flat surface. Pushing a joystick sideways, the user sees the squares lagging behind, the connecting lines lengthening; thanks to motors attached to the joystick, she can actually feel the weight of the cubes resisting her pull, dragging on the other end of what seem to be stretching springs. As the virtual springs reach their maximum extension, they pull the cubes forward, faster and faster, finally slinging them past the user's hand position, so that she feels their weight pulling from the opposite direction. With a few keystrokes, the stiffness of the springs is increased; now the cubes follow the user's hand more closely, neither lagging far behind nor swinging far ahead.

What the user is experiencing are forces derived immediately from the equation that represents them. The harmonic oscillator equation that describes a spring's behavior creates these almost Platonic virtual springs: idealized, unencumbered by material effects. As Margaret Minsky explains, virtual toys like these offer the satisfaction of building tangible constructions that can be experimented with by pushing and pulling, not calculating. But they have advantages over real blocks and springs: their behavior is mathematically and physically straightforward, without the complexities introduced by real materials and their defects. They can be changed, given new shapes and properties, and multiplied without limit. From this virtual bag of tricks would emerge the most exotic, well-equipped, and comprehensive construction set imaginable.

At the future Virtual Museum, the Hall of Forces need not confine its exhibits to the simulation of physical devices like springs and pulleys. Any force that can be represented by a scalar or vector field will be easy to incorporate. Visitors to the Magnetism exhibit will be able to fight the pull of giant magnets, then change the composition of the virtual object they were holding and feel the pull lessen or strengthen. The old-fashioned scale showing one's weight on different planets in the solar system can be replaced by a "Space Executive" exhibit in which visitors attempt to lift a virtual pencil from an office desk on Mercury, Venus, or Jupiter.

Frederick Brooks has suggested that large variations in field magnitude are best perceived through the "haptic" senses of position and pressure. The eye searches for motion and for boundaries, but "one does not readily internalize that 'This density is ten times that one'" using vision; force feedback appears to be superior.[3] If this is true, then haptic comparisons of material properties will be far more enlightening than visual ones - as well as more entertaining. Rather than watching ball bearings fall or air bubbles rise through liquids like water, oil, and glycerine, visitors to the Virtual Museum's Viscosity exhibit will trail their hands through virtual vats of them. At the "Village Smithy", their amplified hammer blows will ring down on virtual metals from iron to iridium, allowing them to experience differences in malleability. Some will be inspired to create their own materials at the "Miracle Matter" exhibit: with guidance, they will specify properties like tensile strength and compressibility, then test their new material by modeling objects or building virtual edifices and witnessing the results. The experience of being virtually crushed by a collapsing mistake will be optional.

## The Hall of Molecules

At the Deutsches Museum in Munich, visitors perform chemistry experiments under glass. Along the walls are dozens of different exhibits, each of which is a demonstration ready to proceed at the touch of a button. Fluids pour and mingle, change colors, evolve gases. Text panels explain the results. But this dazzling effort is monumentally costly, both to create and to maintain. It is no wonder that exhibits of this kind are rare, but it is a pity, because the public seems to be more intimidated by the concepts of chemistry than by any other science. Within the field it has been shown that even university students who can solve standard chemistry problems may not fully grasp the concepts behind them.[14] Virtual exhibits could help this situation in many ways: just one will be described here.

Atoms and molecules are thought of as mysterious, intangible entities by many people. They need not be. Computer simulation of the behavior of atoms and molecules is already far advanced. Electronic, interatomic and intermolecular forces can be represented quite accurately. Programs exist which require only the names of a molecule's constituent atoms and a guess at their arrangement in order to find that molecule's structure and properties. At the Virtual Museum, such programs will be combined with force feedback displays like those in the Hall of Forces to create the Chemistry Construction Set. Using this exhibit, a child will be able to "pick up" two hydrogen atoms and experiment with the creation of a molecule. As she moves the atoms together, they will begin to attract each other, pulling her hands together of their own accord, until they reach the equilibrium bonding distance. By playing with the new molecular bond, pulling on it to test its strength and comparing it with bonds in other molecules, she will learn to understand bonding.

Other visitors will twist substituted ethane molecules to compare their rotational barrier; the difference between repulsive steric effects and attractive dipole forces will be experienced directly. Reaction activation energies will be applied by the visitors themselves, pushing molecules with their own hands up and over the saddle points of potential energy surfaces. Intangible effects that exist only as approximations or models will become real. As a visitor moves a carbon atom into a pool of hydrogen atoms, four of these will automatically arrange themselves in a tetrahedron; if he wants to learn more, he can request representations at various levels of theory. For example, pressing the "Hybridization" button will reveal s and p orbitals on the carbon which he must mix correctly to produce a tetrahedral set of sp3 orbitals. In these exhibits, atoms and molecules will become like any other real objects. Even their most arcane properties will appear in a form that can be literally grasped.

*The Hall of Life*

This may be the field where even a virtual museum will be too small to contain all the possible tempting exhibits. We already have most of the technology needed to create a marvelous Biochemistry alcove. The lock-and-key hydrogen bonding between members of nucleic-acid base pairs is most naturally represented in virtual force feedback; even a child will be able to pull apart strands of DNA and construct a messenger RNA molecule, picking up and fitting together bases like puzzle pieces. Visitors to the "Enter an Enzyme" exhibit will find themselves enlisted as substrates. Visually surrounded by the residues of the active site, they will move substrate functional groups into the correct positions, guided by color coding, force feedback, and perhaps a reassuring voice offering advice. It may be a little intimidating to be trapped within the active site of an allosteric enzyme – watching huge polypeptide chains like the catalytic trimers of aspartate transcarbamylase lift and turn around you, waiting for the reaction to be completed and you, the product, to be released – but it will be unforgettable.

Beyond the biochemistry alcove, visitors will come to a collection of exhibits on botany and zoology. The principles of plant growth and form are already being modeled in an exhibit at The Computer Museum in Boston. This "Graftals" program encourages visitors to create forests of trees from the fractal repetition of branching rules.[15] Higher levels of graphic virtuosity, like those in Prusinkiewicz and Lindenmeyer's book, *The Algorithmic Beauty of Plants*, would allow visitors to create a rose bouquet or a fir branch laden with spiralling cones.[16] Virtual zoology is full of possibilities. Margaret Minsky's "Sandpaper" system lets users feel a virtual texture – bumpy, rough, or slippery – by moving a joystick.[17] When it is possible to transmit these sensations more naturally, to the fingertips and palm, visitors will be able to learn about animals by sight, sound, and touch. An exhibit on the adaptive qualities of skin coverings will illustrate its points by letting visitors sink their fingers into the deep warm coat of a chinchilla, feel the prickles of a hedgehog, or compare the smooth slither of a snake's skin to the pebbly back of a lizard.

In a display on evolution, the "Design a Species" exhibit will help imaginative visitors create new life forms by subjecting simulations of existing species to new conditions. Possible mutations will be explored and their effect on fitness calculated, finally producing a new phenotype. The resulting animal may be strange-looking, but the user will be encouraged to reach out and pet his creation. The visitor to "Another World" will explore one of Stephen J. Gould's lotteries of extinction: by randomly selecting certain fauna of the Burgess Shale to survive, and others to vanish, she will create alternate histories of life.[18] It will require enormously powerful hardware and software, but at some point it will be practicable to view, as in time-lapse photography, the likely evolutionary consequences of different patterns of extinction, and see what sort of life forms might have arisen from species that vanished long ago. Such an exhibit may forcibly make the point that we are lucky to be here ourselves.

In the alcove devoted to medicine and the human body, children may shock their parents by their eagerness to pick up and handle virtual internal organs. Adults can practice surgery on virtual patients – perhaps being guided through an operation they had undergone themselves – although they might find the feel of flesh under their virtual knife disturbing.[13] Some will prefer to set a virtual broken arm. Others will try out the Bodybuilder exhibit. By changing the force feedback defining virtual weights, visitors will experience in advance the muscle strength they would gain after weeks of workouts. Impatient children may want to glimpse themselves as adults: working from their current appearance as sensed by a robotic eye, the "Grow Up!" exhibit will show them what they might look like in a decade or two – with detailed explanations on request. The most daring of any age can try the "Gender Bender" and see themselves transformed into a member of the opposite sex.

## The Hall of the Earth

There will be a clear path from the Zoology alcove in the Hall of Life to the Ecosystem alcove here, for they are intimately related. The massive computational power needed to reconstruct evolution should allow the representation of a complex ecology. In the

"House of Cards" game, visitors will study an ecosystem and attempt to choose a species which would not be missed. The exhibit will show the effects of that species' extinction on the entire ecosystem. Visitors may discover unexpected dependencies, or be surprised by the significance of a less than glamorous plant or animal.

In the geology alcove, visitors will feel mountain ranges rise and erode away beneath their fingers. They will attempt to recreate landscapes, marshalling the forces of earth, water, and wind to simulate the Badlands or the Mississippi Delta. Further on, in the meteorology section, visitors will play the "Weather Game" with a giant map simulating current weather systems. By moving in cold fronts and high pressure regions, they will try to get sunshine at the nearest beach or bring heavy snow clouds over their favorite ski resort. Children will be able to fly through simulated weather; soaring at cumulonimbus height through a thunderstorm, they will feel the vast charges build up around them and hear the crack of lightning as it races for the ground.

## *The Hall of the Universe*

This is the place for grand concepts played out on a grand scale. Graphical simulations of the solar system are available today, but far more will be possible in the Virtual Museum. In "Create a Solar System", visitors will gather interstellar gases together and set them spinning. If they choose the right initial mass and velocity, they will be rewarded with a planetary system; extra points for anyone who manages to create a planet in the "life zone" of its new sun. With permission from George Gamow's estate, alcoves will be set aside for Mr Tompkins' Wonderlands.[19] A town where the speed of light is ten miles an hour, and objects are foreshortened in the direction of relative motion, will be easily simulated in a visual projection. A little more difficult will be the system of force feedback that allows the visitor to feel her hand gaining mass as she tries to move it past the "speed limit". The Virtual Museum may or may not include the baffling quantum jungle, in which predators and prey alike have visibly indeterminate position and velocity; but visitors are sure to appreciate a few minutes inside a miniature expanding universe – with guidance from a simulated companion as knowledgeable as Mr. Tompkins' Professor. In a related exhibit, visitors will learn about the missing mass problem by viewing recreations of the Big Bang and the evolution of the universe over time: some initial conditions will lead to eternal expansion, others to an eventual Big Squeeze and second Bang. This simulation will be projected over most of the Hall of the Universe to take advantage of size. Perhaps it will also entertain visitors in the museum restaurant.[20]

## Conclusion

Only a few potential exhibit concepts have been described here. While speculation is tempting, the Virtual Museum will not really begin its evolution until the first visitors come in, look around, and get to work. With computer tools of any kind, the most significant advances tend to be user-driven. Users evolve unexpected ways to apply new techniques: for example, it was users who applied network technology to create online bulletin boards.[21] At the Virtual Museum, developers will be sure to ask visitors for suggestions. Even better, they will want to spend some time watching what happens at each exhibit, seeing what new ideas visitors come up with. It will be easy for developers to dream up exhibit after exhibit; the most difficult task for the Virtual Museum's designers may be to stop designing occasionally so that they can learn from their visitors.

## Acknowledgements

I would like to thank several people at The Computer Museum: Liz Armbruster and Gail Jennes for help in finding sources, and David Greschler for an enlightening conversation about virtual reality and its users. I would also like to thank Margaret Minsky of the MIT Media Lab.

This article is dedicated to the memory of Miles Pickering, brilliant teacher and patient advisor, who brought the gift of understanding to thousands of students.

## References

1   Semper, R. J. 1990. Science museums as environments for learning. *Physics Today,* **43**(11), 50–56, November.
2   Danilov, V. J. 1982. *Science and Technology Centers.* The MIT Press, Cambridge, Massachusetts.
3   Brooks, F. P. Jr., Ouh-Young, M., Batter, J. J. and Kilpatrick, P. J. 1990. Project GROPE – haptic displays for scientific visualization. *Computer Graphics* (SIGGRAPH '90 Conference Proceedings), **25**(4), 177–185, August.
4   Danilov, V. J. 1982. *Science and Technology Centers,* p.14. The MIT Press, Cambridge, Massachusetts.
5   Danilov, V. J. 1982. *Science and Technology Centers,* p.14. The MIT Press, Cambridge, Massachusetts.
6   Sproull, R. F. 1990. Parts of the frontier are hard to move. *Computer Graphics* (SIGGRAPH '90 Conference Proceedings), **25**(4), 9 August.
7   Minsky, M. (MIT Media Lab.) Private correspondence.
8   Danilov, V. J. 1982. *Science and Technology Centers,* pp.196–199. The MIT Press, Cambridge, Massachusetts.
9   Danilov, V. J. 1982, *Science and Technology Centers,* p.198. The MIT Press, Cambridge, Massachusetts.
10  Exhibits of this kind were first developed by Eva Van Rennes at the Cranbrook Institute in Detroit. See: Sweet, W. 1987. Exploratorium influences science museums new and old. *Physics Today,* **40,** 65-68.
11  Danilov, V. J. 1982. *Science and Technology Centers,* p.33. The MIT Press, Cambridge, Massachusetts.
12  Burcaw, G. E. 1975. *Introduction to Museum Work.* p.146. American Association for State and Local History, Nashville.
13  Bylinsky, G. 1991. The marvels of 'virtual reality'. *FORTUNE,* **123**(11), 138–150.
14  Nurrembern, S. C., and Pickering, M. 1987. Concept learning versus problem solving: is there a difference? *J. Chem. Educ.,* **64**(6), 508–510.

15  For information on this exhibit, contact Thomas A. Defanti at the University of Illinois at Chicago. A. Lindenmayer's 'L- systems' were adapted to computer graphics by A. R. Smith.

16  Prusinkiewicz, P. and Lindenmayer, A. 1990. *The Algorithmic Beauty of Plants.* Springer-Verlag, New York.

17  Minsky, M., Ouh-Young, M., Steele, O., Brooks, F. P. Jr. and Behensky, M. 1990. Feeling and seeing: issues in force display. *Computer Graphics,* **24**(2), March, 235–243.

18  Gould, S. J. 1989. *Wonderful Life: The Burgess Shale and the Nature of History.* W. W. Norton and Company, New York.

19  Gamow, G. 1940. *Mr Tompkins in Wonderland; or, Stories of c, G, and h.* The MacMillan Company, New York; The University Press, Cambridge, England.

20  Adams, D. 1981 (c.1980). *The Restaurant at the End of the Universe.* Harmony Books, New York.

21  Greschler, D. (The Computer Museum, Boston.) Private correspondence.

# The Future of Student Computer Use

**William J. Joel**

*IBM Corporation, T.J. Watson Research Center, Yorktown Heights, NY, USA*

*The computer has not been embraced as an educational tool by the educational community as some have predicted in the past. The reasons for this lack of interest and integration range from the computer's bulkiness to the student's difficulty in using it. In order for students to fully integrate computer use in their education, it must be more than just a simple tool. By examining these present limitations, we can see when and how students will fully embrace the computer as an educational tool.*

## The Computer as a Tool

Where are the little slates that students once used to practice their lessons? Where are the slide rules that students once used to calculate results via logarithmic lengths? Are these tools no longer useful? Or is this a silly question to ask?

Educators and computer professionals have, in the past, been extremely eager to tout the computer as the ultimate magic box for students. In my opinion, computers may be able to perform some incredible tasks, but they are certainly not magic boxes.

The computer is a tool. This is a rather simple statement, and most likely it hides a great deal of information. It does not reflect the nature of the tool, or how people interact with the tool. It does not tell the whole story.

Students use tools, both in the classroom and at home, as they perform their educational tasks. Do students stop to think about why they are using the tool? Perhaps, but more likely they simply want to know how to use the tool in order to finish their work. After all, students have more important things to take care of, compared to school work. Don't they?

Computers are being used in a large proportion of the schools in the United States; however, the computer is still a relatively new tool in the classroom, and it is taking more time to integrate these devices into the educational experience than most have envisioned. Previously, teachers have been encouraged and supported in their efforts to learn as much as they can about this emerging technology. After the initial euphoria died down, educators found that the computer, as it exists today, cannot live up to the expectations for its use. There appears to be something lacking, and if one were to ask teachers just what that something was, you would obtain many intuitive responses but few specific answers.

Immediately, one might ask why. The answer relates to both the nature of the tool and to how students approach its use. Many times we forget that there are real people involved in this scenario, as Alan Kay so eloquently states:

"I don't think the technology is as big as issue [in education] as people's attitudes and values. Putting computers into schools is like putting pianos in every classroom. It's not going to help. Any musician will tell you that music is not in a piano. What I'm trying to say is, if you put computers in every school, it's like pianos in every school.

Everybody wants media and technology to save them, but it's attitudes, [and machines don't affect attitudes]."[4]

We need to study just how students use existing educational tools and then apply our newfound knowledge to the task of creating computers that will also be successful tools. In doing so we will find why computers have failed as tools for our students, and once we know why computers have not been fully embraced by students, predictions can be made as to when this integration will begin.

## Students and Computers

Watch a student use a new tool, such as a non-programmable calculator, and you'll see the student initially play with it, then settle back into a rather routine pattern. This defacto acceptance of such a calculator as just another tool is due in part to the fact that you can't really play with a calculator. Of course you could have fun pressing the *Sin* button several times to see what sort of number you end up with, but these entertainment qualities are limited.

Also, calculators are relatively inexpensive compared with the cost of a computer. In fact, some US school districts can afford to purchase calculators for an entire school, if they wished. These same districts cannot, currently, purchase the same quantity of computers.

Calculators are very portable devices. They can be carried around by the student and used wherever necessary. I remember the time when I was a college student and calculators were first making an impact on students' lives. As Chemistry majors, I and my fellow Chemists carried our calculators around in pouches on our belts. When we whipped out our *electronic sliderules* we looked like gunslingers ready to have a shoot-out at the O-K Chem Lab.

Today, calculators are taken for granted by students, to the point where they are often looked on as just another *thing* you use in school. You could even have one on your wrist, as part of a fancy digital watch. So why doesn't a student *gunsling* a computer?

## Differences

The differences, here, are ones of scale: scale of size, scale of cost, scale of use. In all aspects, the computer is many steps removed from the simple, or even the complex,

**Figure 1**   Nope!

calculator. Most computers are big. They are still essentially tools that are fixed to a single place. Yes, they can be set up on a movable cart, and rolled from place to place, but this mobility is very limited. You do not, yet, carry your computer around on your belt. Not even laptop computers are very portable. Just look at our student's opinion in Figure 1.

Computers are expensive. A simple calculator can be purchased for less than ten dollars, while a simple computer will cost several factors more than this. Parents might easily see the wisdom in buying calculators for their children, but individual computers are still a long way off.

Obviously, computers do more than calculators. Computers can be used for a wide, practically infinite, number of tasks. They are multi-purpose tools, programmable by definition, and most often provide a highly visual interface for the user. A student can play with a computer much more than with any other educational tool. Computers can be used for play even after the student is well on the way to using this tool for educational tasks. Calculators are basically fixed-purpose tools, possibly programmable, but usually to a limited degree. You could figure out a way to play the game *Dragon Slayers of Kalamazoo* with a calculator, but would it really be worth the trouble?

## Needed Changes

The first change that will need to occur, in order for students to fully embrace computers, is to make computers available to all students. Spero[1] states that in order to realize the complete potential of computers as learning tools, students must have access to their own computers, any time the students wish to use them. The calculator is a tool which all students *could* own or make use of. The fact that all students don't use a calculator is not always a negative reflection on the tool. Sometimes it's because the local school district has decided that students would be better off without them - a pedagogical reason.

The size of the computer will need to be reduced. The computer will need to be small enough to be easily carried by the student, just as pens, notebooks, and the like are carried. Fleury,[2] describing an at-home word processing project, states that this project requires a portable computer.

Computers should be small enough that a student could forget it at home. This may sound like rather a simplistic statement, but let's examine its implications.

Pens, pencils, rulers, erasers, notebooks and textbooks, are all taken for granted by the student. They are often forgotten by the student, in preparing for the school day, because they are not at the top of the student's priority list. They are probably somewhere in the middle (hopefully not at the bottom). If a computer were as small, and as easily portable, as say a pencil-case, it could be forgotten.

This leads to the next required factor: the computer will need to be inexpensive, to the point where all students could easily acquire one. This does not mean that the computer will need to be as cheap as a pencil, but a tool that costs at least several hundred dollars is not inexpensive. If the computer were relatively inexpensive, the importance a student would associate with it would be much less than today. Again, it could be forgotten at home.

In some respects this goes against the corporate objectives of large computer companies - to make as much money as possible. Let's face it, there wouldn't be very much of a profit margin for these proposed, inexpensive computers.

## Ease of Use

The last two needed factors are rapidly approaching realization, as our technology improves the size of and the cost of computers. One factor still falls under an area of fervent research: the student will need to be able to use the computer as easily as writing in a notebook or reading a textbook. To use a well-worn phrase, it must be *user friendly*. Kahn and Freye[3] discuss how the insistence of teaching touch typing to young children is a hindrance to the effective use of word processing systems. Considering how most communication skills are taught, today, in the integrated Whole Language approach,[*] it seems archaic to insist that these keyboarding skills be isolated from the other communications skills.

When will we know that a computer is easy enough to use? To answer this, one need only examine how a notebook is written in, or a book is read. To write an entry in a notebook, you merely pick up the book, turn the pages to a hopefully clean page, pick up a writing instrument, and begin writing. Can this be done with today's student computers?

---

[*]The Whole Language approach integrates all communications skill into a single educational goal. Such skills as phonetics, grammar and pronunciation are no longer taught as separate entities.

When a student is asked to read a section from a textbook, the student looks for the book amongst all the other paraphernalia brought to school, opens the text to the appropriate page and begins reading. Can a student do that with today's computers?

At this point in our discussion it could be amusing to imagine what sort of technologies could be used to accomplish these feats with a computer. Some have suggested that a computer, for a student, be turned into an electronic slate, with some buttons or dials on the side, and a corresponding stylus.[7] Okay, this will allow the student to easily write in the *notebook*, but what about flipping pages in the notebook or text?

Possibly, the slate could be programmed to know where the student wants to be in the *book*. That's asking quite a lot from the programmers. It implies that the programming present be many factors more sophisticated than what is available today. It would be simpler to give to student a method for browsing the screenloads (*pages*) until the appropriate place is found.

Maybe we could even provide entire *books* on micro-disks, encased in a protective housing no larger than a credit card. Figure 2 shows what such a bookcard might look like.

Does this really fill the needs of the student? That's to be seen. There are functions which a computer could provide that more traditional tools could not. If a student wished to view all sections of a text relating a specific topic, the slate could search for them and display them in sequence. Educational researchers, today, are developing methods for storing and retrieving information based upon what is termed hypermedia.[5,6]

Our linear approach to information is tied directly to the linear nature of the books we have used. *Hypermedia* allows the student to use a computer to traverse information in a non-linear fashion, much like the way humans naturally approach information. A student could actually create a path through the book, relating to a specific exercise, and then store that path for later traversal. Many of these paths could be created, and they need not all be linear paths.

## Targeting the Problem

If computers can be so beneficial, why are educators not rushing to embrace them fully? There must be something in the traditional tools used in education that would be lost, or not easily replaced, by the use of computers. What are these factors, and are they essential to the educational process? As Cummings[8] states, advanced technologies must not be seen as a separate layer added on top of our educational system. Rather, they need to be an integrated part of the curriculum. Students, and teachers, must have the freedom to choose when to use the computer. They must be able to utilize a computer when it is appropriate and not simply because it is there.

Elmer-Dewitt[9] states that "...children learn their math tables faster, and more effectively, when drilled by fellow students rather than by machine . Some educators are even starting to re-examine such well-established instructional packages as IBM's Writing to Read program."

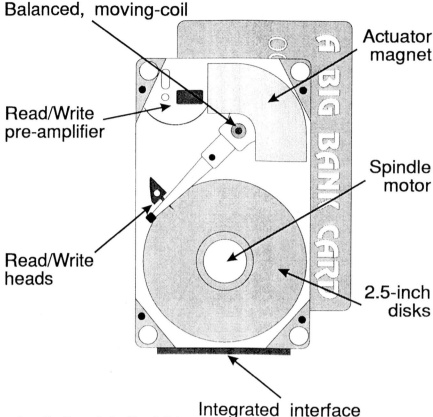

**Figure 2**  *Credit card-sized hard disk.*

Consider the learning process for reading a book. A child first begins by seeing the book as an object, sometimes filled with pretty pictures. Next, the child recognizes that others approach a book as more than just an object. There is some other meaning to it. Soon the child is flipping pages, realizing that the words/images have a sequential nature to them, and after awhile, the child will recognize words. Reading is not far behind.

While this is happening, the child is maturing in many other language areas, as well as physical areas. As stated above, the concept of Whole Language approaches the acquisition of communication skills by the child as an integrated whole. The ability to communicate is a multi-faceted skill, that relies on many sub-skills.

Consider how a child learns to use a computer. At first it is an object that makes pretty pictures and cute sounds, but soon it will be necessary to use the computer to do *something*. The interface for the computer is a bit more complex than that for a book. Even if that interface were simplified, as one could imagine for our electronic slate, it would still require many more sub-skills before the student was sufficiently comfortable with using it.

Looking at the computer this way, one can begin to see why students and the rest of the educational community have not moved into the computer future like other parts of society have. It could be stated that students, in the pre-college years, are just not ready to use computers, but then this would be too simple an explanation.

As Elmer-Dewitt goes on to relate, according to a report by the Center for Technology in Education, computer use seems to be most beneficial to students when they choose to use it themselves. This self-choice can most readily occur in free-form classrooms, which are not easily implemented.

## Just Another Tool

Does this mean that computers will never be embraced by the educational community? So far, we have discussed how computers have not been integrated as fully into education as educators would like. We have shown how computers, though heavily used by business workers and scientists in their daily activities, are not utilized to the same degree by students.

When will students see computers as just another tool? As stated before, when they can forget it on the kitchen table while dashing off to catch the school bus.

This scenario is not too far off in the future, but is most likely more than a decade away. Though many would like to see it so, computers of the level of sophistication we have been talking about will not be here when we celebrate the next millennium. Still, indications that such a device is coming are here already.

Many calculators are already programmable to a limited degree. To increase this capability will require more computer memory in a sufficiently compact size. This area of research is progressing nicely, and will most likely be solved in about ten years. Now that we've taken care of the power and size requirements, how about cost? No problem.

At the point in time where computer memory has been made sufficiently compact, the effect of market demand will drive the pricing for memory down far enough that the computers we are envisioning will be reasonably affordable by the average student, if such a person actually exists. Moreover, we are assuming that the power of these chips will increase concurrently with their decrease in size, so the desired level of ease of use should occur not too far behind. When? Let's say in about another ten years after we've gotten the devices small enough, they will be flexible to use by even the youngest student. In fact, Pickover[10] presents an interesting extrapolation of computing power into the 21st century. If we accept his proposal it will not be until at least the year 2005 before we see personal computers obtain the computer power of today's large mainframe computers (See figure 3).

This means that sometime after the year 2010, if our predictions hold, students will be leaving their computers on kitchen tables by the thousands. Parents of this future generation will simply have something else to remind their children about during the morning schoolday mayhem. Our student in Figure 4 seems to agree.

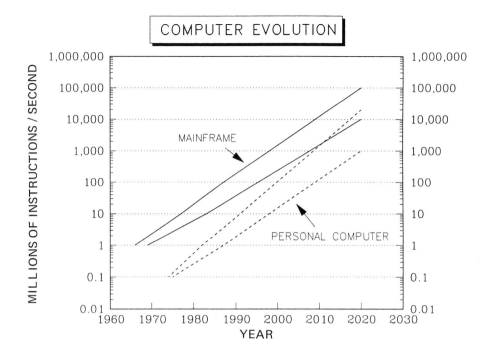

**Figure 3**   *Projected computing power. Each of the bands defines a range of computing power in units of MIPS (millions of instructions per second).* Reprinted from
Pickover.[10] The data for the chart comes from: Peled, A. (1987) The next computer
revolution. *Scientific American.* Oct **257**(4), 57.

## Conclusions

When computers were first introduced in the educational system, many believed we
should put a computer on every student's desk. Intelligent educators, on the other hand,
were justifiably cautious and decided to just sit back  and wait for the fallout. Soon,
these prophecies were found to be lacking, and educators realized that though computers
are and can be very useful, their current use is limited. They also recognized that the
computer as a tool was still evolving.

The fact that there are real people who will be using these computers is often
forgotten by educators. There are students who will use the devices; teachers who will
both use the computers as well as assist students; parents who will help students with
their homework, as well as provide them with other life experiences.

If we truly believe that form follows function, then why do we force our students
to change the way they learn because of an inflexible device? There is no good reason

**Figure 4**   Yes!

to do so, yet there are plenty of good reasons to force computers to adapt to the way students learn. In our case, student learning is the function and computers are the form.

Sometime in the near future, the needed requirements of scale (size, cost, ease of use) will have been attained, and we can begin creating computers that will be suited to the way students learn. Perhaps the computer, as an educational tool, could someday be looked at by students as just another item to tuck into their knapsacks as they prepare to go to school.

## References

1   Spero, S.W. 1987. The Homework Machine. *Collegiate Microcomputer,* **5**(1), 87-93.

2   Fleury, B. 1986. A Family Writing Project. *Computing Teaching,* **14**(2), 29-30.

3   Kahn, J. and Freyd, P. 1990. Touch Typing for Young Children: Help or Hindrance? *Educational Technology,* **30**(2), 41-45.

4   Kay, A. 1990. On Computers in Education. *BYTE,* **15**(9), 232.

5   Layman, J. and Hall, W. 1991. Applications of Hypermedia in Education. *Comput. Educ.,* **16**(1), 113-119.

6   Lehtio, P and Reijonen, P. 1990. Trends in Media Based Learning: Personal Computer Hypermedia. *Educational Computing,* **6**(1-2), 123-127.

7   Mel, B.W., Omohundro, S.M., Robinson, A.D., Skiena, S.S., Thearling, K.H., Young, L.T. and Wolfram, S. 1988. Tablet: Personal Computer in the Year 2000. *Communications of the ACM,* **31**(6), 638-646.

8   Cummings, J.B. 1989. Computers, the Cutting Edge of Learning. *Computers and Graphics,* **13**(1), 111-113.

9   Elmer-Dewitt, P. 1991. The Revolution that Fizzled. *Time,* **137,**(20), 48-49.

10  Pickover, C.A. 1991. *Computers and the Imagination,* St. Martins Press, New York.

# Forging a Career as a Sculptor from a Career as a Computer Programmer

## Stewart Dickson

*The Post Group Digital Center, 6335 Homewood Avenue, Hollywood, CA 90028, USA*

*In this personal essay, I discuss careers for computer programmers in the art world. Topics include computer-designed dress fashions and sculpture. I also suggest how current technology could affect the future of sculpture. By linking the power of computer graphics to the direct formation of a solid-shaped object, a process called stereolithography permits a user to design an object on a computer screen, then generate a 3-D plastic model. The process shows promise as a method to help visualize mathematical shapes and also produce futuristic art forms.*

## Introduction

Scientific and artistic interest in computer graphics has been growing rapidly in the last few years.[1] Today's graphical computer workstation integrates a general-purpose computer with high-performance graphic hardware for visualizing complicated data stored on a computer. The digital computer itself is a recent and radical novelty in human history, and the visual expressions of computer graphics appeal to both artists and scientists. I am a sculptor, and I have found that a career in fine arts is a speculative venture. Often, critical and economic success will never be reached during the life of the artist. The artist develops his aesthetic for a personal ideal, which may or may not match that of a hypothetical audience. This essay details some biographical aspects of my life as they relate to my interest in art and technology.

## My Early Years in Music and Print

I began my career by studying electrical engineering in order to learn how to design and assemble electronic circuits for creating and performing electronic music. Anyone familiar with the history of electronic music between the years 1970 and 1980 will be aware of the impact that the concurrent development of electronic circuit technology had on the field. In the late Sixties, the first Moog synthesizer was built using discrete components.[2] By 1980, synthesizers could be built using a single-chip VLSI (Very Large Scale Integrated) digital circuit which had the power to synthesize the combined timbre, or tonal spectrum, of a symphony orchestra in real time. By 1980 there were also essentially no new circuits required to make electronic music. Today, the major technical work involves assembling and programming modules composed of general-purpose computers.

Around 1980 I invented a strange musical instrument, which I think you will find of interest.[3,4] This instrument combines architecture and environmental sculpture with a study of the acoustics of vibrating strings. The instrument is composed of a small number of very long strings, at least thirty meters in length. The fundamental frequency of vibration of each string is subaudio, and is manifest as rhythmic element in the resulting music. The first audible harmonics are at intervals of microtones, resulting in a continuously playable harmonic series. The string can also be viewed as an acoustical delay line with a linear frequency response. The opposite ends of the string are fitted with stereo driving and pickup transducers, enabling a regenerative mode of playing including possible external electronic signal sources.

I eventually came to the realization that the context in which I had imagined making electronic circuits was in fact an artistic one and not a technical context. The practicalities of artmaking require building a cohesive portfolio demonstrating a focused vision. This usually takes many years.

I then chose the pragmatic approach of entering industry. There are at an engineering office numerous facilities which, with some creative application, are excellent tools for making art. There are also suitable outlets for these media. In 1983, there was an organization called the International Society of Copier Artists (ISCA).[5] This organization was also intertwined with the less-highly organized Anarchist MailArt Network. The activities in this circle involved sending limited-edition art through the postal system, binding collections of copier art into journals, and holding exhibitions of mail and copier art.

The photocopy machine is a resource which is freely available in a large corporate office. A few years ago a computer-interfaced phototypesetter was also a freely available resource to me. This was a physically large precursor to the present-day desktop laser printer. I discovered that it is possible to create sculpture using this machine. By writing a program which uses a software facility for typesetting documents that combines text and graphics, it is possible to calculate and print pages which contain successive cross-sections of a three-dimensional object.[6] Photocopying the stack of laser prints onto acetate results in a block of plastic which has a black, three-dimensional object embedded within it. I call the set of transparencies a "3-D book". Present-day color laser printers and copiers allow for an additional expressive dimension.

In an engineering facility which designs, builds, and tests electronic circuits, there are systems for computer-aided electronic design and manufacturing. The manufacturing of electronic circuitry in the present day is primarily an optical printing process. The manufacturing tools tend to be computer-interfaced graphical output devices. For example, the computer-interfaced film printer produces a high-quality image which is excellent for making visual art. There are also cinematic cameras available for these devices with which one can create computer-animated motion pictures. The resolution of the film printer is even high enough to allow experimentation in computer-generated holography.

The information regarding the operation and method of accessing the commonly-available graphical output devices is available to anyone with the inclination to learn how to use it. It is, therefore, possible to be employed at an engineering facility and to continue making art. The office-place artist is often a corporate guerilla or at least often has a habit of civil disobedience within a corporate community.

## The Turning Point

In 1985, I made a speculative venture into direct three-dimensional output of computer-aided designs using numerically-controlled milling machinery (see Figure 1). The designs were created in an interactive computer modelling environment. I also made fairly realistic computer renderings of the designs to serve as proposals for the sculpture (see Figure 2). The proposals were successful enough to afford admission into an art show on the basis of objects which did not yet physically exist. However, none of the pieces were sold. It is possible that this venture failed in part because this technology has been known since the late 1960s.

The fact that the computerization of this technology is basically in the hands of machinists means that the interfaces are less sophisticated than the computer programmer might desire. The technology is somewhat mundane, and in the past the artistic statement must also have been lacking.

I have also made sculpture from luminance contour graphs of electronically captured or digitized video images (see Figure 3). When a monochrome picture is represented in computer memory, it is actually a three-dimensional system. Visualized spatially, an electronic photograph is actually a graph of brightness against the vertical and horizontal coordinates of the sampled points (picture elements or "pixels") in the picture. When a three-dimensional subject is viewed, the brightest points of the object are generally associated with those which project forward, toward the viewer.

The luminance contour graph can be created as a polygon surface mesh in the computer simply by interpreting the brightness of the image as the Z coordinate, mapping horizontal and vertical to X and Y, respectively (see Figure 4). The fidelity of the luminance graph is associated with the lighting conditions of the subject. It can be observed that when the subject is lit head-on, producing "flat" or even illumination across the object, the luminance graph is also subjectively flat. However, when the subject is attractively lit, with a good range of contrast, then the contour graph is more interesting as well.

## Catching the Wave

In 1988, the first commercially available example of a computer-aided prototyping technology called Stereolithography was announced.[7] This is a process of building a three-dimensional object directly from a computer-resident geometrical description. Stereolithography uses a liquid polymer resin which hardens when exposed to ultraviolet light. Like a three-dimensional laser printer, the apparatus deposits successive layers of hardened material one upon another. Each layer is a successive two-dimensional

**Figure 1**
*Milled aluminium on hardwood
base, dimensions:* 25" × 12" × 15"
(includes base). Milled at Isthmus
Engineering Cooperative, Madison,
Wisconsin. © 1986 Stewart Dickson.

**Figure 2**
*Wavefront Technologies Advanced
Visualizer rendering of the CAD database.*
© 1986 Stewart Dickson.

cross-section of the three-dimensional database which has been calculated by the computer.

In the same year there was also first announced a compiler of a high-level abstract language, called the Mathematica system for doing mathematics by computer.[8] Mathematica, a software package from Wolfram Research in Champaign, Illinois, performs mathematical calculations on a wide range of computers (*e.g.* Apple, NeXT, IBM, Silicon Graphics). The program does symbolic, graphical and numerical calculations at variable precision. It is also a high-level programming language and interactive programming environment for mathematics.

Mathematics is the oldest and most universal language humanity has devised for speaking concisely at high levels of abstraction. Mathematics is the means for condensing the abstraction of a difficult problem to the level at which it can be implemented in a computer program. The Mathematica software automates this implementation and makes it easy for the user. Mathematics has graphical facilities which can transparently

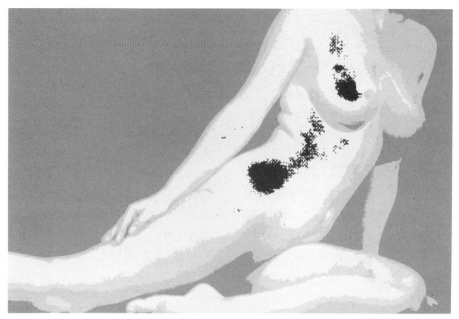

**Figure 3** *Nude, digitally processed electronic photograph.* This is a color-resampling of a digitally captured video camera image of a live model. © 1986 Stewart Dickson.

render a mathematical statement in beautiful color graphics on a two-dimensional screen (see Figure 5, 7 - 10). I have programmed the interfaces necessary to allow Stereolithography to render the abstract mathematical statement in three-dimensional figures that you can touch and hold (see Figure 6).

Visualization in scientific computing has caused a minor revolution in the sciences by allowing researchers to observe, with graphical immediacy, aspects of the system under study which may not be apparent from the numerical results alone. This has produced swift and unforeseen changes in the course of many areas of study. However, even when the spatial representation of the system under study is of dimension three or higher, only a two-dimensional image is available. Three-dimensional computer-aided prototyping tools provide a more immediate experience of the higher-dimensional abstraction.

I have proposed constructing an exhibition of sculpture of direct mathematical objects using Mathematica software and Computer-Aided Prototyping.[9,10] This project has attracted some support from the various industries currently involved in developing these technologies. The manufacturers of computer-aided prototyping equipment find value in beautiful and exotic forms with which to demonstrate their sophisticated hardware. Scientists have interest in this work because of the stated advantages to visualizing higher dimensions.

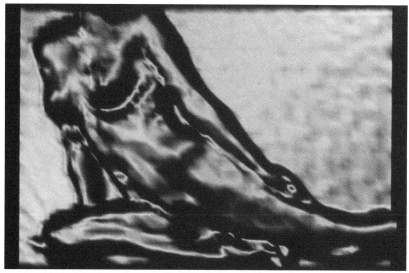

**Figure 4**    *Nude* (photosculpture), This is a Wavefront Technologies Advanced Visualizer rendering of the luminance graph of the source for Figure 3 interpreted as a polygon mesh. © 1986 Stewart Dickson.


There has been a tradition of mathematical influence in the fine arts. The ancients formed philosophies uniting the spirituality of religion with the visual manifestation of abstract logic. Renaissance painters developed the principles of mechanical perspective in order to render three-space on the two-dimensional canvas.

The Russian Constructivists of the early 20th century were lured by the attraction of representing mathematical ideas in concrete form. Max Bill extended this idea by actually proposing a formalism for talking about the proportions of elements in a visual composition.[11] M.C. Esher explored the mechanics of engraving to the point where he was developing mathematical ideas visually at the level at which contemporary mathematicians were thinking abstractly.

I am doing nothing new here in terms of an artistic statement. The mathematics may be as new and revolutionary as the technology. These may be forms which have never been seen before, but the concept is not new. The art critical world has not been favorable toward this work, so consideration of alternate approaches seems indicated.

## Finding a Direction

An element lacking in my previous mathematical work was reference to the human condition. The works expressed abstract concepts regarding pure form, but expressed no sense of life. The luminance contour graphs discussed earlier were made using an electronic photography session and a live model. The subject was the female form. Perhaps this work was simply not promoted by the artist as vigorously as it should have been.

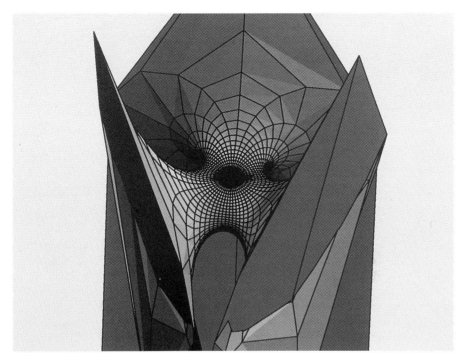

**Figure 5**    *Genus 0, Three-Ended or Trinoid Minimal Surface,* discovered by J.P.M. Jorge and William Meeks III in 1983. Rendered in the Mathematica system for doing mathematics by computer from the Global Enneper-Weierstrass parameterization. © 1986 Stewart Dickson courtesy of The Post Group and Wolfram Research, Inc.

Let's discuss recent technology which may aid the artist now and in the future. There is a device which uses a primitive robot arm, a scanning laser beam, and a synchronized color video camera element to obtain a large number of triangulated measurements of a three-dimensional surface very rapidly. One configuration of this 3-D scanner takes 131,072 measurements of radius against elevation and rotation about a vertical, cylindrical axis. It has been used by sculptor Robert Graham to digitize clay figures of around fifteen inches in height, then to reproduce them in an enlarged wax form using a numerically-controlled milling machine. The wax is finished by hand, and then sent to the foundry for casting in bronze. The digitizing machine works very rapidly, completing 131,072 measurements in about fifteen seconds. The machine can just as easily be used to scan a live subject. The milling machine can produce a facsimile of the subject which is accurate to a few millimeters.

In my opinion, this 3-D model system could be used to fashion custom dressmaking forms for the fashion industry. This would be like a custom mannequin. The surface of this human torso replica would need to have a finish which is rugged and compliant to

**Figure 6**   *Genus 0, Three-ended or Trinoid minimal surface,* Stereolithograph, approximately 8" high. Stereolithography by Hughes Aircraft Company, El Segundo, CA. © 1991 Stewart Dickson.

dressmaking practice (accept pins). It would also have to be of low enough cost to be an improvement over traditional practices. These problems are essentially solved. The measurements are certainly better than previous methods to the point that the 3-D facsimile retains an astounding degree of detail, and it is faithful to the appearance of the subject.

Markets for custom torsos include "theatrical costuming", where the actor's time in costume fitting can be a considerable cost. Imagine the advantages of 131,072 precise measurements in fifteen seconds. It is also conceivable that designers of high fashion could find value in a custom fit using this process, at least for the purpose of exhibition. The sculptor's access to celebrated actors and fashion models could also be an excellent vehicle for advancing his career, as would the experience of collaborating with theatrical and fashion designers.

Ballistic Particle Manufacturing is one method which might be used to color 3-D sculptures.[12] It resembles a high-powered ink-jet printer shooting tiny plastic beads which bond together upon impact. However, speed and size are obstacles to be overcome before computer-aided prototyping can reach its full potential. Another problem is the geometrical limitation of the digitizing device. Currently we are

Steiner's "Quartic" Surface

$$y^2 z^2 + z^2 x^2 + x^2 y^2 + xyz = 0 \text{ ; (1)}$$

(Cundy, H. M. and A. P. Rollett, *Mathematical Models*, Oxford University Press, 1961)

Subtract *xyz* from both sides of *(1)* then divide both sides by *xyz*:

$$\frac{yz}{x} + \frac{xz}{y} + \frac{xy}{z} = -1 \text{ ; (2)}$$

Equate *(2)* with an expression of the form of a sphere of radius *-1*.

$$u_1^2 + u_2^2 + u_3^2 = -1 \text{ ; (3)}$$

Express ( $u_1$, $u_2$, $u_3$ )as a parametric form of a sphere:

(cos*u*cos*v*, sin*v*, sin*u*cos*v* and equate the components to:

$$\left( \frac{yz}{x}, \frac{xz}{y}, \frac{xy}{z} \right).$$

This results in the non-linear system of equations:

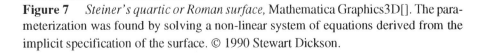

$$u_1: -(\cos u\cos v)^2 = \frac{yz}{x} \text{ ;}$$

$$u_2: -(\sin v)^2 = \frac{xz}{y} \text{ ; (4)}$$

$$u_3: -(\sin u\cos v)^2 = \frac{xy}{z} \text{ ;}$$

*(4)* can be solved for (*x, y, z*) resulting in the following set of solutions for the parametric form of the Quartic Surface:

(*x* = 0, *y* = 0, *z* = 0),

(*x* = –cos*v*sin*u*sin*v*, *y* = cos*u*cos$^2$*v*sin*u*, *z* = cos*u*cos*v*sin*v*),

(*x* = cos*v*sin*u*sin*v*, *y* = –cos*u*cos$^2$*v*sin*u*, *z* = cos*u*cos*v*sin*v*),

(*x* = cos*v*sin*u*sin*v*, *y* = cos*u*cos$^2$*v*sin*u*, *z* = –cos*u*cos*v*sin*v*),

(*x* = –cos*v*sin*u*sin*v*, *y* = –cos*u*cos$^2$*v*sin*v*, *z* = –cos*u*cos*v*sin*v*) (5)

Choose a non-trivial solution, *(5)* for example, to plot over the range:

$$u_0^\pi \text{ ; } v_0^{2\pi}.$$

**Figure 7** *Steiner's quartic or Roman surface,* Mathematica Graphics3D[]. The parameterization was found by solving a non-linear system of equations derived from the implicit specification of the surface. © 1990 Stewart Dickson.

The Global Enneper-Weierstrass representation for Minimal Surfaces:

$$X(\zeta) = \text{Re} \int_0^{re^{i\theta}} \Phi \,.$$

Where:

$$\Phi = (\,1 - g^2, i\,(\,1 + g^2\,)\,, 2g\,)\,\eta.$$

Enneper's Minimal Surface:

$$g = \zeta;\ \zeta = re^{i\theta};\ \eta = 1;$$

Scherk's Second Minimal Surface:

$$g = i\zeta;\ \eta = \frac{4}{1 - \zeta^4}\,;$$

Jorge-Meeks Trinoid:

$$g = \zeta^2\,;\ \eta = \left(\zeta^3 - 1\right)^{-2};$$

Trinoid (Jorge-Meeks):

$$x = \text{Re} \int_0^{re^{i\theta}} \frac{1 - \zeta^4}{\left(\zeta^3 - 1\right)^2}\, d\zeta\,;$$

$$y = \text{Re} \int_0^{re^{i\theta}} \frac{i(1 + \zeta^4)}{\left(\zeta^3 - 1\right)^2}\, d\zeta\,;$$

$$z = \text{Re} \int_0^{re^{i\theta}} \frac{2\zeta^2}{\left(\zeta^3 - 1\right)^2}\, d\zeta\,;$$

$$r_0^4\,;\ \theta_0^{2\pi}\,.$$

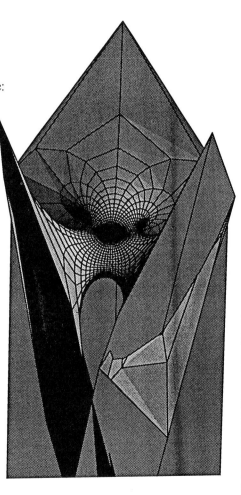

**Figure 8**   *Another trinoid.*

```
(* Klein bottle of Paul Chang, paul@math.ucla.edu *)
<< Graphics/ParametricPlot3D.m
bot = { (2.5 + 1.5 cos[v]) cos[u], (2.5 + 1.5 cos[v]) sin[u], -2.5 sin[v] }
mid = { (2.5 + 1.5 cos[v]) cos[u], (2.5 + 1.5 cos[v]) sin[u], 3v }
han = { 2 – 2 cos[v] + sin[u], cos[u], 3v }
top = { 2 + (2 + cos[u]) cos[v], sin[u], 3Pi + (2 + cos[u]) sin[v] }
us = {u, 0, 2Pi, Pi/8 }
vs = { v, 0, Pi, Pi/8 }
p = ParametricPlot3D
bottom = p[bot, us, vs]
middle = p[mid, us, vs]
topper = p[top, us, vs]
handle = p[han, us, vs]
Show [handle, topper,
middle, bottom]
```

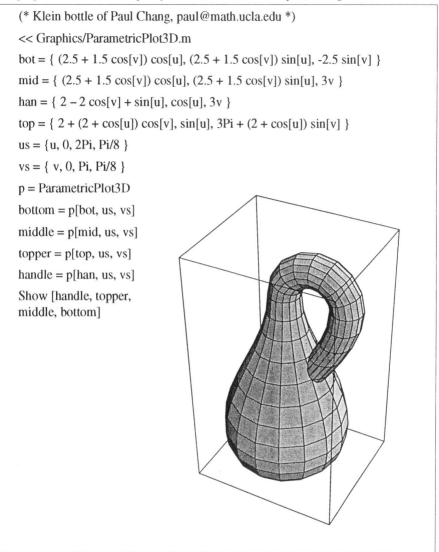

**Figure 9**    *Klein Bottle,* Mathematica Graphics3D[] from the accompanying code.
© 1991 Paul Chang, University of California.

restricted to either a single-valued orthographic or cylindrical mapping of the surface.
In order to digitize a subject's limbs and torso, many separate scans of the torso and
limbs must be made. The subject must be moved to relocate the cylindrical axis of each
scan, and the separate scans must be cut and re-assembled in data form.

Four Kot (of Stewart Dickson):

$X(u, v) = \beta(u) + r\cos v N(u) + r\sin v B(u)$

Where:

$\beta(u) = (10\cos u + \cos 3u + \cos 2u + \cos 4u,\ 6\sin u + 10\sin 3u,$

$$4\sin 3u \sin\frac{5u}{2} + 4\sin 4u - r\sin 6u)\ ;$$

$N(u) = \dfrac{d^2\beta}{du}\ ;$

$B(u) = \dfrac{dN}{du} + \dfrac{d\beta}{du}\ ;$

$u_0^{2\pi}\ ; v_0^{2\pi}\ .$

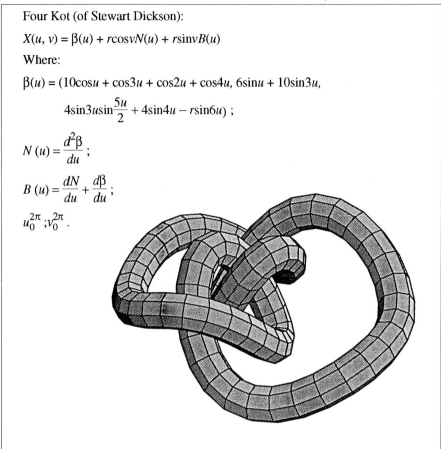

**Figure 10** *Four knot,* Mathematica Graphics3D[]. © Stewart Dickson courtesy of The Post Group and Wolfram Research, Inc.

## Conclusions

Let me sum up this essay by stating some practical uses for my plastic models of mathematical formulas. A physical *stereolithography* model can help researchers understand a complicated mathematical surface better than a picture of it on a two-dimensional screen. They can hold a model at any angle, and even place their fingers into the nooks and crannies. I would assume that my models would be quite useful for blind people attempting to understand mathematical surfaces.

One can hypothesize that in the future, rather than looking at a computer screen to visualize a scientific model, you'll be able to press a button and walk away with a physical model. It's interesting to speculate what this capability would do for both science and art.

# References

1   McCormick, Bruce H. *et al.* (ed.). July, 1987. *Visualization in Scientific Computing,* Report to the National Science Foundation Panel on Graphics, Image Processing and Workstations.

2   Appleton, Jon H. and Perera, Ronald C., (eds.). 1975. *The Development and Practice of Electronic Music.* Prentice Hall, Englewood Cliffs.

3   Dickson, Stewart. 1981. *Stringed Instrument with Electrical Feedback,* United States Patent 4,248,120, February 3.

4   Dickson, Stewart, 1982. "On Electronic Strings in Live Performance: Design and Construction of an Electroacoustic Monochord", *Perspectives of New Music,* Volume 20, Nos. 1 and 2, Fall-Winter 1981, Spring-Summer.

5   *The Quarterly,* Journal of the International Society of Copier Artists, 800 West End Avenue, New York, NY 10025.

6   Kernighan, Brian W. 1982. *PIC – A Graphics Language for Typesetting,* Bell Laboratories Computing Science Technical Report Number 85, Murray Hill, New Jersey 07974, March.

7   Jaques, Beth. 1988. "Desktop Manufacturing" Creates Realistic 3D Models, *BME,* June.

8   Wolfram, Stephen. 1988. *Mathematica: A System for Doing Mathematics by Computer.* Addison Wesley, Redwood City.

9   Dickson, Stewart. Manufacturing the Impossible Soap Bubble. *Iris Universe,* Number 12.

10  Mahoney, Diana. 1991. Art Appreciation. *Computer Graphics World,* **14**(4) April.

11  Bill, Max. 1949. The Mathematical Approach in Contemporary Art, *Werk,* Number 3, Winterthur.

12  Wohlers, Terry, T. 1990. Practical Prototypes. *Computer Graphics World,* March.

13  Muybridge, Eadweard. 1984. *The Male and Female Figures in Motion.* Dover, New York.

14  Partch, Harry. 1974. *The Genesis of a Music.* Da Capo Press, New York.

15  Brooks, Frederick P. Jr *et al.* "Project GROPE - Haptic Displays for Scientific Visualization", *SIGGRAPH '90 Conference Proceedings.*

# The Future of Weather and Climate Prediction

## Thomas T. Warner

*Department of Meteorology and Earth System Science Center, The Pennsylvania State University, 503 Walker Building, University Park, PA 16802, USA*

## Bill Buzbee

*Scientific Computing Division, The National Center for Atmospheric Research, PO Box 3000, Boulder, CO 80307-3000, USA*

*Predicting the weather and climate is difficult because it requires the numerical solution of a complex set of equations that describe atmospheric, oceanic and terrestrial processes. Numerical processing of these equations, as well as the processing of the immense geophysical data sets that are required to define the initial and boundary conditions for the equations, require the use of extremely fast supercomputing systems. We review the computational needs of atmospheric simulation during the next decade, and provide an illustration of this using the requirements for global climate simulation.*

## Introduction

Atmospheric science is a discipline that has traditionally pushed the limits of computing technology. For example, the first electronic computer was constructed at Princeton University in the 1940s for the purpose of numerical weather prediction, and the National Center for Atmospheric Research (NCAR) had the first federally funded unclassified supercomputing facility. Advanced computer hardware has always been needed because the numerical models that are used in the simulation of atmospheric processes are very computationally demanding. The equations that govern the fluid dynamics and thermodynamics of atmospheric motion must be applied over a vast range of spatial and temporal scales, encompassing planetary circulations at one extreme and individual cloud processes and small scale turbulence at the other. Also, numerous physical processes must be treated in the models, either explicitly or through parameterization. These include:

- absorption and emission of radiation by the atmosphere;
- turbulent transfer of heat, momentum and moisture in the planetary boundary layer and the free-atmosphere above;

43

- the atmospheric hydrologic cycle, including the production of clouds and precipitation;

- the thermal energy balance and the hydrology of the surface layers of the earth that exchange heat and moisture with the atmosphere;

- biospheric processes and their effects on the atmospheric and surface hydrologic cycles, and on the chemical composition of the atmosphere; and

- ocean circulations, and specifically their effect on sea-surface temperatures.

These processes can be treated using models of various sophistication. Climate simulations of tens to hundreds of years ideally require calculation of such things as the fluxes of natural and man-made gases at the earth's surface, formation and movement of sea ice, changes in plant type and distribution, and the deep-ocean circulation. Weather prediction models require a detailed representation of the phase changes among the vapor, liquid and solid forms of water in the atmosphere, with attention given to such things as changes in the droplet-size distribution within clouds, conversion from cloud droplets to raindrops, and the chemical and physical nature of the microscopic particles in the atmosphere that serve as nuclei on which cloud droplets condense. Air-pollution modeling applications require the simulation of hundreds of chemical reactions among gases, particles and liquid water in the atmosphere; the turbulent dispersion of pollutants; and the pollution "washout" effects of cloud and precipitation.

Computing power influences the accuracy of atmospheric simulations in two ways. First, physical processes of the sort noted above generally can be more-faithfully represented in the models when relatively sophisticated, but computationally intensive, approaches are used. Secondly, for the purpose of computation, space is usually discretized on a three-dimensional checkerboard-like grid. Decreasing the horizontal and vertical grid increments will reduce numerical error in the atmospheric wave amplitudes and speeds, as well as allow the model to simulate small scale but important weather phenomena. However, the time step used in the numerical integration of the equations is usually linearly related to the spatial grid increment. Thus, if we halve the horizontal and vertical grid increments over a given domain, it will increase the number of grid points by a factor of eight, and increase the computational requirements by a factor of sixteen because twice as many time steps will be needed for each grid point. It is important to recognize here that such improvements in the representation of physical processes or in the spatial resolution cannot be always achieved simply by allowing the model to run for a longer period on the processor. One reason for this is that many applications of these models are for the rapid production of public weather forecasts (*i.e.* operational forecasts), and thus the model atmosphere must evolve much more quickly than the real atmosphere for the output to be useful as a forecast. For example, a 24 hour forecast should be available to the forecaster within one to two hours of the initiation of the forecast cycle. Another reason is that some of the simulations, especially of global climate change, already require thousands of hours of supercomputer processor time. Figure 1 provides evidence of the trend in the forecast skill of the

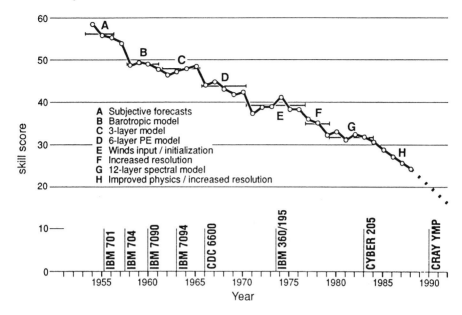

**Figure 1** *Record of the accuracy of 36 hour weather predictions at 500 mb ( 18,000 feet) over North America by the US National Weather Service. The skill score is a measure of the accuracy of the prediction of the height (hence, wind) on the 500 mb pressure surface, where a value of 70 reflects no useful skill and a score of 20 is excellent.[1]*

operational weather prediction models of the US National Weather Service. The graph shows a steady decrease in this representative measure of model forecast error as the increased computing power has allowed for better spatial resolution in the models and more sophisticated treatment of physical processes. The use of improved models, noted in A through H (insert), and the better computers listed on the time axis, have produced a relatively steady increase in forecast accuracy. It is generally believed, however, that there are inherent limits to atmospheric predictability. These limits are related to the chaotic nature of the atmospheric flow and the strong scale interactions that occur. Thus, even though better data for the models, and faster computers, will certainly continue to cause further decreases in the forecast error, it will never reach zero.

## The Next Decade - Atmospheric Simulation On Teraflop Computers

There are two main forces that will govern the computational needs of the atmospheric sciences over the next decade. One is related to the modernization of the U.S. National Weather Service and the operational forecasting services in other countries. This involves the installation and utilization of new radar- and satellite-based remote sensing systems that will provide weather data of unprecedented quality, and spatial and

**Figure 2**   *Photograph of a well-defined debris-filled tornado, near Wheatland, PA, on 31 May 1985, by Richard M. Cione of Farrell – the strongest recorded tornado in Pennsylvania history.*

temporal density. The availability of these data will reduce one of the major historical limitations to the improvement of numerical weather forecasts – that is, the coarse resolution of the upper atmospheric data that are now used as input to the forecast models. However, in order to capitalize upon this large national investment in measurement-system hardware, the spatial resolution of the weather prediction models that use the data will need to be improved significantly. For the reasons noted above, this will require a great increase in computer speed. There is a great economic and human incentive for improving forecast accuracy. For the first time there is hope that we will be able to explicitly predict some of the most life-threatening weather phenomena, such as the thunderstorm complexes that spawned the tornado shown in Figure 2. Unfortunately, these phenomena are often small in scale and difficult to predict. They include heavy-rainfall and flash-flood producing thunderstorm systems, and dangerous windshear zones near airports.

There is a second factor that will drive up the demand for computer resources in the next decade. We will need to make a quantitative assessment of the climate change that is likely to be associated with anthropogenic modifications to our environment. This includes the addition of carbon dioxide to the atmosphere through combustion of fossil fuels, and the release of other optically active trace gases. For this effort, there are a number of well-funded national research programs being planned in numerous countries, and most of these will involve the computationally demanding numerical simulation of the global atmosphere and related physical systems. As explained earlier, in these climate models there are numerous physical processes that need to be accounted for in order that their interaction with the atmospheric system be represented. It is this large number of physical subsystems, and the very-long-period simulations, that make climate prediction so computationally demanding. A good example is the high resolution simulation of basin-scale ocean circulations, a computational feat that was not feasible prior to the availability of the current generation of supercomputers. Such models will need to be coupled to the models of atmospheric climate, even thought they often require thousands of hours of processor time themselves.

Weather prediction in the future will require massively parallel computing techniques. Of historical interest is the fact that Lewis F. Richardson, generally deemed the "father of numerical weather prediction", first proposed the parallel solution of the equations of atmospheric motion over 50 years ago. Before the advent of electronic computers, he formulated the numerical approximations to the differential equations that constitute the mathematical basis of the weather prediction models,[2] and suggested how the equations could be solved in parallel. The system involved the use of a large number of human processors working simultaneously, each assigned the task of calculating the value of a specific term in the equations for a given grid point. A manager of the processors would orchestrate the summing of the terms and the exchange of data with adjacent grid points for each new time step. Even though this vision of modern numerical weather prediction was partially realized some 20 years later when sequential computations were performed on the first electronic computer, it is only now astonishingly evident how far ahead of his time Richardson was with his idea of parallel computations.

## Climate Simulation - An Example of the Computational Needs

Over the next five to ten years, we will advance our ability to model the global climate. Current global models tend to substantially disagree in their predictions about the future climate. This is due in part to a requirement for more computing power than is readily available and to a need for improved treatment of physical processes in models. Improving the treatment of physical processes will require basic research, as well as storage of and access to observational data that are global in space and multidecadal in time.

### Computing Requirements

The computing requirements are dominated by three factors. First, there is a considerable concern that the climate may change on a regional basis and at a relatively rapid rate. If the change is regional and rapid, then obviously the impact on regional economies and ecosystems could be profound. Thus, we need information about climate change on a regional basis, and this implies that our simulations must resolve spatial scales of approximately one degree in latitude and longitude and have some twenty to

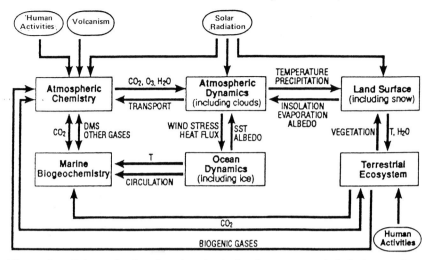

**Figure 3**   *Schematic showing the physical subsystems and their interactions that must be included in a complete model of the global climate. Temperature is abbreviated as "T".*

forty levels in the vertical. Second, the model must also incorporate the interactions among the atmosphere, oceans, land masses, and so forth (see Figure 3). Finally, climate simulation must span at least several decades. Thus, the computational requirements of climate modeling are dominated by the need for regional resolution, the need to couple atmospheric models with models of the ocean and terrestrial systems, and the requirements for decade-to-century-long simulations.

Most climate simulations that have been performed to date:

- couple only the atmosphere and oceans, with no terrestrial systems modeled

- use a simple (*e.g.* single slab) ocean, and

- use low resolution.

Incorporation of the deep ocean into climate models is particularly important because oceans distribute heat and are a sink for greenhouse gases. Due to associated computational requirements, only three 100-year climate simulations have been done using a deep ocean model coupled to an atmospheric model. For example, the Washington-Meehl[3] simulation used the following resolution:

- Atmosphere 5 x 7.5 degrees horizontal grid length

     9 vertical layers

- Ocean     5 degrees horizontal grid length

     4 vertical layers

Clearly, this was a low-resolution simulation, yet about 1,200 CPU hours were required on a CRAY X-MP. (Note that this computation would require over 10,000 years on a personal computer.)

To obtain a perspective on what will be required for high resolution, coupled atmospheric/ocean simulations, let us review the respective computational requirements of high-resolution forecast models and high-resolution global ocean models. The European Centre for Medium-range Weather Forecasts (ECMWF) has extensive experience with high-resolution forecast models. Based on that experience,[4] estimates of computational requirements for high-resolution, multidecadal climate simulations on the CRAY Y-MP are:

- Y-MP/8: 1°grid, 19 levels, 75-150 wall-clock hours/decade simulated,

- Y-MP/16: 1°grid, 19 levels, 15-30 wall-clock hours/decade simulated, and

- Y-MP/16: 0.5°grid, 19 levels, 120-240 wall-clock hours/decade simulated.

(These estimates assume that all available processors are used in parallel. [The Y-MP/8 has eight processors; the Y-MP/16 has 16 processors.]) Note that a calendar week has 168 wall-clock hours. Thus, the above estimates show that, even if the most powerful supercomputers available are dedicated to high-resolution climate simulations, it would take several weeks to complete a single, multidecadal simulation. Also, these estimates do not reflect the additions to models that will have to be incorporated to improve the treatment of physical processes. With respect to computational requirements for ocean simulation, recent work of Semtner and Chervin[5] provides quantitative performance data. Semtner and Chervin completed the first high resolution global ocean simulation. Again, using all available processors in parallel, the associated requirements are:

- Y-MP/8; 0.5°grid, 20 levels, 200 wall-clock hours/decade simulated.

Both the ECMWF and Semtner/Chervin models sustain 1.0–1.5 gigaflops when executing on the Y-MP/8. Based on the above performances, we see that a high resolution, coupled atmosphere-ocean model running at 1.0–1.5 gigaflops will require one-half to one month per decade simulated. Thus, to routinely do such simulations over several decades, and do so within a reasonable period of calendar time (a few days), we will need computers that can sustain about 100 gigaflops. If all the physical process components illustrated in Figure 3 are incorporated, then we will probably need a teraflop computer.

## Use of Highly Parallel Systems

Probably the only way to achieve and sustain speeds of 100–1,000 gigaflops is via highly parallel systems. This is due to the fact that the speed of a single processor is limited by the finite time required to propagate signals within the computer. Fortunately, VLSI technology has made possible very powerful microprocessors and high-density chips, and as a result, parallel systems have been commercially available since the early 1980s. Today, the microprocessors used in these systems deliver from 5 to 25 megaflops on Fortran source code and in 64 bit precision. This performance is expected to double every 12 to 24 months. So by 1995, a system with a few thousand processors may be able to sustain 100 gigaflops. And by the end of the century, sustained performance at one teraflop is feasible. Of course, a key question is whether climate simulation is amenable to parallel computation. Already, substantial research is underway to explore the applicability of highly parallel computers to the climate problem. Decisive results should be available within the next twelve to twenty-four months, and there is considerable optimism among the researchers involved.

## The Data Storage Problem

The NCAR supercomputer center is heavily used by scientists engaged in climate simulation. In recent years, NCAR has observed that its user community is archiving about 0.5 megabytes of model output for every gigaflop executed. Thus, sustained performance at 0.5 gigaflops (*e.g.* the Y-MP/8) necessitates storage of about 7.5 terabytes per year, and sustained performance at 100 gigaflops would necessitate storage of 1.5 petabytes per year. The volume of observational data available in the 1990s may be comparable to the volume of model output data (terabytes per year). For example, storage of data from NASA's Earth Observing System Distributed Information System will require approximately one petabyte per year. It is a common observation that, in most scientific and engineering disciplines, data generation outstrips the ability of scientist and engineers to store and access the information. The data archiving requirements of climate research in the 1990s will far exceed the capability of today's storage technology. Fortunately, in the 1990s, technology is becoming available that will improve storage density, access time, and transfer rate by at least an order of magnitude.

## Data Analysis and Access

It is highly desirable that climate model output and observational data be easily accessible by a large and diverse university research community. Once completed, scientists need the ability to easily compare simulations at various points in time and space. Similar access and analysis capabilities are needed for observational data. Data must be visualized, compared with other datasets,and processed/reduced for distribution to collaborating scientists. In the late 1990s, the workstation will be the center of the computational universe in the sense that the workstation will be the primary tool that scientists and engineers use to carry out and manage their computational work. Workstations will retrieve "sizable chunks" (but subsets) of observed and model-output data from remote archives, and analyze the data. This means that supercomputers and data archives must appear as attached resources to workstations. That, in turn, implies a need for high-speed local and wide-area networks with which to support distributed file systems and distributed visualization (computer graphics). We must also improve the "bandwidth" for information access and exchange by collaborative researchers. For example, we need electronic mail that includes graphics, equations, spreadsheets, voice, and even video. We also need distributed databases that support efficient search and retrieval of a variety of scientific data types. To efficiently accomplish this distribution requires a close coupling of storage, supercomputers, and visualization workstations via high-speed networks.

## *Synopsis*

Over the next decade, we will improve our ability to model the climate over regional spatial scales and decades of time. To realize this opportunity, we must use highly parallel computers. We must also improve the treatment of physical processes in models. Model improvement and validation require easy access to vast amounts of global observations of the climate. Similarly, comparative analyses of simulations require storage of, and access to, large amounts of output from simulations. Fortunately, emerging developments in parallel processing, workstations, data storage, and networking technologies make all of this feasible. In fact, by suitable integration of:

- dedicated, high-performance computers,

- capacious data storage archives,

- powerful, software-rich workstations,

- and very-high-speed networks

we have the possibility of creating a global climate change "distributed laboratory" as shown in Figure 4.

## Summary

The numerical simulation of the global climate system and the improved numerical prediction of weather during the next decade will require substantial increases in computer processor speed, data storage capacity, and network speed and bandwidth. In the case of modern weather prediction, this need is dictated by the order of magnitude increase in the volume of meteorological data that will be available from new sensing systems for use in the numerical prediction models. Effective utilization of these data by the improved, but much more computationally demanding, weather prediction models has the potential to reduce the loss of life by providing better warning of hazardous weather-related events such as flash floods and wind-shears near airports. The simulation of climate change by global models of the atmosphere will allow us to assess the long- and short-term impacts of the many ways in which mankind is modifying the Earth system. For example, we need further information about the possibility of the global warming which may result from the enhancing of the "greenhouse effect" by the anthropogenic release of carbon dioxide and other radiatively active gases.

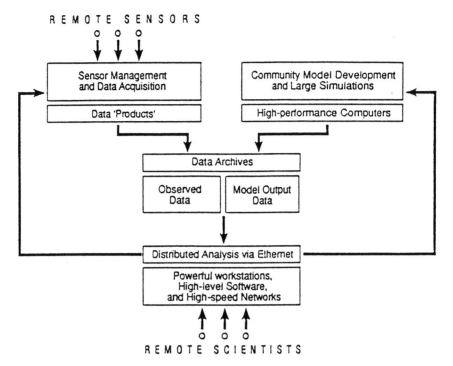

**Figure 4**    *A global-climate change "distributed laboratory" showing how scientists working at diverse laboratories can interact with data and models.*

## Acknowledgements

The first author's (TTW) preparation of this manuscript was supported by the Earth System Science Center under NASA Contract NASA 5-30556. The manuscript was capably typed by Ms Joann Singer.

## References

1    Shuman, F.G., 1989. History of numerical weather prediction at the National Meteorological Center. *Weather and Forecasting,* **4,** 286–296.
2    Richardson, L.F., 1922 (reprinted 1965). *Weather Prediction by Numerical Process.* Dover, New York.
3    Washington, W. and G. Meehl, 1989. Climate sensitivity due to increased $CO_2$; experiments with a coupled atmosphere and ocean general circulation model. *Climate Dynamics,* **4,** 1–38.
4    Burridge, D. (ECMWF), 1990. Private communication.
5    Semtner, A. and R. Chervin, 1988. A simulation of the global ocean circulation with resolved eddies, *J. Geophys. Res.,* **93,** 15502–15522.

# Computers and Human Communication

## Davis Albert Foulger

*IBM Thomas J. Watson Research Center, PO Box 218, Yorktown Heights, NY 10598, USA*

*In this chapter I describe how computers have affected human communication. I also show a graphical method for visualizing the relationships between different types of media such as electronic mail, computer conferences, and electronic bulletin boards. New computer media, such as virtual reality and hypermedia, are discussed. The future of these new ways of communicating will change the way we learn, interact with other people, and seek entertainment.*

## Computers and Human Communication

Today, computers are used to help people talk to one another. In fact, for those who use computers as a routine element of their work, the impact of computer media on communication with others is increasingly obvious. For these individuals, the computer now mediates a large percentage of their daily interaction, in part because computer-based communication brings diversely located people together who might otherwise be unaware of each other. Foulger[1] finds that computer mediated communication is becoming a dominant mode of interaction in IBM, with total use of electronic mail significantly surpassed only by face to face interaction. These results, shown in Table 1, do not represent a complete profile of media use. Survey participants were only asked about two computer media and ten media overall. Still, the media surveyed are certainly those one might expect to be the most important in a information intensive business environment like IBM.

Among these media, face-to-face interaction is used significantly more than any other. Publications, television, and electronic mail are all used at about the same rate, but significantly more than any of the remaining media. Group meetings, computer conferencing, and the radio stand out as a second such cluster. The remaining media, including the telephone, correspondence, and lectures, all record significantly less use. Electronic mail in IBM is barely more than 15 years old. Computer conferencing (*i.e.* publically appendable electronic bulletin boards) in IBM are just coming up to their tenth anniversary. Nevertheless, both electronic mail and computer conferencing are widely used relative to long established media.

These results would not surprise Hiltz and Turoff,[2] who have projected computer conferencing as a revolutionary medium of communication with the potential to make

McLuhan's[3] "global village" an interpersonal reality (p. xxix). Indeed, they surpass Turoff's[4] expectation that computer conferencing will eventually "become as commonly used by the general public as the telephone is today." At least within IBM, both computer conferencing and electronic mail use significantly surpass telephone use. Hence it may well be, as Keisler[5] has suggested, that computer conferencing "has much in common with past technical innovations, like the telephone and the typewriter, that have had great social impact". Indeed, other results detailed in Foulger's[1] study of one particularly successful computer conferencing facility in IBM indicate that the impact of these media inside IBM has been very substantial – arguably even revolutionary.

## Keyboards are Just the Beginning

Today's keyboard-oriented computer conferencing and electronic mail are just two of several computer media that may enhance and possibly change the ways in which people communicate with each other. As yet underdeveloped computer media, including hypermedia, multi-modal documents incorporating combinations of text, graphics, image, voice, video, and other presentation formats, voice-into-text concurrent interaction, and virtual reality (simulated environments in which the user is made to feel as if the simulation is "real"), hold the promise of more radical changes yet to come. It may be that all of these possibilities will be successful. It is more likely, however, that one or a few will attract huge audiences and a large range of applications, that some will be moderately successful in niche applications, and that most will fail.

Many of the proposed futuristic modes of communication just mentioned are often absent in popular portrayals of the future. Indeed, most of these alternatives appear to be largely irrelevant in "Star Trek: The Next Generation". Here painting remains the pinnacle of art, Shakespeare remains the pinnacle of theatre, and face-to-face communication retains its dominance, aided by technology that allows people to "beam" from one place to another and technology that allows city-sized starships to travel across the galaxy at warp speeds. When, for whatever reason, we cannot warp or beam across the space that divides us, we view each other on wall sized videoconference screens. The effect of computer communication in this 23rd century vision of human communication is seen in two venues. First, the computer acts as a repository for human knowledge – a huge multi-modal "memex"[6] that can find source material to answer almost any already-answered question almost instantaneously. Second, the computer creates the ultimate virtual reality in "holodeck" recreations where a viewer can walk through a realistic setting indistinguishable from the real world.

This vision of human communication in the distant future is probably as reasonable as any that can be imagined right now. Shakespeare has weathered 500 years and seems likely to find continuing relevance in a distant future that will continue to value live performance. Although technologies for beaming people across space and eclipsing light speed are unlikely given our current understanding of the way the universe works, face-to-face communication will probably persist in its dominance of all other media. Something like a computer probably will replace libraries as the repository of accumulated human knowledge. Something like a holodeck probably will bring users into remote and alien frames, although perhaps not with the full sensory reality associated with Star Trek's holodeck.

Still, Star Trek's vision of the future of communication does not satisfy, especially given the wide range of media that already exist and the early success of computer conferencing and electronic mail. The question, then, remains: What kind of impact will computer media have on human communication in the foreseeable future?

## Making Tracks through Media Space

I have suggested (in ref. 1) a new way of understanding the ways in which people create and evolve human communication media to meet their needs. This process of media creation and evolution is particularly obvious in computer conferencing but which is clearly evident in many media. The success of a medium, according to this theoretical perspective, is a function of its relative costs and benefits to its prospective users, with key benefits measurable in the distinctive applications to which a given medium is applied. The perspective suggests that media with similar characteristics compete for the same applications, with one medium's success usually obtained at the expense of others.

Media, in this perspective, occupy positions in a "media space" that is directly analogous to the "animal space" proposed by Dawkins.[7] Let me explain. There are an infinite variety of possible media (protomedia), but only a few succeed. Each successful medium is distinguished by its ability to ply one or more "trades" or applications better than its competitors. Computer media, like all other protomedia, must succeed in the face of a variety of existing media, each of which is entrenched in its use for specific applications. Success, in the face of such competition, must come through either displacing other media from applications or creating new trades that do not, as yet, have competition.

Evidence for these ideas can be found in Foulger's[1] typology of 53 media, a representation of which is shown in Figure 1. This representation shows six clusters of media, each of which represents a generalized set of trades. These clusters are depicted in a three dimensional space. Audience size occupies the vertical, with mass media found nearer the top and interpersonal media found closer to the bottom. Bandwidth (the amount of information transmitted via the medium at any given time) occupies the dimension extending to the right from this vertical, with higher bandwidth media found near the left wall and lower bandwidth media found in the right foreground. Dynamism (a combination of interactiveness and message persistence) extending to the left from the vertical, with more dynamic media found near the right rear wall and less dynamic media found in the left foreground.

The six clusters of media occupy distinct vectors through this multi-dimensional space. Face-to-face media are found deep in the media space, extending up from the bottom rear and intersecting, about midway across the bandwidth wall, with an almost perpendicular vector associated with telephone media. Correspondence media occupy the bottom left foreground. Television and radio media occupy the upper right foreground. Publishing media occupy the middle upper foreground. Film and art media

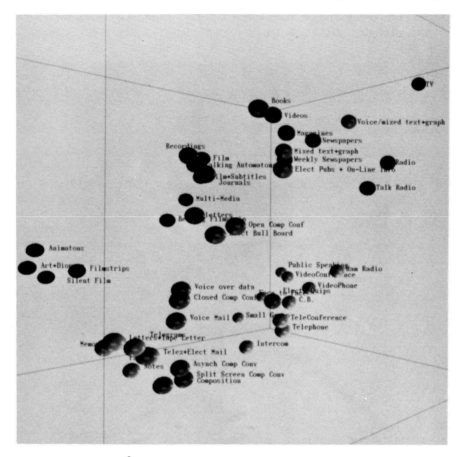

**Figure 1.**  Foulger's[3] typology of media.

describe a vector across the dynamism wall, attracting larger audiences as dynamism increases.

What is interesting, in this depiction, is the relationship of these media to each other and, in particular, the relationship of computer media to these media. Specifically:

- Where two media occupy the same space, as written letters and tape letters do, one (written letters) is highly successful and the other (tape letters) is a comparatively unsuccessful late-comer to the same trades.

- The most successful new media of the last hundred years, which should certainly include telephones, radio, movies, and television, all start out occupying relatively unique niches in the depicted media space. Indeed, what is arguably the most successful of these media, television, retains a highly distinctive niche, well away from all other media, and faces no real competition from other proto-media.

• Current computer media occupy the center ground between four of these clusters of media. Computer media associated with correspondence trend over toward publishing and telephone media. Computer media associated with publishing trend over toward broadcast, correspondence, and telephone media. Computer media associated with telephony stretch toward correspondence.

• Computer conferencing sits alone, almost dead center in this and other representations of media space, indicating that it too has a relatively distinctive position.

• Several locations in the media space remain entirely uninhabited. In particular one notes the absence of high bandwidth, high dynamism media that reach large audiences. One also notes, given the propensity of computer media to find the middle ground between clusters of existing media, that gaps in the direction of face-to-face and film and art media remain unfilled. These gaps may represent an incomplete survey of existing media. They may also indicate opportunities waiting for a new medium.

The first of these observations serve to support the perspective that media with similar characteristics do indeed compete for the same applications. The second supports the notion that the surest route to success for a medium is finding a way to avoid competition. The third suggests that computer media are opening new ground in media space, with the fourth suggesting that computer conferencing is particularly distinctive. The last observation suggests that there is much untapped ground in media space that remains to be occupied by as yet non-existent media. Much of the rest of this paper will be dedicated to exploring computer media that may succeed in these newly occupied and unoccupied spaces.

## Computer Media and the Middle Ground

With the observation that *computer media occupy the center of this media space* we begin to reach a better understanding of the role the computer plays in communication media. Conventional assessments of the characteristics of computer media dwell on such characteristics as asynchrony, written form, transcripts, immediacy, shared memory, and the integration of the communication process with other activities.[8] Perhaps the most important characteristic the computer brings to its media, however, is flexibility. Computer media can create a middle ground between other clusters of media because the mediators associated with computer media can be manipulated to highly specific ends.

Consider, for instance, computer conferencing. Public computer conferencing in the style Foulger[1] observed in IBM occupies the middle ground of Figure 1. One can, however, by simply restricting access to a select group of people, create a variant of computer conferencing that is very correspondencelike in its characteristics. By contrast, one can also create a very publishing-like variant by simply adding a person (an editor) that screen contributions before they are posted and schedule their distribution. One notes that these three variants of computer media form a nearly perfect vector across the media space. The changes entailed in this distribution are small. Indeed, all three variants can be implemented by enforcing different rules using the same software.

Many other variations of computer conferencing, electronic publishing, and electronic mail should also be possible with only small changes in the rules that govern existing computer conferencing software, the interfaces that are available for authoring and viewing computer mediated information, and the filters used in computer media to select, order, control, and systematically modify that information. The flexibility offered in these variations should be such that no computer media need ever exactly match the characteristics or trades of an existing medium. It can be expected, then, that computer media will continue to find success in merging the characteristics of existing media in new ways.

## Multi-modal Documents

Multi-modal documents (sometimes called multi-media or compound documents) combine two or more presentation formats, possibly including text, graphics, image, sound, voice, and video in integrated documents. Such combinations are, of course, hardly new. Newspapers have integrated text, image, and graphics for over 100 years. Magazines, books, movies, television, and multi-media presentations have all combined such formats to differing degrees. Computer media remain relatively young, however, and while the computer has proven to be a valuable tool for producing newspapers, books, and other hard copy documents that combine text, voice, and image, it has yet to achieve any general solution to the problem of sharing multi-modal electronic documents.

The biggest problem for such documents is standards. There are only two generally used formats for computer text representation, the international standard ASCII format and IBM's widely used EBCDIC. These two representations of the English language character set readily translate to each other, moreover, making it possible to automatically translate documents from one format to the other with minimal losses or, more commonly, perfect fidelity. This relatively high level of standardization has made it possible for text based computer media like computer conferencing and electronic mail to become highly successful, at least within IBM.

The same cannot be said of graphics, image, sound, voice, or video storage formats, where a growing variety of often incompatible "standards" contend for dominance, or even for the ways in which these formats are joined to create multi-modal documents. Assuming such standards are agreed upon, and there are at least six major format groups in which agreement needs to be reached, there remain other problems to be solved. Text generation remains a fairly simple task on a computer, and recording voice and facsimile images is probably similarly simple. Generation of graphics, video, and sound, by contrast, remains a more complex enterprise. Each of these elements of multi-modal documents require both substantial storage and transmission capacities (which are just beginning to be realized) and major user interface solutions if they are to become widely used.

Computer graphics tools continue to improve, but are hampered by limited graphic interface devices. Signing your name with a mouse or trackball is an almost impossible exercise that readily demonstrates this need. Video entails even greater complications, and unless one is willing to stay very still, taking a picture of oneself talking requires a second person operating the camera. Here again, interfaces can be improved with intelligent camera control computer software that can recognize the image it should track and then do so. If these problems aren't solved, multi-modal documents that incorporate graphics and, in particular, video will remain largely a mass production medium, more similar in its characteristics to books, newspapers, and Filmstrips than to interpersonal correspondence or telephone media.

Applied to Figure 1, the effect of multi-modal documents should be to increase the bandwidth associated with publication and correspondence media. This appears to be the case for the two multi-modal document media presented in the figure. Voice over data (text with voice annotation) is presented above, to the right, and somewhat behind correspondence media, indicating a movement toward both publishing and telephone media. These general directions indicate larger audiences, increased dynamism, and increased bandwidth relative to other correspondence media.

This appears to be what is happening in what is perhaps the most successful multi-modal media venture thus far, Videotex systems like PRODIGY™. Although neither correspondence nor daily news delivered by PRODIGY are multi-modal, many of its features and virtually all of its advertising are. PRODIGY already has a readership that exceeds that of all but the largest newspapers and features highly dynamic multi-modal features and advertising.

Voice over mixed text and graphics appears to the right and somewhat behind publishing media stretching over in the direction of television. Mixed video, text, and graphics should move even further in that direction, clustering more closely with television and radio media than it does with publishing media. Indeed, if structured into hypermedia (see following), such a medium might make the closest approach to television of any medium yet devised, but with non-linear cross reference capabilities that should create a wealth of distinctive new applications.

## Hypermedia

Hypermedia allows a user to explore text in a non-sequential matter. Let me explain. Hypermedia describes a potentially non-linear mode of document organization that differs strongly from the usual format of books, newspapers, movies, television, and radio formats. Traditional documents, whether letters, books, newspapers, or movies, have a linear, sequential organization. One idea is typically presented at a time, with one following another in some structured manner. If two or more facets of the same idea must be presented, they are sequenced, with one shown before the others. Ideas may be presented together at the beginning of end of a sequence, but will be serialized in a specific author-determined order in the body of the document.

Hypermedia breaks this serialization by allowing a text to be organized in a non-sequential manner. A frame that introduces two ideas together will most likely point to two or more other frames that explain the ideas with additional detail. These frames may themselves point to additional frames of related or detail information. Except for the paths by which frames are joined, the order in which these frames are read, if at all, is left to the reader.

It is helpful, in visualizing hypermedia documents, to think of them as a cave system in which passages diverge and intersect in several dimensions. Getting from the entrance to the cave to a river a quarter mile underground may require use of a series of passages and chambers, with each passage accessible by only a limited number of paths. If you are exploring, the cave system will allow you to stray from the path into interesting side passages. If you have a goal to achieve and know where you are going, you can travel quickly through the minimum number of passages.

It is clearly possible, in such a system, to build highly linear documents in which the side passages are mere footnotes. It is possible to build parallel serializations that occasionally intersect. But it is also possible to build highly convoluted knots of documents in which complex ideas express themselves in complex relationships. The flexibility associated with computers doesn't constrain hypermedia access to cave exploring. Indexes, tables of contents, and search engines can all be added to the viewer's interface possibilities, allowing them, in some sense, to "beam" straight into a given passage.

These structures change the way we view documents in important ways. They change the whole vocabulary of, and quite possibly the authoring style associated with, reading and writing. Letters and books no longer have meaningful page numbers. They simply have parallel frames that cross-reference each other in much the same way different books and articles reference each other. Each frame is, in some sense, a complete mini-document, and the resulting macro-document can be traversed flexibly according to the reader's wishes. The effect of these changes should be to make documents appear more dynamic and to increase their overall content. The effect should be correspondence and publishing related media that stretch across the dynamism dimension of Figure 1 in the direction of telephone and broadcast media, and across the bandwidth dimension in the direction of film and art.

This movement in media space should assure hypermedia some measure of distinctiveness and may prove very challenging, in particular, to newspapers. This trend will only be accentuated if, as will almost certainly be the case, computer hypermedia incorporate graphic, image, and video multi-media document technology. One notes, however, that it remains to be seen if hypermedia composition can be easy enough for hypermedia to be used in any but publication contexts. Given the difficulties currently associated with compound document composition, radical new interfaces appear to be a requirement for hypermedia correspondence applications are to be widely adopted.

## Voice-into-text Concurrent Interaction

Continuing progress in the area of computer voice recognition opens up possibilities for additional computer media including one that might be called "voice-into-text concurrent interaction" in which people talk to each other verbally but read a real time transcript of the text rather than listening. The major advantage of voice over text, given highly accurate transcription of voice into a textual transcript, is the relative speeds with which people can talk and write, read and listen. Other advantages can be found in reduced requirements for synchrony and turn taking and increasing opportunities for review relative to purely verbal (face-to-face and telephone) media.

The speed advantages are fairly obvious. Most people can talk at 140 to 150 words per minute with little effort but have difficulty creating new typewritten text at a rate better than 20 words per minute. By the same token, most people can read at a rate of at least 300 words per minute (and sometimes much more quickly), but are generally unable to listen at speeds much greater than 150 words per minute. In other words, where speed is the measure of a medium, voice is the preferred mode of text creation and reading is the preferred mode of text review.

This speed advantage is accentuated by reduced synchrony requirements, which allow two speakers to literally talk at each other continuously. When interacting via voice-into-text, there will frequently be no need for speaker A to wait until speaker B has finished before replying. Interaction, under these circumstances, becomes parallel and simultaneous in the manner that is usually associated with non-verbal interaction in face-to-face settings. The ability to review text easily may also enhance interaction speed, as the need to ask someone to repeat themselves (all too common in face-to-face and telephone exchange) will be reduced.

These advantages are clearly not obtained without cost. Much of the non-verbal dimension of face-to-face and, to a lesser extent, telephone verbal exchange will be lost in such exchanges, and computer substitutions for such non-verbal elements as pauses (...) and emphasis (boldface text) will be poor substitutes for this element of verbal interaction. Translation accuracy is also a potential issue, and voice-into-text may need to be augmented by an on-demand voice over text option that allows readers to occasionally review an associated voice transcript of the translated text.

Still, the advantages are potentially substantial, especially in contexts where the emphasis is on the sharing of information rather than affect. An individual might participate in several voice-into-text interactions simultaneously, work in a voice-into-text small group interaction environment, converse voice-into-text with one individual while interacting directly with another, *etc.* At extremes of translation, interactants might converse at some reasonable level without being able to speak a common language.

Viewed relative to Figure 1, one would expect media based on voice-into-text to fall somewhere in the gap separating telephone and correspondence media, but with an increased level of dynamism and information bandwidth that pulls it into unexplored media space in the general direction of face-to-face media. Voice-into-text concurrent interaction can be expected, then, to provide the basis for one or more primarily interpersonal media that break new ground in media space. The result should be a truly unique mode of interaction that may well provide the basis for a whole new cluster of what might be called translation media.

## Virtual Reality

Perhaps the most ambitious goals for computer mediation of human interaction are found in recent efforts to create "virtual realities" via computer. Virtual reality is, in some sense, a covering term for a wide range of experiments in computer interfaces, including video goggles, motion sensing data gloves, and other technologies that attempt to bring an observer into a dynamic and high bandwidth frame. Star Trek's "holodeck" is the ultimate virtual reality fantasy in which one can create and recreate alternate realities at will, interacting with real and imaginary others in a world of sight, sound, touch, taste, and smell. We're a long way from this kind of complete virtual reality, but the first steps on this path are being taken.

These first steps are more oriented to presentation than interaction. One direction of such development attempts to bring the viewer more closely into the frame of a video game. A virtual reality golf game would substitute a real golf club for the keyboard or joystick of today's video games. The behavior of the ball would be based on the swing of the club, contact with the ball would create tactile feedback, and a large screen TV or video goggle would create the impression of actually being on a golf course. This kind of recreation is already found in arcade simulations of automobiles and motorcycles, and can be expected to be extended, over time, to encompass a range of games and game activities.

It remains too early to say very much about the future of virtual reality, which will probably emerge as a half or dozen or more distinct mass media, including an individual and small group gaming medium, one or more presentation media, and one or more publishing media. If adequate interfaces and transmission bandwidth are established, moreover, there may be a variety of interpersonal virtual reality media, including a remote small group discussion medium and a virtual reality face-to-face telephone that might allow two people (mom and daughter; grandparents and grandchildren, boyfriend and girlfriend, *etc.*) to interact under the illusion that they were in the same room, perhaps even with some level of tactile interaction extend the possibilities for remote telephone-like interaction into the face-to-face realm.

What is clear is that virtual reality will break new ground in the media space of Figure 1 by occupying the high bandwidth, high dynamism space above face-to-face media. Traditionally, new ground in media space represents new opportunities, as-yet-unimagined applications, and breakthrough media that revolutionize the world in unimaginable ways. Virtual reality, more so than any of the other media described here, appears to have this potential for producing revolutionary media that change our world in fundamental ways.

# Conclusion

It is argued here that the early success of electronic mail and computer conferencing in the face of a wide range of existing media is just a beginning. When projected in a multidimensional media space, today's relatively low-bandwidth text-based computer media cluster with a variety of existing media, including telephone, correspondence, and publishing media (Figure 1). Interestingly, however, they form what can be thought of as a "seventh" cluster of media, a middle ground between existing clusters of media that unifies these clusters and creates new opportunities for mass interpersonal communication and more interactive correspondence. This middle ground gives computer media a distinctiveness, relative to other media, that probably helps to account for the rapidly growing success of electronic mail, computer conferencing, and electronic publishing.

New computer media, including multi-modal media, hypermedia, voice-into-text concurrent interaction, and virtual reality, appear to have characteristics that may make them even more distinctive. Multi-modal computer media should increase the bandwidth and, to a somewhat lesser extent, the dynamism associated with correspondence and publishing media, thus extending the possibilities associated with these media in the direction of both film and art media and television. Hypermedia should have a similar effect in increasing the dynamism and, to a lesser extent, the bandwidth, of these same media, thus pulling these clusters in the direction of television and telephone media. Voice-into-text concurrent interaction should increase the dynamism and, to a lesser extent, the bandwidth and audience sizes associated with telephone and correspondence media, thus stretching these clusters in the direction of face-to-face interactive media. Finally, the high bandwidth and dynamism associated with virtual reality promise to stretch the limits of face to face interaction and create a new cluster of interactive mass media in the empty space above face-to-face interaction.

The effect of these media, broadly stated, will first be to expand and fill in the computer mediated middle ground between existing clusters of media, and then to explore new ground. The effect of hypermedia, multi-modal media, and voice-into-text will be to expand this middle ground to encompass broadcast media (including computer mediated television and radio variants), film and art media, and, to a limited extent, face-to-face interactive media. Complexities of multi-modal and hypermedia production argue that such media will, at least initially, more likely be oriented to mass audiences. The general structure of voice-into-text argues that it will produce interpersonal media. Virtual reality, by contrast, promises to expand into the unexplored regions of highly dynamic, high bandwidth media space above interpersonal media.

I argue that the role of the computer in human communication is one of an integrator. Where there were once clearly interpersonal media that were obviously different from what were clearly mass media there is now a growing continuum that allows any individual to interact, almost as if on a one-to-one basis, with a large audience. The effect of this growing range of media will be an increasingly complex media environment in which individuals will have many choices depending on the kind of interaction they want to have or are constrained to having, the kind of message they want to deliver or receive, and the kind of audience they want to reach or be a part of.

## References

1   Bush, Vannevar. 1945. As we may think. *Atlantic Monthly*, July, 101-108.
2   Dawkins, Richard. 1986. *The Blind Watchmaker: Why the evidence of evolution reveals a universe without design.* W.W. Norton and company, New York.
3   Foulger, Davis. *Medium as Process: The structure, use, and practice of computer conferencing on IBM's IBMPC computer conferencing facility.* (Doctoral Dissertation, Temple University, 1990). U.M.I. Dissertation Services, Order Number 9107898, 1991.
4   Hiltz, Starr Roxanne, and Turoff, Murray. 1978. *The Network Nation: Human Communication via Computer.* Addison-Wesley, Reading, MA.
5   Kiesler, S. 1986. The hidden messages in computer networks. *Harvard Business Review,* January-February, pp. 4660.
6   McLuhan, Marshall. 1964. *Understanding Media: The Extensions of Man.* McGraw Hill, New York.
7   Turoff, M. 1989. The Anatomy of a Computer Application Innovation: Computer Mediated Communication (CMC). *Technological Forecasting and Social Change*, 107-122.
8   Turoff, M. and Hiltz, S.R. 1987. Computer Mediated Communications and Developing Countries. *Telematics and Informatics*, 1987.

# The Universal Robot

**Hans Moravec**

*Robotics Institute, Carnegie Mellon University, Pittsburgh, PA 15213, USA*

*Various robots and machines are becoming smarter, and a loose parallel with the evolution of animal intelligence suggests one future course for them. "Computerless" industrial machinery exhibits the behavioral flexibility of single-celled organisms. Today's best computer-controlled robots are like the simpler invertebrates. A thousand-fold increase in computer power in the next decade should make possible machines with reptile-like sensory and motor competence. Properly configured, such robots could do in the physical world what personal computers now do in the world of data – act on our behalf as literal-minded slaves. Growing computer power over the next half-century will allow this reptile stage to be surpassed, in stages producing robots that learn like mammals, model their world like primates and eventually reason like humans. Depending on your point of view, humanity will then have produced a worthy successor, or shaken off some of its inherited limitations and so transformed itself into something quite new.*

Instincts which predispose the nature and quantity of work we enjoy probably evolved during the 100,000 years our ancestors lived as hunter-gatherers. Less than 10,000 years ago the agricultural revolution made life more stable, and richer in goods and information. But, paradoxically, it requires more human labor to support an agricultural society than a primitive one, and the work is of a different, "unnatural" kind, out of step with the old instincts. The effort to avoid this work has resulted in domestication of animals, slavery and the industrial revolution. But many jobs must still be done by hand, engendering for hundreds of years the fantasy of an intelligent but soulless being that can tirelessly dispatch the drudgery. Only in this century have electronic sensors and computers given machines the ability to sense their world and to think about it, and so offered a way to fulfil the wish. As in fables, the unexpected side effects of robot slaves are likely to dominate the resulting story. Most significantly, these perfect slaves will continue to develop, and will not long remain soulless. As they increase in competence they will have occasion to make more and more autonomous decisions, and so will slowly develop a volition and purposes of their own. At the same time they will become indispensable. Our minds were evolved to store the skills and memories of a stone-age life, not the enormous complexity that has developed in the last ten thousand years. We've kept up, after a fashion, through a series of social inventions – social stratification and division of labor, memory aids like poetry and schooling, written records stored outside the body, and recently machines that can do some of our thinking entirely without us. The portion of absolutely essential human activity that takes place outside of human bodies and minds has been steadily increasing. Hard working intelligent machines may complete the trend.

Serious attempts to build thinking machines began after the second world war. One line of research, called Cybernetics, used simple electronic circuitry to mimic small nervous systems, and produced machines that could learn to recognize simple patterns, and turtle-like robots that found their way to lighted recharging hutches.[1] An entirely different approach, named Artificial Intelligence (AI), attempted to duplicate rational human thought in the large computers that appeared after the war. By 1965, these computers ran programs that proved theorems in logic and geometry, solved calculus problems and played good games of checkers.[2] In the early 1970s, AI research groups at MIT (the Massachusetts Institute of Technology) and Stanford University attached television cameras and robot arms to their computers, so their "thinking" programs could begin to collect their information directly from the real world.

What a shock! While the pure reasoning programs did their jobs about as well and about as fast as college freshmen, the best robot control programs took hours to find and pick up a few blocks on a table. Often these robots failed completely, giving a performance much worse than a six-month-old child. This disparity between programs that reason and programs that perceive and act in the real world holds to this day. In recent years Carnegie Mellon University produced two desk-sized computers that can play chess at grandmaster level, within the top 100 players in the world, when given their moves on a keyboard. But present-day robotics could produce only a complex and unreliable machine for finding and moving normal chess pieces.

In hindsight it seems that, in an absolute sense, reasoning is much easier than perceiving and acting – a position not hard to rationalize in evolutionary terms. The survival of human beings (and their ancestors) has depended for hundreds of millions of years on seeing and moving in the physical world, and in that competition large parts of their brains have become efficiently organized for the task. But we didn't appreciate this monumental skill because it is shared by every human being and most animals – it is commonplace. On the other hand, rational thinking, as in chess, is a newly acquired skill, perhaps less than one hundred thousand years old. The parts of our brain devoted to it are not well organized, and, in an absolute sense, we're not very good at it. But until recently we had no competition to show us up.

By comparing the edge and motion detecting circuitry in the four layers of nerve cells in the retina, the best understood major circuit in the human nervous system, with similar processes developed for "computer vision" systems that allow robots in research and industry to see, I've estimated that it would take a billion computations per second (the power of a world-leading Cray 2 supercomputer) to produce the same results at the same speed as a human retina. By extrapolation, to emulate a whole brain takes ten trillion arithmetic operations per second, or ten thousand Crays worth.[3] This is for operations our nervous system do extremely efficiently and well. Arithmetic provides an example at the other extreme. In 1989 a new computer was tested for a few months with a program that computed the number $\pi$ to more than one billion decimal places. By contrast, the largest unaided manual computation of $\pi$ was 707 digits by William Shanks in 1873. It took him several years, and because of a mistake every digit past the 527th was wrong! In *arithmetic,* today's average computers are one million times more powerful than human beings. In very narrow areas of *rational thought* (like playing chess or proving theorems) they are about the same. And in perception and control of movement in the complex real world, and related areas of common-sense knowledge and intuitive and visual problem solving, today's average computers are a million times less capable. The deficit is evident even in pure problem solving AI programs. To this day AI programs exhibit no shred of common sense - a medical diagnosis program, for instance, may prescribe an antibiotic when presented a broken bicycle because it lacks a model of people, diseases or bicycles. Yet these programs, on existing computers, would be overwhelmed were they to be bloated with the details of everyday life, since each new fact can interact with the others in an astronomical "combinatorial explosion." [A ten year project called *Cyc* at the Microelectronics and Computer Consortium in Austin Texas is attempting to build just such a common-sense data base. They estimate the final result will contain over one hundred million logic sentences about everyday objects and actions.[4]]

Machines have a lot of catching up to do. On the other hand, for most of the century, machine calculation has been improving a thousandfold every 20 years, and there are basic developments in research labs that can sustain this for at least several decades more. In less than 50 years computer hardware should be powerful enough to match, and exceed, even the well-developed parts of human intelligence. But what about the software that would be required to give these powerful machines the ability to perceive, intuit and think as well as humans? The Cybernetic approach that attempts to directly imitate nervous systems is very slow, partly because examining a working brain in detail is a very tedious process. New instruments may change that in future. The AI approach has successfully imitated some aspects of rational thought, but that seems to be only about one millionth of the problem. I feel that the fastest progress on the hardest problems will come from a third approach, the newer field of robotics, the construction of systems that must see and move in the physical world. Robotics research is imitating the *evolution* of animal minds, adding capabilities to machines a few at a time, so that the resulting sequence of machine behaviors resembles the capabilities of animals with increasingly complex nervous systems. This effort to build intelligence from the bottom up is helped by biological peeks at the "back of the book" - at the neuronal, structural, and behavioral features of animals and humans.

The best robots today are controlled by computers just powerful enough to simulate the nervous system of an insect, cost as much as houses, and so find only a few profitable niches in society (among them, spray painting and spot welding cars and assembling electronics). But those few applications are encouraging research that is slowly providing a base for a huge future growth. Robot evolution in the direction of full intelligence will greatly accelerate, I believe, in about a decade when the mass-produced general purpose, *universal* robot becomes possible. These machines will do in the physical world what personal computers do in the world of data – act on our behalf as literal-minded slaves.

## The Dumb Robot (ca. 2000-2010)

To be useful in many tasks, the first generation of universal robots should navigate efficiently over flat ground and reliably and safely over rough terrain and stairs, be able to manipulate most objects, and to find them in the nearby world. There are beginnings of solutions today. In the 1980s Hitachi of Japan developed a mobility system of five steerable wheels, each on its own telescoping stalk that allows it to accommodate to rises and dips in uneven terrain, and to climb stairs, by raising one wheel at a time while standing stably on the other four. My laboratory at Carnegie Mellon University in Pittsburgh has developed a navigation method that enables a robot equipped with sonar range measuring devices and television cameras to build probabilistic maps of its surroundings to determine its location and plan routes.[6] An elegant three-fingered mechanical hand at the Massachusetts Institute of Technology can hold and orient bolts and eggs and manipulate a string in a humanlike fashion.[6] A system called 3DPO from SRI International in Menlo Park, California can find a desired part in a jumble seen by special range-finding camera.[7] The slow operation of these systems suggests one other element needed for the universal robot, namely a computer about one one thousand times as powerful as those found on desks and in robots today. Such machines, able to do one billion computations per second, would provide robots approximately the brain power of a reptile, and the personality of a washing machine.

Universal robots will find their first uses in factories, where they will be cheaper and more versatile than the older generation of robots they replace. Eventually they will become cheap enough for some households, extending the reach of personal computers from a few tasks in the data world to many in the physical world.

As with computers, many applications of the robots will surprise their inventors. Some will do light mechanical assembly, clean bathrooms, assemble and cook gourmet meals from fresh ingredients, do tuneups on a certain year and make of cars, hook patterned rugs, weed a lawn, run robot races, do detailed earthmoving and stonework, investigate bomb threats, deliver to and fetch from warehoused inventories, and much more. Each application will require its own original software (very complex by today's computer program standards), and some may also need optional hardware attachments for the robot such as special tools and chemical sensors.

## Learning (2010-2020)

Useful though they will be, the first generation of universal robots will be rigid slaves to simple programs. If the machine bangs its elbow while chopping beef in your kitchen making Stroganoff, you will have to find another place for the robot to do its work, or beg the software manufacturer for a fix. Second generation robots with more powerful computers will be able to host a more flexible kind of program able to adjust itself by a kind of conditioned learning. First generation programs will consist primarily of

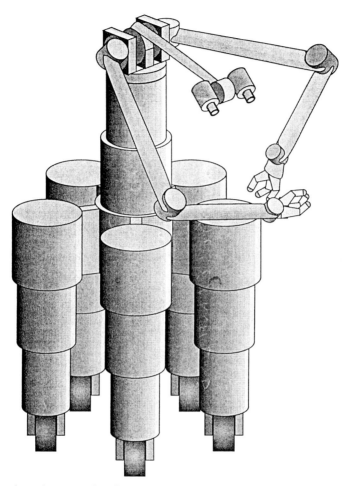

**Figure 1**   *A caricature of a first-generation universal robot, showing wheels on telescoping legs, arms with dexterous hands, camera eyes for object-finding and an implied spatial awareness and navigation system, all operated by a billion operation per second onboard computer.*

sequences of the type "Do step A, then B, then C ...." The programs for the second generation will read "Do step A1 or A2 or A3 ... then B1 or B2 or B3 ... then C1 or C2 or C3 ...." In the Beef Stroganoff example, A1 might be to chop with the right hand of the robot, while A2 is to use the left hand. Each alternative in the program has a "weight," a number that indicates the desirability of using it rather than one of the other branches. The machine also contains a "pain" system, a series of programs that look out for problems, such as collisions, and respond by reducing the weights of recently invoked branches, and a "pleasure" system that increases the relevant weights when good conditions, such as well charged batteries or a task efficiently completed, are detected. As the robot bangs its elbow repeatedly in your kitchen, it gradually learns to use its other hand (as well as adapting to its surroundings in a thousand other ways). A program with many alternatives at each step, whose pain and pleasure systems are arranged to produces a pleasure signal on hearing the word "good" and a pain message on hearing "bad" could be slowly trained to do new tasks, like a small mammal. A particular suite of pain- and pleasure-producing programs interacting with a robot's individual environment would subtly shape its behavior and give it a distinct character.

## Imagery (2020-2030)

Adaptive robots will find jobs everywhere, and the hardware and software industry that supports them could become the largest on earth. But teaching them new tasks, whether by writing programs or through punishment and reward, will be very tedious. This deficiency will lead to a portentous innovation, a software *world-modeler* (requiring another big increase in computer power), that allows the robot to simulate its immediate surroundings and its own actions within them, and thus to think about its tasks before acting. Before making Beef Stroganoff in your kitchen, the new robot would simulate the task many times. Each time its simulated elbow bangs the simulated cabinet, the software would update the learning weights just as if the collision had physically happened. After many such mental run-throughs the robot would be well trained, so that when it finally cooks for real, it does it correctly. The simulation can be used in many other ways. After a job, the robot can run though its previous actions, and try variations on them to improve future performance. A robot might even be configured to invent some of its own programs by means of a simpler program that can detect how nearly a sequence of robot actions achieves a desired task. This training program would, in repeated simulations, provide the "good" and "bad" indications needed to condition a general learning program like the one of the previous section.

It will take a large community of patient researchers to build good simulators. A robot entering a new room must include vast amounts of not directly perceived prior knowledge in its simulation, such as the expected shapes and probable contents of kitchen counters and the effect of (and force needed for) turning faucet knobs. It needs instinctive motor-perceptual knowledge about the world that took millions of years of evolution to install in us, that tells us instinctively when a height is dangerous, how hard to throw a stone, or if the animal facing us is a threat . Robots that incorporate it may be as smart as monkeys.

## Reasoning (2030-2040)

In the decades while the "bottom-up" evolution of robots is transferring the perceptual and motor faculties of human beings into machinery, the conventional Artificial Intelligence industry will be perfecting the mechanization of reasoning. Since today's programs already match human beings in some areas, those of 40 years from now, running on computers a million times as fast as today's, should be quite superhuman.

Today's reasoning programs work from small amounts of clear and correct information prepared by human beings. Data from robot sensors such as cameras is much too voluminous and too noisy for them to use. But a good robot simulator will contain neatly organized data about the robot and its world. For instance, if a knife is on a countertop, or if the robot is holding a cup. A robot with simulator can be married to a reasoning program to produce a machine with most of the abilities of a human being. The combination will create beings that in some ways resemble us, but in others are like nothing the world has seen before.

## First Generation Technicalities

Both industrial robot manipulators and the research effort to build "smart" robots are twenty five years old. Universal robots will require at least another decade of development, but some of their elements can be guessed from the experience so far. One consideration is weight. Mobile robots built to work in human sized spaces today weigh too many hundreds of pounds. This dangerously large mass has three major components: batteries, actuators and structure. Lead-acid batteries able to drive a mobile robot for a day contribute about one third of the weight. But nickel-cadmium aircraft batteries weigh half as much, and newer lithium batteries can be half again as light. Electric motors are efficient and precisely controllable, but standard motors are heavy and require equally heavy reducing gears. Ultrastrong permanent magnets can halve the weight and generate high torque without gears. Robot structure has been primarily aluminum. Its weight contribution can be cut by a factor of four by substituting composite materials containing superstrength fibers of graphite, aramid or the new material Spectra. These innovations could be combined to make a robot with roughly the size, weight, strength and endurance of a human.

The first generation robot will probably move on wheels. Legged robots have advantages on complicated terrain, but they consume too much power. A simple wheeled robot would be confined to areas of flat ground, but if each wheel had a controlled suspension with about a meter of travel, the robot could slowly lift its wheels as needed to negotiate rough ground and stairs. The manipulation system will consist of two or more arms ending in dexterous manipulators. There are several designs in the research labs today, but the most elegant is probably that of the so-called Stanford-JPL hand (mentioned above, now found at MIT), which has three fingers each with three controlled joints. The robot's travels would be greatly aided if it could continuously pinpoint its location, perhaps by noting the delay from a handful of small synchronized transmitters distributed in its environment. This approach is used in some terrestrial and satellite navigation systems. The robot will also require a sense of its immediate surroundings, to find doors, detect obstacles and track objects in its workspace. Research laboratories, including my own, have experimented with techniques that do this with data from television cameras, scanning lasers, sonar transducers, infrared proximity sensors and contact sensors. A more precise sensory system will be needed to find particular work objects in clutter. The most successful methods to date start with three dimensional data from special cameras and laser arrangements that directly measure distance as well as lateral position. The robot will thus probably contain a wide angle sensor for general spatial awareness, and a precise, narrow angle, three dimensional imaging system to find particular objects it will grasp.

Research experience to date suggests that to navigate, visually locate objects, and plan and control arm motions, the first universal robots will require a billion operations per second of computer power. The 1980s have witnessed a number of well publicized fads that claim to be solutions to the artificial intelligence or robot control problem. Expert systems, the Prolog logical inference language, neural nets, fuzzy logic and massive parallelism have all had their spot in the limelight. The common element that I note in these pronouncements is the sudden enthusiasm of group of researchers experienced in some area of computer science for applying their methods to the robotics problems of perceiving and acting in the physical world. Invariably each approach produces some simple showcase demonstrations, then bogs down on real problems. This pattern is no surprise to those with a background in the 25 five year research robotics effort. Making a machine to see, hear or act reliably in the raw physical world is much, much more difficult than naive intuition leads us to believe. The programs that work relatively successfully in these areas, in industrial vision systems, robot arm controllers and speech understanders, for example, invariably use a variety of massive numerical computations involving statistics, vector algebra, analytic geometry and other kinds of mathematics. These run effectively on conventional computers, and can be accelerated by array processors (widely available add-ons to conventional machines which rapidly perform operations on long streams of numbers) and by use of modest amounts of parallelism. The mind of the first generation universal robot will almost certainly reside in quite conventional computers, perhaps ten processors each able to perform 100 million operations per second, helped out by a modest amount of specialized computing hardware that preprocesses the data from the laser eyes and other sensors, and that operates the lowest level of mobility and manipulation systems.

## Mind Children (2050+)

The fourth robot generation and its successors, with human perceptual and motor abilities and superior reasoning powers, could replace human beings in every essential task. In principle, our society could continue to operate increasingly well without us, with machines running the companies and doing the research as well as performing the productive work. Since machines can be designed to work well in outer space, production could move to the greater resources of the solar system, leaving behind a nature preserve subsidized from space. Meek humans would inherit the earth, but rapidly evolving machines would expand into the rest of the universe. This development can be viewed as a very natural one. Human beings have two forms of heredity, one the traditional biological kind, passed on strands of DNA, the other cultural, passed from mind to mind by example, language, books and recently machines. At present the two are inextricably linked, but the cultural part is evolving very rapidly, and gradually assuming functions once the province of our biology. In terms of information content, our cultural side is already by far the larger part of us. The fully intelligent robot marks the point where our cultural side can exist on its own, free of biological limits. Intelligent machines, which are evolving among us, learning our skills, sharing our goals, and being shaped by our values, can be viewed as our children, the children of our minds. With them our biological heritage is not lost. It will be safely stored in libraries at least; however its importance will be greatly diminished.

## References

1   Norbert Wiener, 1961. *Cybernetics, or Control and Communication in the Animal and the Machine,* (2nd edn.), MIT Press, Cambridge, Massachusetts.
2   Feigenbaum, E. and Feldman, J. (eds.), 1963. *Computers and Thought.* McGraw-Hill Inc., New York.
3   Moravec, H. 1988. *Mind Children: The Future of Robot and Human Intelligence.* Harvard University Press, Cambridge, Massachusetts.
4   Lenat, D. and Guha, R. 1989. *Building Large Knowledge-Based Systems: Representation and Inference in the Cyc Project.* Addison-Wesley Publishing Co., Reading, Massachusetts.
5   Moravec, H. Sensor Fusion in Certainty Grids for Mobile Robots, *AI Magazine,* 9(2), Summer 1988, pp.61-77.
6   Mason, M. and Salisbury, K. 1985. *Robot Hands and the Mechanics of Manipulation.* MIT Press, Cambridge, Massachusetts.
7   Bolles, R., Horaud, P. and Hannah, M.J. 1984. 3DPO: A Three-Dimensional Part Orientation System, In: Brady, M. and Paul, R. (eds.), *Robotics Research: The First International Symposium.* MIT Press, Cambridge, Massachusetts, pp 413:424.

# Materials Science:
# One Morning in the Year 2079

## B. D. Silverman

*IBM Research Division, T. J. Watson Research Center, Yorktown Heights, NY 10598, USA*

*Materials Science is the study of the physical properties of materials such as metals, ceramics, and plastics. Typical physical properties that are often studied include the electrical, corrosive, elastic, and thermal characteristics of a material. Here is my personal vision of the state of Materials Science in the 21st century.*

Materials Science is one of the fastest growing and most promising scientific fields today, especially in the area of ceramics (which includes the study of superconducting materials). Let me tell the story of Materials Science as I sit in my office and look back from the year 2079. As background, Materials Science is the study of the fundamental properties of matter that shape our daily lives. Since the 1990s there were numerous advances in computer technology that enhanced the capabilities of scientists involved with material science. The present report details the morning's work of a typical scientist in the year 2079.

The garage door flips open, and my car backs out onto the street as the door closes effortlessly. The auto negotiates the next several turns before reaching the highway that will be the major part of my trip to work. All the time, echoing in my mind, are the words, "we really should attempt to understand how water interacts with PI". PI is a multi-purpose material that is used in thermally insulating the exterior of the daily rocket shuttle to the moon. It is also used in electrically insulating the angstroelectronics in space ship communication devices as well as providing the tough lifting surfaces for subsonic home-use flight devices. Indeed, water has been a problem since, as one could say about PI, "the good usually comes with the bad". The "good" is that PI material can be deposited, formed, and shaped almost effortlessly since it starts out in solution and only hardens into the desired form after thermal processing. The "bad" is that during thermal processing, water is driven off in some complicated chemical reaction and, as a result, forms convenient pathways for ambient water molecules to reenter the material after it has been processed into a hard mechanically tough substance. Such reentrant water can cause havoc with the function of a device having PI as its active part. In fact this hard, generally impervious material, scavenges water so effectively that it has been used in devices configured to detect ambient humidity.

My auto nears a more slowly moving van, pulls out into the left lane and accelerates to pass before returning to the middle lane of this three lane segment of highway. I am not driving the car. It is automatically controlled from garage to parking at work. This is surely a convenience. Actually, speculation[1] concerning the feasibility of such an automatic control system had been around for years before final implementation. I am truly fortunate that it had been finally implemented about 90 years ago. I only wish that the agency that is responsible for the system would give us control in programming the driving profile. That poor sucker in the van couldn't have been driving faster than 465 kilometers per hour. Maybe next year I'll invest in one of those local flight devices. That would reduce the duration of my trip by minutes.

Anyhow, let us return to our thoughts of water and PI. This is a project that we have just initiated. As a result, our experience of previous work in the field is somewhat limited. It would be useful to find out what others have learned in the past. The flat panel display has already been activated, ready and waiting. This display has been on since I had turned on the master switch initiating the processes that would eventually transport me to work. I pull the panel into a more convenient position to address it more easily. Now, what might be several key words that would identify previous literature that could be of interest to me concerning this subject? Hesitantly, I softly speak aloud, "water, PI, diffusion, water uptake". I guess it makes more sense to search for such words in the titles and abstracts rather than in the full text. So let's try searching for the concatenation of several of these words to see what we get. The computer has found 76 entries by scanning titles and abstracts. There's something that looks interesting. Let me display the full text. Let's see... The measurements described have not been performed on the exact material we are interested in, but the material is sufficiently similar to be of interest. Yes, these are the type of properties that we would be interested in obtaining information about. Do they really understand what they have measured? Let me open another window on the auto's computer display to scan the other references I have found that were published at a later date than this paper. At the same time I'll continue to scan the text of this paper. Now, of these references, published at a later date, do any of them refer to the previous paper I have been looking at? Yes. Two refer to it. In another window I'll scan what these later works have to report. Let's access and display one of the papers. There it is. Okay. fine. Now we'll search the text of this paper to find the place which refers to the earlier paper. Got it. What do they say?

"Smith and colleagues have measured the sorption of water in PI3491843 (see Figure 1) and have obtained a nonmonotonic increase with ambient relative humidity. While the data we obtain are similar to the results of Smith, we believe his interpretation of the origin of the sorption curve to be erroneous".

Ooops. The car has stopped. I have arrived at work. The door opens and I emerge from the auto and step onto the people-mover which transports me to my office. As the door to my office opens upon my arrival, the lights come on, and messages accumulated in my absence begin to play. Actually, things could be configured so that I would receive messages instantaneously on my personal monitor as they are sent to me, but that has not been my preference. You never know what you might be doing at any moment, and

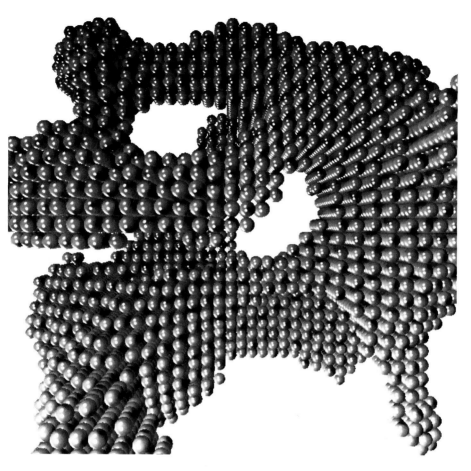

**Figure 1**   *Sorbed water in the substance P13491843 (produced by computer simulation).* Figure produced by C. Pickover on an IBM RISC System/6000 using rules for generating cellular automata similar to those described in *Computers, Pattern, Chaos, and Beauty.* St Martin's Press, New York, 1990.

being distracted by an incoming message could be a little upsetting. Even in this present age, I don't use what has evolved from the so called early days of "call waiting". Remember, this allowed one to interrupt the present conversation and to direct attention to someone attempting to make connection. Somehow I always believed interruptions were in poor taste and a certain amount of screening of calls was a plus. Also, if the communication was sufficiently important it would be established at some later time. Now seated at my desk, and having dealt with the messages that had accumulated, I can turn my thoughts back to PI. Several displays flick on and duplicate the screen environment that I had prior to alighting from my auto.

Interesting, it works. This is part of an experimental project to sense brain wave patterns and to enable them to communicate with the external environment to bring about desired effects. At the moment not much has been achieved, however, if I am sitting at my desk, and oriented properly with respect to the sensing devices, concentrate sufficiently, I am able to activate the visual displays. Actually while in the auto I had been inputting data and making queries vocally. Speech recognition by the computer has been around for a long time. It's even hard to fool it with colloquial usage. Even if you let loose with a string of epithets because things haven't been going well, it will respond with a soothing message. It's like having your own Chinese fortune cookie message tailored to your mood. Now in the confines of my office I'll type for a while, and when I get tired of this I'll write on a tablet. It's convenient to be able to choose these different modes of input to call upon. Now back to Smith *et al.* Interpretation erroneous... what do they propose? Hmmm... nothing really. Let's look at the second paper that refers to Smith *et al.* It doesn't say much either about interpretation. We'll let's do a quick search on everything published after these two papers to see if they are referenced. Who are the authors? Got them... Now search... Yes. There are five papers that refer to one or the other of these two papers. Of these five papers, do any refer to either of the words, "simulation", "theory", "calculation", or "interpretation"? Good, one does. Let's scan its text. Okay, where does the word "simulation" appear in the text? There it is. It says that the water take-up data can be simply explained by a theory proposed by Relhof 144 years ago which appeared in a book several years later by Relhof and Heimgen. The paper also uses expressions from the book to fit their data. Let's bring up, on the display, the Relhof-Heimgen book. There it is. Now we input a few key words to get us to the appropriate part of the book. Good. These people were really before their time. Yes, there is the equation. And there is a figure they have generated to display the take up of various substances as a function of the several parameters of their theory. It doesn't seem as if either the figures shown in the book or in the other papers I have examined have evaluated this equation for the set of values that would be of interest in my present work. Let's see what sort of behavior is predicted by this equation if I use a set of values more appropriate to the situation we are interested in. Let's access the formula-graphics generator. Good. Now we put the cursor on the equation in the book and press the button once. Oh yes. We must choose the units. We will choose cgs. units. Now it will prompt me to input the parameters in the equation, ask what range over which I want it evaluated and displayed. Good. There is the prompt. Let's type in the values. Not bad, but the high humidity value doesn't really look like the behavior that we had measured. perhaps a generalization of this theory is required. No. First let me change the values of some of the parameters in the equation to see what changes we'll get. I'll put the cursor on the value that I want to input. Click once. And type in the new value. Interesting. this curve looks like the previous one except that the high humidity behavior appears to be somewhat different. Let's try another value. Click. Interesting. This game is yielding small changes that don't seem to reproduce the type of saturation we have found at high relative humidity. Let's read on in the book to see what other expressions have been derived and discussed. Here's something of interest. If the water molecules interact with each other as well as with the substrate, then the expression for take-up looks somewhat different. Here's the equation. Let's evaluate it in the same manner as previously. Inputting parameters... Generating a figure. Interesting. Somewhat closer to the sort of behavior we are observing. Let us click on one of these parameters and this time let the calculated curves and corresponding figures cycle through a set of parameters to see what we get. Wow. Here is a range of interaction energies that seems to generate the sort of behavior that we have been seeing.

Since the Relhof work seems so relevant to what we have been doing, let's do a quick check to see if any of the 76 references that were previously unearthed refer to the Relhof book. None. Strange that this sort of analysis hasn't been extensively discussed within the context of this sort of problem, namely sorption in a uniform but random medium. I wonder if people in other areas of investigation have used a similar expression to interpret their data. Let's see. We should already be linked to the formula citation index. If I recall correctly this covers publications over only the past 97 years, however, it should be good enough for our purposes. Let's click on the equation and wait.

It is really aggravating to have to wait seconds for a response as the system is searching. Someday there will come a time when the only limitation will be the imagination of the person who queries the computer. Instantaneous response. You could ask anything, do any simulation, search for any type of information, anywhere, and have the information instantaneously. Of course you still wouldn't be able to get an exact closed expression for the solution to something like a quintic algebraic equation, but you could approximate such solution to any degree of accuracy. You could, say, in principle be able to solve the Schrodinger equation for all the cells, molecules, and atoms in the brain – for something like that it seems that formatting the input to such problem would be a task in and of itself. I wonder if you would need all of the atomic coordinates? With the new imaging techniques we have, however, perhaps one might be able to scan the brain and automatically generate input to the computer so that it could solve the Schrodinger equation – something like we do today with X-rays on crystalline materials. Would one ever want output from the solution to such problem? Just think, you'd have a list of eigenvalues several miles long. That is the problem with most of these computational tools – they give you a ton of information that isn't really directly relevant to what you are interested in. Now if I had a wave function for the brain... even if it wasn't stationary. I'd really like to know how all of the electrons dancing around, and nuclei vibrating, where somehow related to the thoughts one was having. But from the little I know, this is somehow related to chemistry, so the solution to the Schrodinger equation would then have to be fed into some other program that would make connections between fundamental quantities involving electrons and nuclei and some consequent higher lying chemistry going on and its connection to behavioral patterns. It would be nice if all this could be done automatically. It would be fun playing with this sort of program but I guess its still in the future.

Well, while I have wasted time on these speculations, my computer search has ended. It seems that just about everyone has used this equation over the past 97 years. And not one of the original 76 papers I had found in my initial query with respect to water take-up in PI apparently appreciated the relevance of this approach. It seems strange that no one else interested in this water take-up problem has identified the Relhof approach to be of importance. Anyhow, let me print out the results of all of these searches so that I can look at them in some greater detail sometime. Perhaps I will look at it when I am seated in an easy chair at home with proper nourishment nearby. At present, however let's play a few computational games. Let's check the applications solutions library to see what simulation programs are available. I'll type in a few key words to see if any of the programs that are listed will do what I am interested in. I'll use similar key words to those used in my initial literature search. Actually I could have looked at any particular reference I had previously obtained to see if an appropriate simulation was available that was related to the subject matter in the reference, but the present search will give me all such available programs. Here we go. Well, not too much – only 12 programs. Let's look at a brief description of what each does. Only one of these programs appears to calculate the take-up in a manner that is relevant for my particular problem. Let's look at certain details of the simulation. Interesting. Let's try it.

Actually the only difference between using this particular program and the formula-graphics generator is that this program will solve a set of nonlinear partial differential equations. It also will not only print out a list of numbers but graphically display the results in what it has determined to be the most informative manner. I don't quite understand how it determines what I'd like to look at and the range over which I am interested but it guesses right most of the time. For time dependent phenomena it provides some really nice animation. So let's set up the input. This time we'll just let it read input from a file previously configured, and let it go. Nice. These sets of equations generalize the early Relhof expression. The Relhof equation is essentially a macroscopic rate equation. I'd like to do a more microscopic type of calculation that treats an actual polymeric structure of PI... Oh yes. PI is a polymer and its structure is partially disordered as well as being partially ordered. It would be useful to examine how a water molecule wends its way through relatively complex molecular structure. So we'll have to let the program know something about PI structure. First, I'll construct the repeat unit of the polymer and tell the program to show me what a single strand looks like. Good. Next, let's generate a perfectly ordered crystalline type structure - inputting primitive cell information and space group. There it is. Well I have created some kind of molecular crystal. Let's see what the density is for such structure. 1.53 g cm$^{-1}$. Not bad; experimental values are somewhat less.

Now let's ask the program to cleave this crystal along an easy direction, to show a surface. There we go. Look at that - the surface is automatically cleaved with no covalent bonds broken. Let's reorient the surface so that we are looking at it at some angle to the top. Good. I can see a distribution of active sites associated with oxygen atoms. By clicking appropriately let's find out how many such sites per unit area on this surface.

I can also ask for the adhesive energy with a particular metallic or other species. Now let's start all over again in generating the polymeric structure by asking the program for a disordered structure. We'll also ask it to maximize the degree of disorder. Actually it does this by constructing a large number of such structures and checking certain spatial correlation functions. There is the disordered structure. Now lets bring up a surface that is a mixture of both regions, *i.e.* ordered and disordered regions... Interesting. I could go thru this again to find a new structure that would be representative of some mixture of phases.

I wonder how much free volume such a mixture has. Well let's query the system concerning this and ask it to compare this value with the value for the previous crystalline structure it had generated. Furthermore, let's check the structure data base to see if a similar structure has been previously reported in the literature. Yes. Two such similar structures have been previously reported. I'll check these structures later but for the present let's see if a water molecule fits into the structure. First we will ask for the largest free channels that will accommodate one molecule as well as distances to the various polymeric atomic constituents as we move the water molecule about. There we go. Quite a large degree of free volume in this region near a carbonyl group. Let's see. If we hydrogen bond water to the carbonyl group how will the remainder of the molecule adjust to the local environment? Good. What is the binding energy for such arrangement ? 1.78 kcal mol$^{-1}$. Good. Now let's choose a value for the the the relative humidity above the substrate and examine how the water molecules penetrate PI as a function of time. This time, as water enters the polymer we'll let the polymeric structure relax to accommodate the take-up of water. In a little window to the side we'll examine a plot of take-up as a function of time as we visually examine how the water molecules penetrate the polymer. We will also overlay the results of our measurements and compare with the results of the simulation. Good, the dynamics of the sorption tracks experiment at least qualitatively. Now, while this simulation is running lets see what I might expect from an ultraviolet photoemission experiment (UPS), *i.e.* if we doused the surface with UV light and looked at the electrons kicked out of the valence orbitals of the polymer and water structure. Examining the emitted electrons yields a measure of these higher lying electron orbitals. Good, there is the UPS spectrum as a function of electron energy; and there is the water band superimposed on it. Let's also check how photon energy variations and consequent electron mean free paths affect such results. Let us also overlay available experimental data.

This data generation feature has been extremely useful. Years ago when one ran a simulation such as this – involving molecules, atoms, and dynamics – and one wanted to see some quantity related to chemical or physical behavior, it was necessary to do the programming oneself or to find the package that would convert structural data to the quantity or quantities one would be interested in. This is not true any more. Now, for any structural simulation, we have the capability of having displayed, almost instantaneously, any related physical or chemical quantity of interest – and we can bring up, not only data obtained locally but data previously published to compare with the results of the simulation. Furthermore curve plotting, fitting, and visualization of 3-D structures are done with the simplest of commands. Also, all simulations are completely interactive, and if I wish I can override any of the program defaults. For example, what if the hydrogen bond formed between water and the carbonyl group is twice the true value. So I simply change this interaction energy in the simulation to play any kind of thought game that I might find appropriate to generate a deeper understanding of what might happen in some phantom world. Furthermore, the terminal I sit at is a window on an external world being connected to a vast network coupled to remote locations. While performing this current simulation, everything that I have generated at my terminal has appeared in a window of a colleague of mine 7,500 miles away. While he views the sort of mental gyrations I have been performing he is playing his own set of games, the results of which I have been monitoring on this small window down in the left hand corner. If either he or I see something of interest we can query the system to find out in greater detail what is being displayed. I also have online instantaneous access to every data base imaginable. I can not only search for key words in Materials Science publications, but for key words in the text of all fictional material printed within the past 70 years, *i.e.* if you want to do that sort of thing.

It looks like the simulation I have been running has achieved a steady state since all averages are only varying slightly with time. So let's find out how water has affected this material. Let's pull on it to see at what value of stress it will fail and what the nature of the failure is. There it goes. It looked like salt water taffy before it finally gave way. Now let's see what would have happened to the material in "dry ambient", that is with no water take-up. Yes, as expected, it requires higher stresses to fracture the material, and the failure mode is not so taffylike. Let me see. What did Joe find during the fracture tests ? Joe is an experimental co-worker of mine. I remember the general trend but I don't recall the exact value at which he found that the material was pulled apart. Let's bring up Joe's lab notebook on the screen and search for fracture at the latest entry. Here we go. I am glad I asked Joe for permission to search his notebook whenever I wanted to. Anyhow he'll know that I've been snooping so he'll probably want to know what I've been up to. Here we go. The simulation result is not that bad – just about 10 percent below the measured value required for fracture. I'll have to play some more with the simulated materials structure to see if closer agreement is possible. Perhaps inputting structural data obtained from the X-ray scans will modify the structure and change material strength. We should complete these scans in a few days. The disordered PI structure still creates difficulties after all of these years. Now if the material was crystalline and cleaved in absolute vacuum, the simulation would tell us almost everything with great accuracy about the interface it forms with most other materials.

It is surprising how much we have learned by performing simulations. For example, the cost of medicines would be astronomical compared with present costs if drug firms weren't able to reduce these costs dramatically with the latest advances in computer-aided-drug-design. Also, since the complete sequencing of the human genome, there have been a number of advances in drug design that involve molecular interactions with DNA itself. Yes, our understanding of biological processes has significantly been enhanced. Many of the protein structures now can be calculated from first principles, *i.e.* with only knowledge of the primary amino acid structure or sequence. A few lengthy proteins still have not yielded to simulation. This apparently will be one of the last bastions to yield to computation, *i.e.* large numbers of degrees of freedom unrelated by symmetry requiring search algorithms just a little beyond the capability of our present machines. On the other hand, not all drug design problems involve protein structure. Some relate directly to DNA sequences that are what people called "junk" DNA years ago. At that time it wasn't clear what role was played by the introns, or the DNA sequences between protein coding regions. Today we know many specific details related to the control exerted by special sequences in these regions. High speed search algorithms can find pathological sequences and modern biological techniques can generate an array of synthetic repair enzymes to go to work fixing up such sequences.

Oops. Joe wants something. Let me display his image in the first quadrant. Hi Joe. You look disturbed. What's up? What! You want to know why I was snooping in your notebook. Remember you gave me permission. Oh. You just are curious about what I was up to. Well you see I was doing these fracture simulations and wanted to see where you found the material to fail when you stretched it. You were speaking to who ? Oh. Steve at Mewaska U. about such simulation. What did he say? He's been running similar simulations? What did he find ? Wait a minute. Let's see if he is around. Steve, are you there ? You are. (I'll bring Steve up in the 2nd quadrant.) Steve, how come you are in this early and why are you wearing a tie ? Oh, you are in because you are preparing for a visit from your funding agency. Same reason for the tie. I see. Joe tells me you have been running structural simulations similar to the ones I have been running. You have, and you say you are convinced they probably yield results better than the ones I have done. Why is that? Oh, you are using X-ray scattering data to assist the program in it's PI structural determination. Sounds like what we were planning to do. I see. I only have to let my simulation address your input data to modify my structural simulation. Good. I'll try it.

Steve has started talking to Joe, and while I listen in on this conversation I'll turn off my terminal input response click so they won't be able to hear me. Strange that I require this sound when I touch the keys. I tried it without sound but somehow the reassuring response is required by my psyche. Have you ever communicated with someone while you heard their typing clicking away in the background? Really annoying. Even if they reassure you that they are listening to what you are saying, the clicking in the background makes you think that they aren't giving you the attention that the conversation deserves. Talking to the computer doesn't help since that is also heard. Soon if things proceed along schedule one will be able to work by just thinking appropriate thoughts to activate a detailed computer response, not to just activate terminals. That will really be something – holding a one-way conversation while reserving some of your thought processes in directing the computer. I guess this is what we are doing essentially when we talk to someone and type away at the same time. Well, from their conversation it sounds like Joe really wants to keep up with the ins and outs of the simulation. Oops. Query from Debra – third quadrant – now what does she want? Oh yes. The results of a calculation I did for her last week. Let's bring them up in another monitor, the 3-D one, with holographic display. There they are. Looks good. Let's ship them out to her. Good. there they go. I think I've had enough of this Joe-Steve conversation so I'll sign off and at the same time remind Steve that I need the address of the input he referred to. Just great this online access to input info. Several years ago Steve would have had to ship his data over the network to my machine and I would have to rearrange the input format. The present rapid online access as well as standardization really have made things, as they used to say in the olden days, not-so-golden-days, "user friendly".

Standardization took quite a while to develop. Now everything communicates easily with everything else. Hardware-hardware, software-hardware, software-software, people-hardware, and people-software interfaces are all standardized these days. Today the concept of operating system is only discussed in the closed door meetings of representatives from all of the hardware and software vendors. Printed literature concerning the relative merits of different systems also appears only in trade journals selectively distributed to system developers. Gone are the days when popular magazines devoted significant space to the wild opinions and prognostications of a small select uninformed vociferous cadre of computer columnists. Well, it really took a strange revolution to bring all of this about. As things grew more and more complex the user became more and more frustrated. Departments at the major universities actually started granting degrees prior to the PhD called the CpuD. This was an advanced degree, a pre PhD degree, called the doctorate for the computer user. It wasn't that PhD's came out of school not really knowing how to wend their way through the complex computer jungle; just that those who were the best at this sort of thing usually ended up performing larger and larger calculations on problems of lesser and lesser significance. So at that time there was a reversion, motivated predominantly by elderly faculty, to go back to educational fundamentals, *i.e.* to a certain degree of emphasis on significance, direction and thought. There was a bitter battle between faculty members over initiation of this new degree with small groups arguing for greater emphasis on larger and larger calculations of marginal significance. Finally granting of the new degree was approved. Less emphasis on utilization of the computer was encouraged during actual Phd study and the final formal years of study, *i.e.* PhD study, were primarily devoted to figuring out what was accomplished during the years of CpuD study.

This worked for a while and things seemed to be getting better, when there was a grass roots revolution inspired by Jeremy Kirnif, a long-shoreman who attempted, with use of a miniature hand-held newly introduced computer, to keep track of the cargo he was unloading. Kirnif realized immediately that drastic action was called for. Consequently, he was able to mobilize the entire active user community to essentially total inaction in the purchase of anything having to do with computers unless a single operating system was adopted with total standardization, interoperability, etc. As you might imagine this created quite a bit of economic turmoil for a while, but after the dust settled, out of the chaos and debris emerged a serenity in the world of computer usage that few would have been able to imagine. As a result, the technical user of the present can do most anything with relative ease. He/she can also train junior people almost immediately to exhibit impressive strengths in computer utilization. Well, enough of this mental rumbling. It's time to eat lunch. I have wasted so much time this morning in speculation. Let me bring up the menu and order something that is simple and will appear at my desk momentarily.

## References

1   K. Jurgen, R.K. 1991. Smart Cars and Highways go Global. *IEEE Spectrum,* **28,** 26.
2   Gordon, J.E. 1968. *The New Science of Strong Materials or Why You Don't Fall Through the Floor.* Penguin Books (First published in the United States by Walker & Co., New York, 1968).

# Current Techniques and Development of Computer Art

## Franz G. Szabo

*Sechshauserstrasse 59/19, A-1150 Vienna, Austria*

*In this chapter, I discuss different approaches to produce computer art prints, in color and black and white. Laser art prints are shown as illustrations. These are made with the help of software for painting and drawing, image manipulation, and programs for the creation of mathematical (fractal) forms and patterns.*

## Introduction

In this chapter I give a general account of the possibilities of computer art as it applies to the special subfield of graphic art. This is only a small but important part of the rapidly growing complex of computer art, which includes such interesting fields as animation, virtual reality and computer aided composing. The obvious future for these fields is limitless. The view in this chapter, of course, will be a very personal one, based on experiences acquired from five years of doing artistic work with the help of a computer. Other artists not only will have experienced completely different approaches to the subject but also will have a different view of computer art as a whole. This is one of the reasons that make it such an fascinating field for unlimited creativity. After the more technical part of the chapter, I shall explain briefly how the illustrations have been created.

## How does the image get onto the screen?

At exhibitions, where I show computer-made art prints in black and white or color, most people are completely astonished that art can be done by means of a computer. I have noted this reaction since I started to show my work, and it has not changed at all, even though one should have thought that within these last five years people would have grown used to the idea of doing creative tasks by computer. Word processing, calculating, or maybe CAD (Computer Aided Design) is the kind of work that most "educated" people know about and usually associate with computers. If one takes time to look up the definition of art in Webster's Collegiate Dictionary – "the conscious use of skill and creative imagination especially in the production of aesthetic objects" – suddenly there seems not to be the slightest doubt left why art should not also be done with the help of a computer. In the coming decade, this will be more apparent.

Once people have accepted that art can be produced using a computer, the problem arises of explaining how it is done, something almost unimaginable without having seen it. The computer only acts as a tool. The process of creativity and imagination has to take place in the artist's fantasy as always. But the electronic tools, consisting of hardware and software, differ enormously from traditional techniques.

## Pixels, Dots and Bits

The monitor picture, the artist's working space, has a certain size and resolution, in my case 640 pixels horizontally and 480 pixels vertically. Every pixel (or "picture element") will be printed as a point by the printer that turns the virtual image on the screen into something that you can hold in your hand and look at on paper. A picture the size of a screen will therefore consist of 307,200 pixels. It is possible to work on and adjust every single one of them. Using simple black and white systems, the pixel can either be black or white. The pixel can assume two ($2^1$) different states, a so called 1 bit system. An 8 bit system offers the choice of 256 ($2^8$) different shades of gray or colors per pixel.

The actual size of the printout depends upon the resolution of the printer used. Printing with 72 dpi (dots per inch) turns the 640 pixels horizontally into 8.8 inches, printing with 300 dpi results in 2.1 inches horizontally. The picture becomes smaller and shows less grain, to speak in photographic terms. Pictures, of course, can be smaller or larger than the display area of the monitor screen. If they are larger, one only sees a small part of them, as if looking through a window that can be moved all over the canvas. In addition, it is possible to enlarge or reduce the size of the picture's representation on screen, but then the correspondence between "one pixel on screen is equal to one point of the picture" will temporarily be lost.

## Special Software

Pictures are not created by typing on a keyboard, as many people believe. The movement of an input device called a mouse moves a cursor on the screen that acts like a drawing tool. The MacPaint program on the Apple Macintosh computer was the first commercial program allowing a computer user to paint in black and white. In the early 1990s, the software industry furnishes the user with fantastic software for painting, drawing and image manipulation. Examples include the pixel oriented drawing and painting programs PixelPaint Professional and Studio/32, the image processing programs Adobe Photoshop and Letraset ColorStudio, or object oriented drawing tools, like Aldus FreeHand or Adobe Illustrator. All of these run on the Macintosh and are tools which computer artists heavily rely on.

In contrast to what people might imagine, one can draw or paint quite well with an input device like a mouse or a graphics tablet. One of the most regularly repeated questions at exhibitions is: "Did you really paint this or was the picture captured by scanning?" If the answer is "paint", people melt with disbelieving admiration; if it is "scan", one can almost feel their satisfaction about having brought the artist's work down to earth again. Both methods are on equal standing, but the artist should be fair enough to tell how he has done his work. Scanning is not automatically the easy way out: scanned images usually require a lot of additional manual labour until they reach the quality that can be used for further work. Only a few people today would deny photography the status of art simply because these pictures have not been drawn. The viewer should not forget that copying techniques have been a legitimate artistic tool for centuries. The use of scanners allows artists who cannot draw as well as a gifted painter to use photographic images for their work. Computer art, in one of its numerous varieties, is offering a new electronic approach to the art of collage. Interest in computer collage, including the negative aspects of photographic picture manipulation, will continue to grow in the next century.

## How to Draw with a Computer

The techniques of drawing with a program are completely different from conventional art methods. I do not attempt at all to claim that electronic brushes, pencils and airbrushes are better than their real counterparts, but they are much more versatile. One can adjust form, size, color flow and colour variation while drawing, take parts of a picture to draw with and adjust transparency of colours in a way that never will be possible in reality. There is no real brush you can tell to make a transparent stroke at one moment and a covering one the next. The latest generation of graphics tablets, such as those Wacom offers, enables one to use a pressure sensitive electronic stylus. The harder you press the more color you get onto the screen. For example using such a stylus in a charcoal setting almost makes it possible to draw as if on a piece of paper. But then, the most dramatic advantage after having drawn the work is to be able to set and change the attribute of every single point of the picture. At a resolution of 72 dpi (dots per inch), which I momentarily use for color work in order to keep the size of the files as small as possible, one square inch holds 5,184 points. At 300 dpi one square inch contains 90,000 points.

The hardware industry offers high-resolution computers, monitors, printers and scanners for color or black and white graphics. In the early 1990s, 300 dpi have become a standard for black and white laser printers. Color thermal transfer printers are many times more expensive but now offer the same resolution. The variety of colors is even more impressive. Eight bit color systems offer 256 colors on screen simultaneously, out of a palette of 16,777,216 different colours, and 24-bit systems offer the complete palette of 16,777,216 colors on the color monitor. "Eight bit color" means that every pixel on the screen can have one of $2^8$ (= 256) states (= colors). One can immediately try out $2^{24}$, which results in 16,777,216 different states or colors per pixel. Photorealistic work can be achieved with these 24 bit systems. Still, even a black and white art print by itself can be stunning at 300 dpi. I have seen professional artists standing in front of some of my black and white laser prints on handmade paper, not being able to decide with which kind of technique they had been made.

Producing art work with the aid of a computer has some major advantages. One of them is the artist's ability to work at different levels of magnification. PixelPaint Professional on the Macintosh, and other drawing and picture processing software, allows the user to employ most of the tools at various magnification levels, up to 16 times. At this (16 ×) magnification, every point of the 300 dpi print can be easily modified, for example, colored in one of the 16,777,216 possible colors. Another great advantage, compared with conventional working strategies, is the possibility of making changes in a piece of work without damaging it. If the changes fail to please the artist he can always go back to the latest, saved copy. This certainly encourages the artist to take a greater risk. Boldness can often add a new dimension to the artist's work. Parts of previous work can easily be used again for another picture if the artist so decides. Printing with color inkjet and thermal transfer printers is probably a cleaner method for producing a limited edition than producing art in a conventional way.

## Software and Hardware

Let us look at some interesting methods of changing a picture that demonstrate a few computer-aided capabilities. First of all, the paint on an electronic piece of art never dries. It can be altered as often as the artist wants. Every color that appears in the work can generally be exchanged with another one. Mathematical transformations easily allow deformations of the picture. Stretching, superimposition and blurring operations are possible. Special tools enable the user to pick almost any part of the picture and let it respond to changes and actions. In a drawing of a summer meadow, there might be ten different shades of green. Let me pick three of them and select all pixels of these greens. This action produces tiny active islands of certain green shadings all over the picture. To these islands, I could apply practically every trick that can be thought of in photographic darkroom and much more. Solarization, posterizing, softening, sharpening, changing contrast, brightness, hue and saturation are but a few of them. It is possible to surround such active areas with lines of certain thickness and color, to deform, resize or rotate them. Mac Cheese, a color paint program for the Macintosh, offers a special tool called transmogrifier that sprays subtle color changes upon an area of pure color, like adding an impressionistic texture. PixelPaint Professional offers a variety of paper and canvas structures to work on, and these structures always remain in the picture.

These examples demonstrate how computer graphics allows non-conventional ways of painting and drawing. Drawings are only the starting point for a journey into the infinite land of fantasy, and the most exciting thing about it is, that in spite of meticulous planning, you don't always know where it is going to take you. Today's computer graphics allow us to combine 'conventional' painting and drawing on the screen – using brush, airbrush and pencil with a mouse cursor, or a graphics tablet as an input medium – and 'computerised' painting and drawing techniques – using special effects like variant color flow in a brush or defining a part of the picture as a new brush. Practically everything that can be done in a photographic darkroom can be achieved with image processing software. The addition or incorporation of scanned images in black and white or color has become possible in high quality. One can either use flatbed scanners or very expensive systems ($10,000) that scan photographic slides. Objects from nature often are even more interesting to integrate into a picture than photographs. Leaves and ferns add very exotic structures and colors.

In 1991 scanners for three-dimensional objects are reaching the market. (Canon's Visualizer is one example.) Digital pictures captured by video or still video cameras become more interesting from year to year. Sony's latest model, the Ion still video camera RC-260, saves pictures on a still video floppy disk. Using a Canon Laser document copying machine with a video interface, one can perform electronic image manipulation and then print color copies in different sizes. If somebody only needs small prints, a video printer will do as well. Pictures produced by the Ion can be transferred to TV or video tape. The new optical film adapter offers by far the least expensive way to transfer slides or color negatives to a computer. Of course with this kind of setup, you always need an additional frame grabber card to do the job. Another new still video camera, the Dycam Model 1, uses a chip for saving the black and white pictures it can take and only needs to be connected to the computer via the RS-232 port. The computer's software produces a screenshot of all the pictures, and the selected one is transferred and saved in the universal TIFF (Tagged Image File Format) format, which high quality graphics programs can read. If Kodak's picture CD reaches the market in two or three years, you can have every slide of your collection put on that CD in highest quality, and you will be able to use it for computer graphics purposes.

## Incorporating elements from mathematics

The use of mathematically generated objects (like fractals, function plots, and simulations of natural forms such as flowers, trees, plants and seashells) adds a completely new dimension to art. Benoit Mandelbrot's Mandelbrot and Julia sets, Clifford Pickover's Julia set biomorphs, and Aristid Lindenmayer's L-systems, or string rewriting systems, are well known approaches used to generate fantastic forms and colors. Iterated function systems (IFS) are used to rebuild natural forms like clouds, landscapes, seashores, trees, leaves, and ferns. Many consider these objects as art by themselves, especially since the process of creation – sometimes compared with fishing in the infinite ocean of mathematics – not only needs mathematical 'artistry' but includes choosing the colors of the objects as well. I especially like to use such mathematical objects as a starting point for a picture that in the end often does not resemble the starting form.

## The Battle with too Large Files - Picture Compression

Color computer art often results in very large stored files on disk. This is often a problem. Working with 24-bit quality, one can easily end up with files of a few megabytes or even more. Two approaches used to solve this problem are available now, and a combination of approaches should be completely successful within the next five years. One is picture compression and the other is the use of erasable optical disks for data storage. Picture compression can be done by software, by hardware, or with a combination of both. The speed of compressing and expanding is becoming so fast that the user doesn't even realize that it occurs while he is saving or loading the file. Many different ways of image compression exist. One almost universally accepted method has been defined by the Joint Photographic Experts Group (JPEG) and works with chrominance and luminance data instead of RGB (red, green, blue) descriptions. The image is compressed by applying three different mathematical algorithms to individual 8-by-8 pixel squares. This does require a lot of computation. A screen of 24-bit color information will require approximately half a minute to compress or decompress. Today's compression amounts range from 2:1 (Huffman or Lempel Ziv encoding) to about 80:1 (JPEG, Kodak Colorsqueeze).

Another new compression scheme uses fractal theory. Using mathematical transformations of very simple elements like rectangles or triangles, it is possible to build up a complex picture. If one is able to find these transformations for a given picture the amount of data that is needed to store the picture's information is reduced most drastically. Michael Barnsley is developing such a fractal algorithm for picture compression that, as he says, will be able to reach a compression factor of 300:1.

Erasable optical discs with 600 megabytes storage capacity have been used for some years, but the drives still cost above $3,000. With increased propagation and higher sales numbers, the new 3 1/2 inch CDs, that will hold about 150 megabytes, should come down to harddisk price ranges in the next few years.

## Advances in Speed

When I started working with a computer, I could never understand why faster and faster processors were needed for computer art. Later on, working with large color files, I suddenly understood the everlasting demand for speed increases: the speed of software manipulation and displaying 24-bit images on the screen is needed because the larger the screen, or the more bits, the slower the processing becomes. Megabytes of data have to be rapidly moved when dealing with these photorealistic images. Accelerator boards like the Radius Rocket and CPUs using Motorola's new 68040 processor, which has begun to be shipped in sufficient quantities in early 1991, will substantially speed up this kind of work. Workstations with RISC (reduced instruction set computer) processors (*e.g.* the products from Sun and IBM) are becoming less expensive - comparable to the high end prices of Macintosh's, NeXT's and MS-DOS machines. Another one of the still remaining price problems is the high cost of color monitors. A 24-bit color monitor of approximately 20-inch size costs about 5,000 dollars. Few technical trends can be seen that would lower their cost. But industry offers interesting advances in color depth and the number of colors on the screen. 32-bit graphics is the current standard on the newest generation of NeXT machines, and some developers are already working on 64-bit color graphics. The number of colors possible with such systems then reaches the astronomical figure of 18,446,744,073,709,551,616. The eye probably cannot distinguish eighteen quintillion different colors, but with this capacity, one can produce superrealistic gradient fills (where two different colors blend very smoothly). This race for producing the greatest number of colors might seem unnecessary to those people not involved with computer art, but 64-bit color graphics is an important milestone on the stony road to achieve outstanding photorealistic picture quality with computers.

Although computer artists can manipulate and display millions of colors on their machines in the early 1990s, accurately printing those colors has been practically impossible. Impossible, until Kodak recently unveiled its new dye sublimation color print technology. For the first time it is possible to reproduce the subtleties of a color photograph in absolutely stunning picture quality. The Kodak XL7700 Digital Continuous Tone Printer produces prints that are virtually indistinguishable from the original photographs. Instead of dithering the different shades of colors by printing individual dots, the machine heats the cyan, yellow and magenta dye layers on its ribbon into a gas. These gaseous dyes are blended into a true color and diffuse into the surface of the paper. Finally a protective coating is applied to the print. Printing time is a few minutes only, due to the most surprising fact that Kodak reaches this incredible picture quality with a resolution of 200 dpi. The XL7700's list price is approximately $25,000 and the cost of a 8.5 × 11 inch color print is $3.84.

I hope I have not alienated the reader with so many technical facts and outlooks in an article about art, but computer art is deeply involved with the technical aspects of its electronic tools. The tools will change in this decade, not the ideas and works of art that artists bring to paper, canvas, video screen, video tape, etc. Only after the new tools have become widely spread and accepted, will new ideas become strong enough to achieve deep changes in our fundamental understanding of art. The pioneers of today may never become the real trendsetters of tomorrow. This certainly need not discourage or disappoint anybody! I always consider computer art as a fantastic new game to play using the help of the newest technology possible. Many of today's buyers of art tend to be suspicious when they hear about computer art, but the ones that like it are certainly worthwhile to work for.

## Illustrations

Figure 1 ("Nymphe") actually consists of three separate pictures: the girl, the trees and the ferns. They have been drawn using scanned photographs as a model and finally assembled by transparently copying them onto each other. The ferns were first drawn in black and then used as a fern-shaped eraser applied to the composition of girl and trees. The final work was done using different electronic drawing tools.

Figure 2 ("Rotation") began as line drawing done by hand, which I rotated six times to produce one of the picture's nine elements. Then the line drawing was converted to a pixel oriented object and partially filled with black. Two different shadings of the object and one not filled original were combined to give the final picture. The last step was to apply a black fill to the center for reasons of balance.

To produce Figure 3 ("Hommage an Duerer") I started by scanning an engraving by the famous artist called "The Devil and the Fool as Treasure Seeker". Solarization (a photographic effect that reduces different shades and areas of gray to thin surrounding border lines) was applied to the whole picture and the resulting outlines were filled with black to produce the thick lines. First, of course, some of the drawing's outlines were removed with an eraser to clarify the picture, and all the rest of the outlines had to be closed by using a black pencil so that the area-filling was not going to flood the whole

**Figure 1**    *Nymphe.* A transparent copy of a girl, trees and fern.

picture with black. It is essential for this kind of work to use different stages of magnification, since all these pictures' resolutions are 90,000 points per square inch! The gray shadings were applied with a brush tool, and corrections drawn with pencils of different sizes. Finally, differently scaled down and rotated copies were assembled to produce the picture, implying that the fool will search for ever.

Figure 4 ("Beta") was drawn by filling outlines with different shades of gray and including the picture of a strange attractor (a mathematical object) that I had found in beta-waves of an electroencephalogram. The picture of the head was first completed as a whole and then cut apart, and both parts rotated outward. The attractor was copied into the picture after adjusting its size.

To produce Figure 5 ("Venezia") I started by scanning a black and white photograph. The resulting image was solarized and partly filled with black. A delicate veil

**Figure 2**   *Rotation.* Multiple rotation of a line drawing, shaded in different grays.

was produced by taking a window element of the building's front and duplicating it many times to produce a tiled pattern. The veil was copied transparently onto the picture.

Figure 6, ("Joching", a farmhouse in a small town in Lower Austria) was scanned from a photograph and posterized (reduced to a small number of gray levels) to achieve a concentration of the picture. Then the original was solarized, unnecessary lines were removed with an eraser, and the lines were enhanced in thickness. This solarization was copied onto the posterized image, and finally some noise was added to produce the grainy appearance of etchings.

The combination of inverse Mandelbrot sets, rotated at different angles, produced Figure 7, ("Inverse Mandel Art"). A pseudocode in Basic for the inverse Mandelbrot set is given in the appendix.

**Figure 3**    *Hommage an Duerer.* Solarization and manipulation of "The Devil and the Fool as Treasure Seeker".

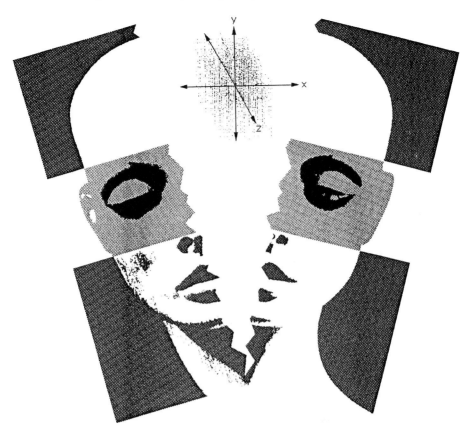

**Figure 4** *Beta.* A split head incorporates a strange attractor of beta-waves.

Original, autographed art prints of the illustrations on handmade paper can be ordered from the author at a price of $100 per print.

## Equipment Used

Here is a short description of the equipment used for the technically interested reader. Black and white work, which was the beginning of my love affair with computer art, has been done with an Atari Mega ST4 computer and an Atari laser printer. Now I mostly work with a color system that consists of a Macintosh IIcx and a Hewlett Packard Paint Writer XL, a color inkjet printer. The different painting, drawing and image processing software which I use is offered by the rapidly growing software market. I have written my own programs for the generation of mathematically based forms, like fractals, IFS- and L-systems. Computer art is much more expensive than pencil and paper art. For a black and white computer system one has to spend approximately $5,000

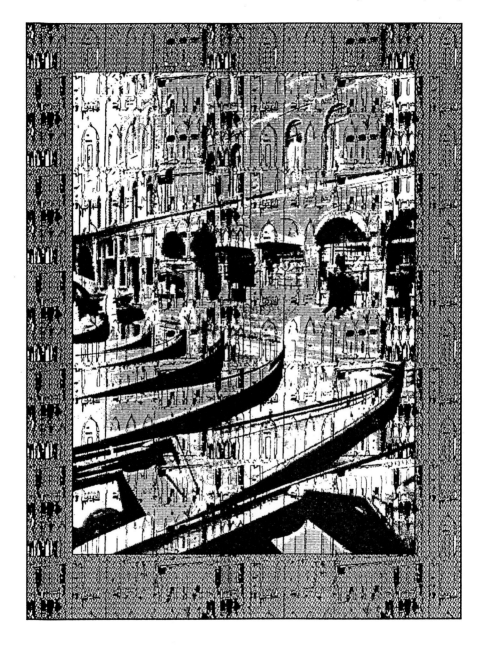

**Figure 5**    *Venezia.* A delicate electronic veil adds new structures to a Venetian view.

**Figure 6**     *Joching.* Posterization of a farmhouse in Lower Austria.

for the hardware and $1,000 for the software to be able to make laser printouts of size A4. For a color system that enables one to produce prints up to the format of A3, using an inkjet printer, one has to at least double the price. In the early 1990s thermal transfer color printers for A4 size paper are slowly coming down in price with $6,000 corresponding to the cheapest models. One should not forget, though, that about fifteen years ago not even a millionaire could have bought such equipment for home use. The

**Figure 7**    *Inverse Mandel Art.* Symmetric tiling of an inverse Mandelbrot set.

simplest graphics in black and white were only possible then in scientific research centers using machines of great size and tremendous power consumption.

## Appendix

The algorithm used for the inverse Mandelbrot set is the same as computing the traditional Mandelbrot set, with only one exception: Instead of the complex numbers $z$ and $c$ one uses the inverse complex numbers $z' = 1/z$ and $c' = 1/c$. In the computation one has to take precautions for the case that $z$ or $c$ are equal to zero.

```
INPUT "Left border of complex plane=";Cx_Min
INPUT "Right border of complex plane=";Cx_Max
INPUT "Lower border of complex plane=";Cy_Min
INPUT "Upper border of complex plane=";Cy_Max
INPUT "Maximum iteration of pixel=";Maxiter
```

```
Pixel_Horizontal=640
Pixel_Vertical=480
X_Step=(Cx_Max-Cx_Min)/Pixel_Horizontal
Y_Step=(Cy_Max-Cy_Min)/Pixel_Vertical
FOR I=0 TO Pixel_Horizontal
  Cx=Cx_Min+I*X_Step
  FOR J=0 TO Pixel_Vertical
    Cy=Cy_Min+J*Y_Step
    Denominator=Cx*Cx+Cy*Cy
    IF Denominator=0 THEN
      Cx_New=1000000
      Cy_New=Cx_New
    ELSE
      Cx_New=Cx/Denominator
      Cy_New=Cy/Denominator
    ENDIF
    X=0
    Y=0
    N=0
    REPEAT
      X_New=X*X-Y*Y+Cx_New
      Y_New=2*X*Y+Cy_New
      X=X_New
      Y=Y_New
      N=N+1
    UNTIL (N=Maxiter) OR ((X*X+Y*Y>4)
    IF (N=Maxiter) OR (N MOD 2<>0) THEN DRAW
      (I,Pixel_Vertical-J)
  NEXT J
NEXT I
```

## References

1 Franke, Herbert W. 1985. *Computer Graphics - Computer Art*. Springer Verlag, Berlin Heidelberg New York Tokyo.
2 Mandelbrot, Benoit B. 1983. *The Fractal Geometry of Nature*. W.H. Freeman and Company, New York.
3 Peitgen, H.-O., Richter, P.H. 1986. *The Beauty of Fractals*. Springer Verlag, Berlin Heidelberg New York Tokyo.
4 Pickover, Clifford A. 1990. *Computers, Pattern, Chaos and Beauty*. St. Martin's Press, New York.
5 Verbum. *Journal of Personal Computer Aesthetics*. PO Box 12564, San Diego, CA 92112.
6 Leonardo. *Journal of the International Society for the Arts, Sciences and Technology*. 2030 Addison Street Suite 400, Berkeley, CA 94704.

## Hardware and Software

1    Atari Mega ST4, Atari Corporation, Sunnyvale, CA 94086.
2    HP PaintWriter XL, Hewlett-Packard, 19310 Pruneridge Ave., Cupertino, CA 95014.
3    Macintosh IIcx, Apple Computer, 20525 Mariani Ave., Cupertino, CA 95014.
4    Kodak Colorsqueeze picture compression software, Kodak XL 7700 Digital Continuous
     Tone Printer, Eastman Kodak Co., Customer Information Center, 901 Elm Grove Road,
     Rochester, NY 14653-6224.
5    PixelPaint Professional, Supermac Technology, 485 Potrero Avenue, Sunnyvale, CA 94086.
6    Radius Rocket, Radius Inc., 1710 Fortune Dr., San Jose, CA 95131.

# Computer War Games in the 21st Century

## James J. Perry

*Regional Operations 9306, IBM Poughkeepsie, Poughkeepsie, New York 12601, USA*

*This chapter introduces the challenges facing computer game programmers who create sophisticated software opponents for complex strategy games. The basic methods and rules of table-top, or miniature, war games are presented and used to show complexities and obstacles in strategy game design. The miniature war games are contrasted with conventional board games, highlighting the more complex programming problems. Future computer war games are discussed at the end of this chapter.*

## Introduction

The inexpensive microcomputer has brought computing to the home, and the computer game market has since flourished. The success of game software created interest in problem-solving algorithms and a market for commercial chess playing programs of near master strength. These programs raise expectations that other types of strategy games will enjoy similar successes in the future. Military simulation software, particularity the scale miniature genre, is likely to benefit from the current research of strategy game algorithms. (Scale miniature games are described in the next paragraph.) Outlining the differences between traditional board games, like chess, and scale miniature games will help clarify the complexities of military simulations and the software problems they pose.

Most strategy games are played on a board. Scale miniature battles can be played on any flat surface, but are often played on specially prepared surfaces that are crafted to look like the terrain of a battle-field. The varied terrain effects the movement and combat abilities of each unit. (Units are made up of one or more miniature figures that move and fight together on the playing surface.) The free-form play area complicates the design of legal move generators and combat result prediction.

Games like chess and checkers have very simple combat resolution methods; pieces are captured by landing on the opponents square or jumping. Miniature war games have varying rules for combat resolution. Often a unit will be able to use more than one method of engagement. These methods are usually based on a *combat resolution table (CRT)* unique to the game. Some of these tables are simple enough to be solved with elementary game theory, others are more complex. All combat resolution contains a random element that effects the outcome. Miniature war game software must be able to adjust to the unpredictable combat results.

Chess pieces have different moves, but their combat value is fixed, and one piece is allowed to move each turn. Board war games allow a player to move some, all, or none of his units during a turn, but the units have a fixed combat strength. Miniature war game players are allowed to move multiple units each turn, and a unit's combat ability erodes as casualties are inflicted. Multiple unit movement causes the move tree to expand quickly, and eroding combat strength makes combat outcomes difficult to predict. (A move tree is a way of organizing movement options in the computer so that they can be searched quickly.) Combined these effects make it nearly impossible to use traditional tree search techniques. Forward pruning is a method of reducing the number of branches in the game tree by eliminating bad moves, or moves that create equivalent positions. Forward pruning is needed to make the tree manageable.

## Influences

Miniature war game playing surfaces are not usually the simple checkerboard worlds which a computer can efficiently handle. Work has already been done to overcome this problem[1]. Jones' algorithm of *scatter mapping* is a multiple step method of assigning weighted values to terrain used in the influence mapping described later. Briefly, scatter mapping is a method of superimposing a grid coordinate system on a map to simplify solving terrain problems and to assign weighted values to unique features. This grid is then used to compute the cost of movement and the most direct path from one point to another.

The original algorithm was used primarily to resolve fixed terrain features and movement problems; however, in this discussion it will be applied to variable battlefield conditions and unit abilities other than movement. The mechanics of the application are not covered. The maps will represent the various influences that terrain, units and other conditions exert on the battlefield. An influence is a scatter map representation of an effect of a terrain feature, unit, or scenario condition on an area of the battlefield. Some battlefield influences are fixed, for example terrain, and other influences are variable. Variable influences are usually derived from a unit's (friendly or enemy) manoeuvrability or combat abilities. Each will be described in turn.

Terrain is the most prominent but not the only fixed battlefield feature. Each side in a battle must have some method of measuring its success. These victory conditions may be a hill top to claim, forcing an enemy retreat, or eliminating the enemy. If these goals are tied to a specific battlefield area they should have a plotted influence.

A typical starting position is shown in Figure 1. The scenario might define occupying the hill top and bridge as the victory condition. Before the game it is a simple matter to plot influences representing how the fixed conditions affect various aspects of the game. Terrain influences might be plotted for movement, line of sight or LOS (what can be seen), line of fire or LOF (what can be fired on), charging (some terrain can not be charged through), or similar activity.

Variable battlefield influences reflect the effect a unit has on the battle. A unit simultaneously influences the surrounding battlefield in several ways and influences change during the battle. The type of influence a unit exerts depends on the combat

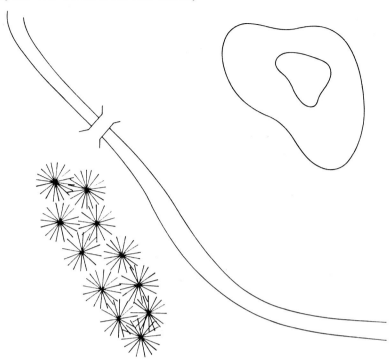

**Figure 1**   *A battlefield.* This battlefield has a number of terrain features. A swift river (parallel curves) cuts the area in two, and can only be crossed by the bridge (the ][ shape across the river) in the center of the battle. Below the bridge is a forest (collection of *). In the upper right hand corner is a hill (kidney shapes).

abilities of the unit. This discussion will briefly consider four common types of influence: melee combat, movement range, missile combat, and future influence; other types of influences can defined based on these examples.

Melee is the hand-to-hand combat common in games of the American Civil War period and earlier. The rate and volume of fire available to a unit during the period was not great enough to turn an attacking enemy before hand to hand combat was joined. A common tactic was to rush an enemy position hoping to overwhelm the less numerous defenders in the ensuing fighting. Melee is often simulated in miniature games by moving the attacking unit into contact with one or more sides of a defender. An opposing unit is in the attackers melee-influence if the target unit can be attacked during the attackers next movement. The rules of the simulation determine the shape of the melee-influence. The influence covers every part of the battlefield that can be attacked during the next movement phase. Usually melee-influence and movement-influence are exactly the same. In the instances they are not, the influences should be mapped separately. Terrain influences movement. Some types of terrain are impassable. Deep or swift rivers, for example, and forests or marshes slow movement. When mapping melee or movement influences, terrain effects must be included.

Missile-influence represents a unit's ability to engage a unit that is not in contact, and it simulates archers, cannons, firearms or other missile weapons. Missile-influence mapping is analogous to melee-influence mapping; every area that can be reached by the missiles is in the missile-influence. Determining if an area of the map can be reached by a unit's missiles requires the analysis of two elements: line of sight (LOS) and line of fire (LOF). Before a target can be hit it must be spotted. LOS is a simple task: can a unit see the target through the intervening terrain? LOF is similar to LOS, instead of determining if terrain will block the sighting of the enemy, LOF determines if the units can fire its missiles over the intervening terrain. In ancient or medieval settings line of sight and line of fire are often the same thing. But, simulations of modern battlefields are more complicated because units can spot the enemy for each other and radio the target's position to the firing units. Modern artillery can compute trajectories over mountains to hit the enemy on the other side. Terrain then is an important factor in missile combat, but its effect will vary greatly from game to game.

A unit's future-influence on the battlefield is the least concrete of the variable influences. Future-influence can be loosely defined as an area a unit will have another form of influence on after its next moves. Several factors must be taken into consideration when determining future influence:

(1) How many types of influence does each unit have?

(2) How far reaching are the influences?

(3) How many moves ahead is it practical to plot future influence?

Experience and experimentation is the best way to apply these questions because simulations that appear similar can often be different in practice. These questions help define a starting point for the experimentation.

Each unit on the battlefield should be mapped. Figure 2 shows an infantry unit on an area of the battlefield. First the melee/movement-influence was plotted to show that the unit can move six inches on the battlefield during the next turn. (The scale distances in miniature war games are usually expressed in the actual distance, in inches, measured on the playing surface.) Note the effect of the swift river: the unit is prohibited from entering the river, and this is reflected in the movement influence. This unit can charge an enemy that is 3-9 inches away. Charging is not one of the basic influences described above, but it is a simple task to read a simulation rule book and choose an analogous influence type. A careful reading of this simulation's rules reveals that charging is a specialized form of melee combat. Next the missile capability of the unit is plotted considering how the forest blocks line of sight. The river has no effect on missile influence because the unit can simply shoot over the river. Lastly, the unit's future influence is mapped. Applying our questions from before:

(1) How many types of influence does each unit have? This unit has three types of influence: Melee, Charge, and Missile. Another influence will refine the information for the unit, although it does add more complexity.

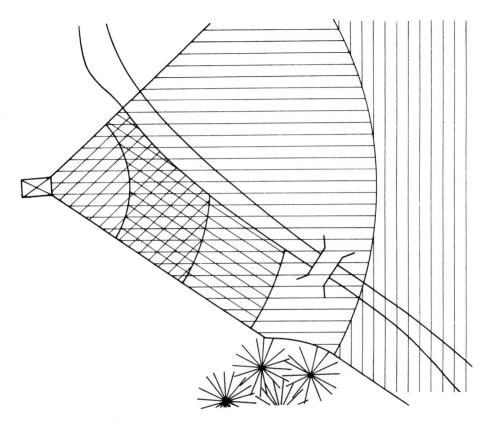

**Figure 2** *A unit's influences.* This unit influences the battlefield several ways. The area marked //// is the melee/movement-influence. The charge-influence is marked with \\\\. The missile-influence is marked with ⚏; and the | | | | area is the future-influence.

(2) How far reaching are the influences? This unit does not have far reaching influence. A far reaching influence would effect more of the battlefield, and reduce its ability to prune the move tree.

(3) How many moves ahead is it practical to plot future influence? In this example we will plot the influences one turn in the future, plotting more than one move ahead would make the influence too far reaching.

Mapping the several variable influences for a unit provides a more precise definition of how it interacts with the battlefield and other units, friendly and opposition. The several overlapping influences can be used to determine the strengths and weaknesses of each side's position, and generate and prune the move tree.

| Turns Occupied | Bridge | Hilltop | Both |
|:---:|:---:|:---:|:---:|
| 0 | 0 | 0 | 0 |
| 1 | 10 | 20 | 40 |
| 2 | 10 | 20 | 80 |
| 3 | 10 | 20 | 100 |

**Figure 3**  *Percentage of victory conditions.* This table lists the value of partial completion of the victory conditions. A score of 100 shows the game has been won.

## Evaluating the Battlefield

Before discussing how to manage the move tree it is important to understand how to evaluate battlefield conditions. A subset of the evaluation functions can be used to determine when to prune the move tree. Miniature war games are zero sum games. A zero sum game is a game in which all gains made by one player must be at the expense of the other players. The discussion below shows how to evaluate one side. The evaluation criteria can be categorized into three groups: victory conditions, unit positions, and outcome prediction.

A successful player can not forget a scenario's victory conditions. Often victory conditions are tied to a terrain feature, but sometimes are less concrete. A short, but not exhaustive, list of common victory conditions:

(1) Occupy terrain features for several turns.

(2) Eliminate enemy units.

(3) Exit a certain board edge with a specified number of units.

(4) Capture or eliminate a specific enemy unit.

(5) Prevent the opponent from meeting his victory conditions for several turns.

An evaluation function should provide a means of quantifying partial completion of the victory conditions. Consider victory condition 1, and Figure 1. A possible victory condition for this battlefield would be: a player wins if he has a unit occupying the bridge and the highest elevation of the hill simultaneously for three consecutive turns.

A glance at Figure 3 reveals one way of approaching the problem of partial completion of the victory conditions. In this example the designer determined the bridge was easier to occupy than the hill top, and since both of the features must be simultaneously occupied for three turns, no advantage is gained for occupying one of the features for multiple turns. A greater value is assigned for holding both, and this value is increased as victory nears with each turn of occupation. This value is represented as Vc in formula 3. Ideally these values could be adjusted by the software based on playing experience.

Terrain and enemy units effect the strength of a unit's position. The exact effect of terrain on a unit varies from game to game, but the following examples are typical:

*Forests:* block line of sight, slow troop movement, prevent charges, and give the defender added protection.

*Elevation:* increases missile range, slows troops climbing the incline, stops charges, eases the defense.

*Rivers:* stop the movement of units.

Other terrain and terrain effect definitions are possible, but the current ones will be used to outline unit position evaluations. The effect that terrain has on mobility, line of sight, *etc.* are accounted for by the influence mapping described earlier. A value can be assigned to an influence by finding the total area of the battlefield affected by the influence and multiplying by a suitable weighting factor. All of the influences of the unit are then totalled to find the unit position value with the formula:

$$Up = (Fi \times Fw) + (Ei \times Ew) + (Ri \times Rw) + (ni \times nw) \tag{1}$$

Where: $Up$ = Unit Position value, $Mi$ = Movement Influence, $Fw$ = Movement Weighting Constant, $Ci$ = Combat Influence, $Cw$ = Combat Weighting Constant, $Ri$ = Missile Influence, $Rw$ = Missile Weighting Constant, $ni$ = Other Influence, $nw$ = Other Weighting Constant.

When a unit's combat influences overlap an enemy position there is the potential for combat. The outcome of combat in a miniature game is less predictable than a capture in chess. Combat in chess consists of landing on an enemy piece and removing it from the board. Combat in miniature war games can have several outcomes, for example, loss of figures from the defending or attacking unit (or both), forced retreat, *etc.,* and the outcome is based on a random element. The random element is used to enter a combat resolution table (CRT) provided with the game. The mean outcome is used to evaluate a unit's strength with the formula: $Ep = (Fs - Os)$ (formula 2). Where: $Cv$ = Combat Value, $Fs$ = Mean friendly combat strength after combat, $Fe$ = Mean enemy combat strength after combat. Some simulations have CRTs with large deviations from the mean, and software written to play them would have to account for the deviations.

The three evaluations are then weighted, and the value for a player's position is determined with the formula: $Pv = (Vc * bv) + (Up * Wu) + (Cv * Wc)$ (formula 3). Where: $Pv$ = Position Value, $Vc$ = Victory Condition Value, $Wv$ = Victory Condition Weighting Constant, $Up$ = Unit position value, $Wu$ = Position Weighting Constant, $Cv$ = Combat Value, $Wc$ = Combat Value Weighting Constant.

## The Tree Search

The square-less nature of the board gives players a greater freedom to deploy their forces. If a grid were superimposed over the battlefield and the scale was small enough to realistically show the options that a player has, the move generator would create a legal move list that is unmanageable for a microcomputer. For example, a 4 foot by 8 foot table must be divided into squares no larger than 1/4 inch to accurately reflect the freedom a player has to move his units creating grid of 192 by 384. A unit allowed to move anywhere within a twelve inch square has 2,304 possible moves. If each player has six of these units the number of combinations for a player's move and all his opponent's responses is 191,102,976. This calculation accounts only for the unit's movement, not other forms of attack or combat, and the tree is already too large to be searched easily. The tree must be reduced to a more manageable number.

The tree management strategy is to identify all of the positions that are tactically equivalent and investigate them once. A *tactically equivalent area (TEA)* is a contiguous area of the battlefield under a common set of influences. All points in a TEA are considered to be equal and are evaluated as if they were one point. The influences plotted earlier are used to discover TEAs. First, all the fixed and variable influences created for the terrain features and units are plotted for the battlefield. Some of these influences will overlap and create smaller areas of combined influence. Each area bounded by an edge of the table or an influence line is a separate TEA. Each unit has its movement, combat, and missile fire plotted to the respective TEAs creating a list of legal moves for the unit, then combined with the legal moves for all other units on the side to generate all of the branches at that node.

Figure 4 shows an abbreviated battlefield map with the TEAs plotted for two units labeled x and y. Each unit has a missile influence and a combat/movement influence. The infantry unit, marked x, is on the move. The figure shows 9 TEAs. The branches for x are created by determining which TEAs it can move to, and the TEAs that are in the units missile range. Unit x can move to the TEAs numbered 5, 6, 7, and 8, and can fire its missiles into 3, 4, 6, and 8. Totaling these, we find that we have pruned the tree to 11 branches.

## General Application

This discussion of miniature war game software would not be complete with out mentioning some general design considerations. Not all influences need to be plotted to accurately reflect the battlefield position and evaluation factors must be properly weighted. Several factors affect the design of influence plotting and battlefield evaluation.

### Scale

The scale of the scenario determines the amount of detail that should be simulated by the software. The details should replicate the concerns that the battlefield commander might experience. For example, in a tank versus tank simulation each commander might have to manage his fuel and ammunition, but would not be concerned with the detailed planning of resupply routes and schedules. Conversely, a theatre size scenario should not try to simulate every tank or infantry company.

### Battlefield Effect

Each attribute of a unit must be considered before including it in a scenario or creating a separate influence for the attribute. If the attribute will have little or no impact on the

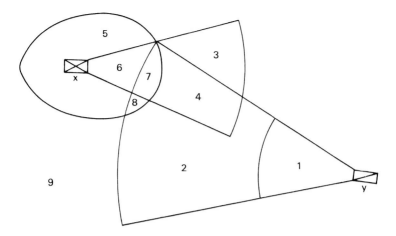

**Figure 4**    *Overlapping influences.* When units approach each other, their influences overlap.

accuracy of the simulation then it is best to exclude it. Sometimes the attribute should be included for historical purposes, but it has little impact on the outcome of the battle. Now, the designer should consider plotting the influence only in specific circumstances, or perhaps not at all.

### *Fluctuation Level*

Battles are sometimes fought in static positions with limited unit movement and combat, and other times are fluid and chaotic. It is easier to apply this design to static battles because the TEAs reflect the current state of the battle, and a rigorous evaluation function can be applied. Fluid battles are not likely candidates for a rigorous evaluation. Fluid battles require a greater depth of tree searching and a well constructed forward pruning algorithm.

These factors should be considered before beginning to design the software of a miniature war game, with careful emphasis the algorithm can be modified to provide a balance between tree searching and evaluation.

### Future Strategy Game Software

The future of strategy game software is limitless. In part the interest and usefulness of combat simulations is their complexity and detail. The victor is often the player who can best decipher the position and create a plan to take advantages of his opponents weaknesses. Unlike chess, the fluctuating nature of war games is more suited to an algorithm that sets goals and creates plans to meet them, rather than exhaustive tree searching techniques. This paper has emphasized the evaluations that will be needed to analyze the battlefield to provide input to a goal setting algorithm.

The programming of strategy games is a good candidate for multitasking operating systems. Each unit could be a separate task managing its own movement and combat. If care were taken to provide the task with the same type of information that is available to a unit's commander in the field, the realism of the units actions would be enhanced.

Many of the lessons of a miniature war game algorithm are applicable to a broader range of problems. The military and naval commands stage elaborate, full scale, war games to teach strategy and tactics to officers that are expensive in both time and money. The training of military and naval officers is an expensive process. Recently the military has begun to use computer simulation to reduce the cost of training. If technically accurate and complete software is written to simulate battlefield decisions, the costs of teaching of military history can be reduced, allowing a more comprehensive course of study. When coupled to *virtual reality* hardware, resembling airplane flight simulators, future officers will have ultra-realistic visions of battles. The effect of this may be more efficient and effective war strategies, or even emotional reactions to the horrors of war made more evident in realistic war games in the 21st century.

## Acknowledgements

I would like to thank Sam Duke for his fine line drawings.

## References

1    Jones, S.T. Solving Problems Involving Variable Terrain. *Byte Magazine,* **5**(2), 58–68 and 5(3), 74–82.

# Will Computers Really THINK in the 21st Century?

## Ira Glickstein

*IBM Federal Sector Division, 0902, Owego, NY 13827, USA*

*Today's computers have given us the wonderful panoply of automated devices that permeate our lives. While these tools do a fine job of simulating narrow aspects of intelligence in some domains of knowledge, they have, so far, failed to achieve anything like the* general *intelligence humans are capable of. Progress towards duplicating intelligence on a non-organic substrate will remain stymied until we understand the relationship between computation and thinking. In this chapter, I give my personal views on how computers, capable of thinking, may be constructed in the 21st century.*

## The Need for Insight

Each of us has experienced the phenomenon we call "insight." Faced with a novel situation, we search our repertoire of responses but sometimes cannot find a solution to the problem. Later, we are struck by a sudden "flash of insight" and instantly know the answer. From a subjective point of view, we are unaware of any sort of "trial and error" search process. Unlike "normal" problems, where we know a solution method that, given sufficient effort, will inevitably bring us to the answer, insight problems appear impervious to any amount of effort, but then suddenly yield an answer without any apparent human effort at all.

Herbert A. Simon, an artificial intelligence (AI) pioneer, explains the "aha!" aspect of insight as resulting from a change in representation as we heuristically search a hierarchy of "search spaces."[1] (Let me give some definitions. AI is the branch of computer science that deals with computers to simulate human thinking. "Heuristic search" is an AI term for computation methods that find satisfactory answers without exploring every possibility. For example, one could play unbeatable chess by considering every possible sequence of moves by both players and making only moves that lead to victory. Such a strategy, called "exhaustive search," could be used for a simple game but would be impractical for chess and for most real-world problems. Therefore, heuristic search must be utilized.)

The search paradigm, which is rooted in the AI interpretation of the Church–Turing (CT) thesis (defined below), conceives of all solutions as pre-existing in a hierarchy of search spaces, and the basic problem of intelligence being the application of heuristics that constrain search so we may find solutions more rapidly. Haugeland (ref.2, p.137) states the CT thesis as follows: "For any deterministic, automatic formal system whatever, there exists a formally equivalent Turing machine." (A Turing machine is a very simple digital computer.) Hofstadter (ref. 3, p. 578) gives what he calls the "AI version" of the CT thesis: "Mental processes of any sort can be simulated by a computer program whose underlying language is [one] in which all partial recursive functions can be programmed." If this interpretation of the CT thesis is valid, anything that is computable by any machine, including mental processes in a brain (if we accept, as I do, that the brain is a machine) is also computable by your personal computer (if you have the time and are willing to flip diskettes to achieve necessary storage).

Given this mind set, we can understand why AI pioneers like Simon seized on "means-ends analysis" and other heuristics they thought were generally applicable to all search problems. The apparent success of programs such as General Problem Solver (GPS) lead Simon[4] to proclaim: "... there are now [1957] in the world machines that think, that learn and that create. Moreover, their ability to do these things is going to increase rapidly until – in a visible future – the range of problems they can handle will be coextensive with the range to which the human mind has been applied." This proclamation was accompanied by four predictions, expected to be true in a decade. A computer would: (1) be world chess champion, (2) discover and prove an important new math theorem, and (3) write critically acclaimed music. A fourth prediction was that most theories in psychology would take the form of computer programs.

Two decades later, although only the fourth prediction was (arguably) true, Newell and Simon[5] boldly stated the Physical Symbol System Hypothesis which holds that a physical machine that can manipulate symbols (e.g., an ordinary digital computer with an appropriate program) "has the necessary and sufficient means for general intelligent action." Elaine Rich, in her authoritative AI text (ref.6, p.3), calls this hypothesis "the underlying assumption ... at the heart of research in artificial intelligence." "Strong AI" is the belief, subscribed to by many AI and computer scientists today, that all brains and all computers, regardless of differences in material and architecture, are equivalent for any mental process whatsoever. I believe this idea will come to be understood as a serious failure of insight, bordering on mass delusion.

Simon's first three predictions remain unfulfilled to this day, but does this mean the CT thesis is wrong? Not necessarily, as Dietrich (ref.7, p227–228) points out: "Turing's conclusion is simply that intelligent thought can be captured in a recipe ... [but] this fact is useless in helping us find the correct program." According to Haugeland (ref.3, p.183), "GPS was a dream come false ... [because] the basic plan presupposes that, under the skin, all problems (or at least all solutions) are pretty much alike. Thus, once a problem is suitably formulated, it should succumb to the same general techniques – means-ends analysis or whatever – as any other." For Reeke and Edelman (ref.8, p.146), "the problem requiring intelligence is the original one of finding a representation. To place this problem in the domain of the system designer rather than in that of the designed system is to beg the question and reduce intelligence to symbol manipulation." The strong AI interpretation is not the only way the CT thesis may be understood. Indeed, Hofstadter (ref 3, pp.566–580) provides nine additional versions, including "At bottom, all mathematicians are isomorphic [of similar shape, form, or structure]," "All brain processes are derived from a computable substrate," and "Computers are ridiculous. So is science in general."

The total failure of AI research with respect to anything approaching human level *general* intelligence reminds me of a (much less monumental) failure of insight. When my Dad taught me the rules of chess I concluded that pawns were worse than useless because they blocked my stronger pieces. My "insight" was "confirmed" by a few games with my girlfriend, which I won by reckless blitz attacks. Needless to say, when I tried these tactics on my father, he hunkered down behind his pawns, arranged along diagonals, and watched with amusement as I wasted my resources on a wild and hopeless attack. That experience taught me insight could be wrong as well as right. This is exactly what has happened with the supposed insight of the AI pioneers. Symbol manipulation worked on relatively simple "toy" problems, in narrow domains of knowledge, for which researchers already knew the answers or had a formal method guaranteed to find the solution by searching in a pre-defined space. However, when applied to more difficult problems, these "insightful" solutions have failed to work.

## So What is Missing from Today's Computers and Programs?

Today's computers, made of silicon semiconductors interconnected via copper wires, utilize what is known as a "serial von Neumann" architecture, named after computer pioneer John von Neumann who invented them about 50 years ago. In this architecture, the hardware consists of a central processing unit (CPU), memory storage unit, and input and output devices such as keyboards and displays. The software consists of a program of computer instructions and data, stored as discrete symbols (strings of "1's and 0's"). The sequence of instructions executed by the CPU is governed by the stored program and by input commands and data from a keyboard or disk drive (or a sensory device such as a mouse, microphone or TV camera). Execution of certain instructions may modify the stored data or instructions. Certain sequences of instructions control outputs to the display screen and disk drive (or effector devices such as a speaker, printer or motor).

This combination of hardware and software is known as the "serial, symbolic" computational paradigm. Automated systems based on this paradigm have proven to be very good at executing effective procedures (solving a familiar problem with novel parameters using a step-by-step procedure and "turn the crank" effort). They do this at blinding speeds, without logical error or boredom, to the point where they often surpass their creators at tasks considered to require intelligence when done by humans. However, we must not confound this type of computation with thinking at the human level of general intelligence. The latter requires an ability to discover effective procedures (solve truly novel problems by means of "insight."). Brains can do this but serial, symbolic computers cannot.

From what we know of the architecture of the human central nervous system and brain, it consists of billions of active organic cells (neurons), each with a pattern of interconnections to thousands of others. Some of these neurons connect the brain to sensory cells and others to muscle cells. Neurons "fire" (generate electrical impulses) at rates that vary according to internal processes and stimulation or inhibition due to electrical and chemical signals from other neurons and sensory cells. The flow and sequence of impulses in the brain is governed by the stimulai and the pattern and strength of neuronal interconnections. A complex feedback system causes certain spatial and temporal firing sequences to be reinforced. This is accomplished by dynamically varying the strengths of some of the interconnections between neurons. Certain sequences of neuronal impulses cause stimulation to be conducted via the nervous system to control the muscles.

What is present in organic brains and missing from serial, symbolic computers? One could list several things, including: (1) live organic material, (2) continuously-variable, non-synchronous processing, (3) multi-dimensional architecture, (4) self-organizing "software" embedded in hardware, and (5) seamless integration of sensors, processors, and effectors.

The first element, live organic material, is characteristic of 100% of "truly" intelligent organisms on Earth at this moment. We may therefore not dismiss out of hand the possibility that there is something unique about live organic material that is necessary for general intelligence at the human level. However, we should not cease trying to reach the ultimate goal of AI research on that account.

The second element, continuously-variable, non-synchronous processing, could be provided, if necessary, by asynchronous analog networks fabricated of copper and silicon. However, digital processing can match the precision of analog processes (since analog processes are inherently limited by noise).

That leaves us with the final three elements. As described later in this chapter, these elements are characteristic of a new computational paradigm called "connectionism," which is based on subsymbolic processing on massively parallel devices. Such devices may be implemented on a copper and silicon substrate using a combination of discrete-level, neural-like networks and/or cellular automaton architectures. (Artificial neural networks are an attempt to replicate, in copper and silicon, something like the networks of organic neurons in the brain. Cellular automata are arrays of processors whose output state depends upon the state of its neighbors in the previous time cycle. Cellular automata are sometimes called "the other von Neumann architecture" because he invented them too.)

In the sections that follow, I provide supporting references and justify my belief that these three connectionist elements are at least necessary for the practical implementation of general intelligence on a non-organic substrate. Perhaps they are both necessary and sufficient to make such implementation possible.

I wish to distinguish my views from those of John Searle and Roger Penrose who have also been critical of the claims of strong AI. I agree with them to a point – namely that serial computers running symbolic algorithms will not yield insightful thinking. However, they go much further, each in his own way. Searle, who originated the term "strong AI",[9] focusses on what he calls the "causal" properties of the material substrate. While not excluding the possibility that some configuration of silicon chips might constitute a thinking machine, he specifically rejects the connectionist paradigm as the solution.[10] Penrose appeals to Godel's theorem to argue that "insights, from outside the system ... cannot be systematized – and, indeed, must lie outside any algorithmic action!" (ref.11, p.110). (Godel showed that any formal mathematical system of sufficient complexity contains truths that are neither provable nor disprovable within the system.) Penrose then applies arguments from quantum gravity, a new theory that introduces time-assymmetry to overcome fundamental problems with quantum theory, to argue that there is an essential non-algorithmic ingredient to conscious thought processes in brains. Since computers, by our design, may only execute algorithmic processes, they are incapable of conscious thought, which is essential to true intelligence (ref.11, p.404, p.407). Penrose rejects parallel processing as any more capable of intelligence than serial processing, citing their Turing equivalence (ref.11, p.398.)

## True Multi-Dimensional Modeling/Intercommunication

The AI entity must have the ability to create a true model (not simply an analysis) of the environment in multiple dimensions, with sensors, processors, and effectors connected to each other via multi-dimensional channels.

We should be troubled by the fact that serial, symbolic computers can handle problems in any number of dimensions, while humans run into serious limitations in understanding problems with greater than three dimensions. We are forced to use graphical and analytic methods to solve problems of greater dimensionality, which is very different from solving a problem by "picturing" it in the "mind's eye." Serial computers are inherently limited to a single dimension plus time, and programmers are therefore forced to utilize analytical algorithms, rather than true multi-dimensional modeling to solve problems of greater dimensionality.

In Figure 1, I have indicated how, on a log scale, serial computer execution time increases linearly with the number of dimensions (*i.e.,* in direct proportion to the quantity of data). Human execution time, however, exhibits a breakpoint at 4-D. At 4-D and below, we are often able to picture the solution. Indeed, for some problems, such as finding a path from one point to another, some people prefer a 3-D picture or sketch to a 2-D map. At 5-D and above, we are forced to make use of graphical or mathematical analysis techniques, and solution difficulty appears to increase much more rapidly than the quantity of data. While using such analytical techniques, I feel that I am just "turning the crank" and blindly following procedures, like a human automaton. If insight is "inner vision," then humans have insight up to 3-D plus time, while serial digital computers are limited to 1-D plus time. No wonder they cannot solve insight problems as well as we do – they have severely limited insight.

There is strong evidence that humans utilize mental images as a mechanism to solve certain types of problems, not just as a means of representing the problem and the solution (ref. 2, p. 221). Evidence that we actualize images in solving problems is provided by Shepard and Metzler's 1971 mental rotation experiment, in which subjects had to mentally rotate objects shown to them as 3-D sketches, (reported in ref. 2, p.

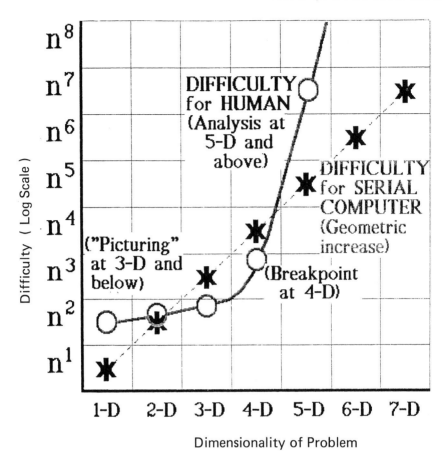

**Figure 1**  *Difficulty vs dimensionality for human "picturing" and computer solution.*
Humans have difficulty in understanding problems with greater than 3 dimensions.

225). Reaction time, minus a small constant, was directly proportional to the amount
of rotation needed. Also, more complex images took longer to rotate. The possibility
that time and mass may also be actualized in mental images is supported by the fact
that heavy objects, when mentally rotated, take longer to speed up, and to slow down,
as if they actually had inertia. Evidence from microscopic examination of the brain
indicates that neurons are arranged in multiple 2-D sheets to reflect the natural geometry
or informationally significant dimensionality of the sensory data.[12]

Interconnection must also be multi-dimensional to support true communications.
For example, imagine we are in radio and TV communication with a far-off galaxy that
has excess manufacturing capacity. We order a large quantity of screws, described in
complete detail, and even include a TV picture. The delivered product is perfect in every

way, but we are flabbergasted to discover they won't work because we needed screws that engage by turning the screwdriver clockwise and they delivered counterclockwise ones! How could this miscommunication occur? If we only exchange serial strings of symbols, there is no way we can communicate the distinction between clockwise and counterclockwise. Even the TV picture might not distinguish the correct configuration of the screw threads, because they may scan their TV sets the opposite way we do.

The point of this is that language (exchange of sequences of symbols) is a 1-D means of communications, and filters any information in higher dimensionality. The only way to convey information by language is if the recipient already knows what you are talking about! Cummins (ref.13, p.4) distinguishes "*cognition" from "cognition," but here he might have used the words "re-cognition" and "cognition." All we can accomplish via 1-D communication links is re-cognition, that is getting the recipient's mind's eye to see something it has seen before, or a combination of things it has seen before. So long as our computers take as input 1-D strings called "programs" they will be limited to re-cognizing tasks, that is tasks that have been done before and for which there is an effective procedure that can be expressed in terms of a symbol string. Waltz (ref.14, p.197) considers this an essential defect of Newell and Simon's physical symbol system hypothesis, because strings of symbols are hopelessly coarse and vague and lack "subsymbolic" distinctions. Churchland (ref.15, p.85) stresses the need for multi-dimensionality to account for and transmit meaningful information, since "any declarative sentence to which a speaker would give confident assent is merely a one-dimensional projection–through the compound lens of Wernicke's and Broca's [brain] areas onto the idiosyncratic surface of the speaker's language – a one-dimensional projection of a four- or five-dimensional 'solid' that is an element in his true kinematical state." Dimensionality of the processing and communication medium must match that of the situation. Churchland asks us to recall the 2-D shadows of 3-D objects projected on the wall in Socrates "Parable of the Cave." As Plato recounts the story, these subdimensional projections were unfit to represent reality in all its aspects.

## Self-Organizing Embedded Soft/Hardware

The software and hardware of the AI entity must be one and indistinguishable. If there is any separation we have simulation, not duplication. Furthermore, the system, at some level, must be self-organizing, otherwise it will be a mere extension of the designers and programmers.

One of the most troubling things about today's computers is their ability to unerringly, and at blinding speeds, do tasks humans find difficult, such as long division. Yet things we find easy, such as recognizing faces, are done poorly and slowly (if at all). The separation of software from hardware, which allows the same program to run on multiple hardware, and the same hardware to run multiple programs (Figure 2), is what gives computers their tremendous power, and at the same time, robs them of anything like insight.

For example, I might write a program to control an automobile factory, and you might write a program to play the game Parchesi, and by chance, both programs, symbol for symbol and bit for bit might be identical. This would be possible because representations in symbolic computation are not related to the physical world except accidentally. If we load the program into a game console, it plays Parchesi; if we load it into a computer at the factory, it orders the assembly of cars. It can do either task without any real understanding because it has no idea what it is doing. According to Reeke and Edelman (ref.8, p.170), we must abandon the separation of hardware from software and design machines that work without programs and adapt to the environment, as biological organisms do.

The software must be embedded in the hardware at the very basic substrate level, as it is with organisms made from biological cells. This substrate must in some sense be self-organizing. The cell of a cellular automaton (or the node of an artificial neuron), would be a start in the right direction both for embedding software at a low level and for providing self-organization as a basic operating mode. However, the cellular automaton and artificial neural nets in today's laboratories are mostly simulated within serial, symbolic computers. Even today's massively parallel computers, such as the Connection Machine, and analog neural networks are far from what will eventually be required to create such AI entities.

## Seamless Integration of Sensors, Processors, and Effectors

The AI entity must have relationships with the environment that are truly meaningful, not just to us, the designers, programmers, and observers of its behavior, but to the AI entity itself.

For example, when I give an orange to a robot, the robot may recognize it, test it for quality, provide agricultural and nutritional details, and even "eat" the orange by using it as fuel for generation of electricity. However, even if the robot says "Yum, yum" and drools a bit, no one believes there is any real understanding, by the robot, of the concept of " orangeness" (of the type a person, or a baboon, would have). The difference is obvious! Every organic cell knows, in physical, not merely-syntactic ways, what it means to obtain nourishment, to sense various chemicals, to react to impinging pressure, light, or electrical energy – in short, what it means to "eat" something.

In the case of the robot, the TV camera module simply generates a stream of modulated electrical impulses that may be reduced to discrete symbols, describing shapes and colors. In another context, that same stream of impulses could represent financial data or a telephone conversation! These arbitrary symbols are transmitted to the computer module which matches them against stored symbols, gets a match on "orange" and, following a formal program, instructs the robot arm module to place the object in the chemical analysis module where the object may be checked for chemical content and then used as fuel by the furnace/electrical generator module. Symbols sent to the loudspeaker module cause it to say "Yum, yum," and the process complete flag is set.

How may we create copper and silicon entities which have meaningful relationships with their environment? We might begin by asking how Nature bridges the gap between mere organization of symbols (syntax) and real meaning (semantics)? Howard

**Figure 2** *Pick a program, ANY program! In today's computers, hardware is separate from software, and real meaning is separated from symbolic representations.*

Pattee (ref.16, pp.338–339) suggests it is the biological cell that is the first natural level of what he calls semantic closure of the syntactic-semantic loop. Organic cells transform molecules into the strings of symbols we call DNA, and also are capable of converting these strings back to meaningful information, namely the primary sequence of a protein. Following this model, we have to design a basic, low-level, self-replicating copper and silicon unit that, like the organic cell, is capable of generating and transforming symbols that are meaningful to it. These elemental units must have embedded processing and multi-dimensional interfaces.

As we combine billions of elemental units to create entities that are capable of artificial cognition at higher levels, we must take care to create collectives, rather than mere aggregations. The interfaces must have consequences for the parties involved. They must be seamless such that the various parts really care about the welfare of the entity as a whole. Thus, we will need the robot equivalent of feelings and emotions. I have previously considered the role of feelings and emotions in assuring the survival of super-organisms, and possible implementation in copper and silicon of the robot equivalent.[17] Any modularity in the design must be carefully examined to assure semantic connection. One may argue that the human brain is modular, with brainstem, thalamus, cerebellum, and cerebral cortex, and within the cortex, the various lobes and areas such as Wernicke's and Broca's. However, these distinctions are merely convenient symbolic labels, conventionally applied by those humans who study brain organization. Complex and multi-dimensional connections and relationships exist between and among each of these "modules." The world is an unlabelled place. As Democrites said long ago: "By convention there is color, by convention there is sweetness, by convention bitterness, but in reality there are atoms and space."

## Implementing the Missing Elements

The key problem with the serial, symbolic computational paradigm that has dominated the first fifty years of the computer age may be summarized in one word: separatism. We have separation of hardware from software, sensors from processors, processors from effectors, multi-dimensionality from communications, and, therefore, separation of symbols from meaning. So long as we place *discovery* of effective procedures solely in the realm of the system designer and programmer, and only the *execution* of these procedures in the realm of the computer, we will continue to suffer from the practical and theoretical consequences of separatism. We have had an awfully good time creating automated tools that simulate aspects of intelligence in facinating and even commercially useful ways, but will continue to fall short of creating anything like *general* intelligence until we face up to the problem.

The answer, in a word, is connectionism, see Figure 3. This term has been used by Smolensky[18] and others to describe a new computational paradigm based on subsymbolic elements, massively parallel networks of concurrent processors, and self-organization of "software" embedded within the hardware. Here's how I, a systems engineer and logic designer, would approach the problem of achieving general intelligence on a non-organic substrate in light of the new connectionist paradigm:

- *True Multi-Dimensional Modeling and Intercommunication.* This may be the easiest part of the solution if we assume that packing densities for microchips will continue to grow, and fabrication costs continue to fall. However, even with a speed advantage of a million or more for microchips compared to organic cells, we have a long way to go before we can match the raw processing capabilities of the human brain's 10-100 billion neurons, each connected to an average of about 10 thousand others.

- *Self-Organizing Soft/Hardware.* The hardware/software distinction may be eliminated by making use of the self-organizing capabilities of artificial neural networks and cellular automata. My main worry about self-organization is that, even with the speed advantage of silicon circuits over organic cells, and help from us based on organic models, it may take many thousands or millions of years for them to self-organize to achieve human levels of general intelligence.

- *Seamless Integration of Sensors, Processors and Effectors.* Signals may be wired directly from sensor transducers to the processing elements, in parallel, and from

Massively Parallel

Seamless, Multi-D
Sensor Interfaces

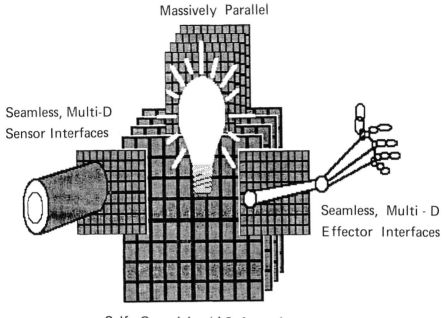

Seamless, Multi - D
Effector Interfaces

Self - Organizing ' ' Software'
Embedded within Hardware

**Figure 3** *21st century computers, designed according to the connectionist paradigm, may be capable of insightful thinking.*

the processing elements to the effectors. This is a start, but I'm worried that guaranteed power to each processing element, and the fact that a processing element cannot "die" from the consequences of its actions, may limit its ability to really care about what is going on. Perhaps the answer is a hierarchical organization, where "watchdog" processors, of lower complexity but higher loyalty to the superorganisms that own the entity, enforce the robot equivalent of feelings and emotions to keep the other processors in line.

The first century of the industrial age was dominated by the steam engine, which is characterized by the separation of fuel combustion from thrust generation. This turned out to have both practical and theoretical consequences. It took the internal combustion engine to make air travel practical, and rocket engines to make space travel possible. In both cases, combustion and thrust generation are inseparably interconnected! Perhaps there is a lesson here that may be applied to the computer age.

## Conclusion

An important paradigm shift, from serial, symbolic computation to massively parallel, subsymbolic computation will characterize computing in the 21st century. This new connectionist paradigm will prove to have both practical and theoretical consequences. The practical consequences, which we will see early in the 21st century, will include much greater flexibility, as well as a geometrical increase in speed and power as we learn to program these new machines (or, more likely, set them up to self-organize). Personal computers will give way to ever-present mental co-processors, at first worn like portable radios or TVs, but later surgically implanted in our bodies like heart pacemakers. While not capable of general intelligent action on their own, these aptly named THINKmans (Asimov) will prove invaluable in automating tasks we find boring or dangerous, helping us visualize complex information, and intimately connecting us to the mental processes of other humans to solve difficult problems.

The theoretical consequences, which may include the ability of copper and silicon machines to exhibit human-like general intelligence, will take much longer to achieve, and may not occur in the 21st century, despite our best efforts. After much effort, and considerable success in ever expanding but still limited domains of knowledge, we may decide on an alternative approach to designing and engineering AI entities capable of insightful thought. We will let a large number of self-replicating robots loose on some uninhabited planet, and plan to come back in a few billion years, expecting to discover (if their decendants still exist) what copper and silicon entities, capable of real insightful intelligence, actually look like!

## References

1   Kaplan, C.A. and Simon, H.A. 1988. *In Search of Insight.* Carnegie-Mellon University.
2   Haugland, J. 1987. *Artificial Intelligence, The Very Idea.* Bradford Books, The MIT Press, Cambridge, MA.
3   Hofstadter, D. 1979. *Godel, Escher, Bach: An Eternal Golden Braid.* Vintage Books, NY.
4   Simon, H.A. 1957. Address to Operations Research Society of America (crediting Newell, A. as co-author), Nov. 14, 1957.
5   Newell, A. and Simon, H. 1976. Computer Science as Empirical Inquiry: Symbols and Search, Tenth Turing Award Lecture. *Communications of the Association for Computing Machinery,* March.
6   Rich, E. 1983. *Artificial Intelligence,* McGraw-Hill, New York.
7   Dietrich, E. 1990. *Programs in the Search for Intelligent Machines: the Mistaken Foundations of AI in The Foundations of Artificial Intelligence.* Partridge, D. and Wilks, Y. (eds.).
8   Reeke, G.N. and Edelman, G.M. 1988. *Real Brains and Artificial Intelligence in The Artificial Intelligence Debate* Graubard, S. R., (ed.). MIT Press, Cambridge, MA.
9   Searle, J.R. 1980. *Minds, Brains, and Programs, Behavioral and Brain Sciences,* 3(3), 417–458.
10  Searle, J.R. 1990. Is the Brain's Mind a Computer Program? *Scientific American,* January.
11  Penrose, R. 1989. *The Emperor's New Mind.* Oxford University Press, Oxford.
12  Schwartz, J.T. 1988. *The New Connectionism: Developing Relationships Between Neuroscience and Artificial Intelligence in The Artificial Intelligence Debate.* Graubard, S.R., (ed.), MIT Press, Cambridge, MA.
13  Cummins, R. 1983. *The Nature of Psychological Explanation.* MIT Press, Cambridge, MA.
14  Waltz, D.L. 1988. *The Prospects for Building Truly Intelligent Machines, in The Artificial Intelligence Debate,* Graubard, S.R. (ed.). MIT Press, Cambridge, MA.

15 Churchland, P.M. 1981. Eliminative Materialism and the Propositional Attitudes, *J. Philos.,* LXXVIII, No. 2, Feb. 1981.

16 Pattee, H.H. 1982. Cell Psychology: An Evolutionary Approach to the Symbol-Matter Problem. *Cognition and Brain Theory,* **5**(4), 325–341.

17 Glickstein, I. 1990. Role of Feelings and Emotions in a Future Just Society Consisting of Humans and AI Entities, July 1990, Proceedings of the 34th Annual Meeting, International Society for the Systems Sciences, Portland, OR.

18 Smolensky, P. 1988. *On the Proper Treatment of Connectionism, Behavioral and Brain Sciences,* No. 11.

# Fractals and Genetics in the Future

## H. Joel Jeffrey

*Computer Science Department, Northern Illinois University, DeKalb, Illinois 60115, USA*

*Fractals are intricate patterns which today appear in computer art books and serious physics journals. Will graphics and analysis tools in the field of fractal geometry provide useful scientific insight in the 21st century? This chapter describes an application to the study of genetic sequences and English text sequences. This is one novel application of fractals – just one example of the kinds of methods which will be increasingly used in the next century.*

## Introduction

It is very difficult for us to develop an understanding of long sequences of letters and numbers. As humans we seem to be very good at identifying patterns within compact structures, but comparatively poor when dealing with long sequential presentations. (You can find a unique discussion of this fact, with some very far-reaching implications, in ref. 5.) Converting a sequence, which is basically a one-dimensional set of inputs, into a graphical form that presents the data in ways that allow us to visually grasp the overall patterns expands our abilities as investigators in two ways. It makes standard investigating easier and more efficient, and it allows entirely new questions and areas of investigation to develop. An excellent example of this phenomena is the Mandelbrot set, that now-famous intricate fractal object in complex mathematics. The graphical representation of this set (Figure 1) is highly motivating and provokes many questions that quite literally could not occur without the picture. (For example: At what position and angle do the tiny copies of the heart-shaped object occur in this set?)

## The Chaos Game

The Chaos Game is an algorithm which I developed for studying linear sequences, which is based on "iterated function systems".[1] The method allows one to produce pictures of fractal structures, using paper and pencil or, obviously, a computer. In simplest form, it proceeds as follows:

(1) Locate three dots on a piece of paper as the vertices of a triangle, and label them with the numerals 1 through 6 (1 and 2 for the first vertex, 3 and 4 for the second, 5 and 6 for the third).

**Figure 1**    *The Mandelbrot Set.*

(2)  Pick a point anywhere on the paper, and mark it. This is the initial point.
(3)  Roll a 6-sided die. Since the vertices were labelled, the number that comes up on the die is a label on a vertex. Place a mark half way between the previous point and the indicated vertex. For example, if 3 is rolled, place a mark on the paper half way between the previous point and the vertex labelled "3".
(4)  Continue to roll the die, on each roll marking the paper at the point half way between the previous point and the indicated vertex.
     This procedure is the *Chaos Game.*[1] After several thousand repetitions the resulting pattern, known as the *attractor*, is called the Sierpinski Triangle (Figure 2).
     The result of the Chaos Game on other than three points is not, as one might think, a four-, five- *etc.*- pointed Sierpinski-like figure. For five, six, or seven initial points the chaos game produces a figure with visible patterns (pentagons within pentagons, a striated hexagon, or heptagons within heptagons), but for eight or more points the game yields essentially a filled-in polygon, except that the center is empty.
     With four initial points, however, the result is different: it is a square uniformly and randomly filled with dots.

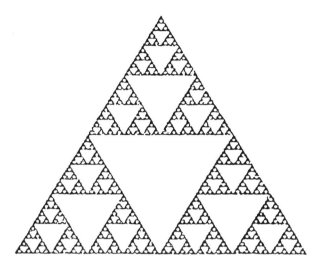

**Figure 2**   *The result of the Chaos Game on three points.*

## Iterated Function Systems

Mathematically, the chaos game is described by an *iterated function system* (IFS). An IFS is a set of pairs of linear mappings, each pair of the form $x = ax + by + e$, $y = cx + dy + f$. Each pair of maps gives the function for computing the new value of the x and y coordinates. If vertices are at (0,0), (0,1), and (1,0) and 3 is rolled, vertex 2 is indicated, and the coordinates of the new point are given by $x = 0.5 \times (x + 0) = 0.5x$, and $y = 0.5 \times (y + 1.0) = 0.5y + 0.5$.

With three vertices, and one map per coordinate, we need six maps. We can write the maps in a compact tabular form as follows. We let $w(x,y) = (ax + by + e, cx + dy + f)$, and then the map is given by the six coefficients $a$ through $f$. For the Sierpinski triangle, the maps are:

| | | | | | | |
|---|---|---|---|---|---|---|
| $w_1$ | 0.5 | 0 | 0 | 0.5 | 0 | 0 |
| $w_2$ | 0.5 | 0 | 0 | 0.5 | 0 | 0.5 |
| $w_3$ | 0.5 | 0 | 0 | 0.5 | 0.5 | 0.5 |

If the probabilities of the maps are not equal, the shape of the attractor is unchanged, but the shading of the attractor may be.[1]

In tabular form, including the probabilities, we can use the following compact notation, which is known as *the IFS code*:

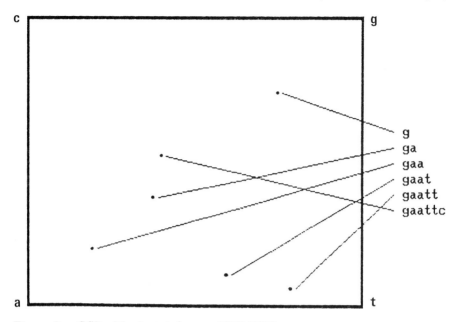

**Figure 3**    *CGR of the first six bases of HUMHBB.*

**Table 1** *IFS Code for the Sierpinski Triangle*

| w | a | b | c | d | e | f | p |
|---|-----|---|---|-----|-----|-----|------|
| 1 | 0.5 | 0 | 0 | 0.5 | 0   | 0   | 0.33 |
| 2 | 0.5 | 0 | 0 | 0.5 | 0   | 0.5 | 0.33 |
| 3 | 0.5 | 0 | 0 | 0.5 | 0.5 | 0.5 | 0.33 |

## Non-random Sequences

Quite by chance, the author and a colleague, (G.M. Henry) discovered that the random number generator used to select vertices can make a very significant difference. With a good random number generator, the Chaos Game on 8 points produces an almost-filled octagonal. However, when the game is played using Turbo Pascal 3.0, which has a flawed random number generator,[6] elaborate patterns are visible, resembling a circle within a circle, the circles connected by 8 (or, respectively, 16) spidery lines.

Since intuitively non-randomness means that a sequence has "structure", or mathematically a non-uniformity of subsequences,[6] we speculated that using successive elements of a known sequence, rather than a random number generator, might produce a useful visual representation of the sequence. We tested this speculation by investigating DNA sequences. Since a DNA sequence can be treated formally as a string

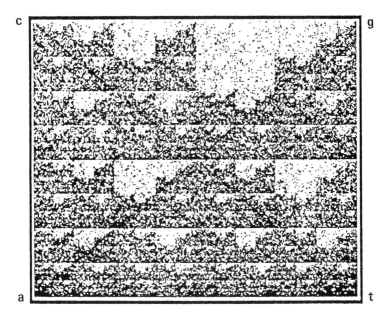

**Figure 4**    *CGR of human beta globin region on chromosome 11 (HUMHBB) (73,357 bases).*

composed from the four letters "a", "c", "g", and "t" (or "u"), it was an obvious candidate for testing the CGR to see whether visually interesting features were present.

We wrote a program (for a PC) to draw a square on the screen labelled with the bases "a", "c", "g", and "t" (clockwise beginning at the lower left corner) and then plot successive points according to the Chaos Game algorithm, using successive bases of a user-specified DNA sequence to pick successive vertices.

Example: The first six bases of the human beta globin region on chromosome 11 (abbreviated HUMHBB[2]) are "gaattc".

(1) The first "g" is plotted half way between the center of the square and the "g" corner.
(2) The next base, "a", is plotted half way between the point just plotted and the "a" corner.
(3) The base "a" is plotted half way between the previous point and "a" corner.
(4) Next, "t" is plotted half way between the previous point and the "t" corner.
    *etc.*

Plotting these six bases, we obtain Figure 3.

As with the initial points of the Sierpinski triangle, little significance is visible. However, if we continue for the entire 73,357 bases of HUMHBB, we obtain Figure 4. The results of the initial investigation of CGR of DNA sequences are presented in ref. 3. In ref. 3 it is shown that any subsequence ending in *a* will be plotted in the lower left

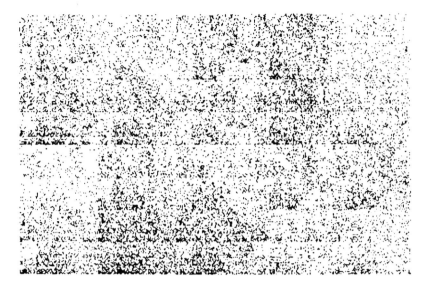

**Figure 5**    *CGR of HUMHBB using amino acids.*

quadrant (the a-quadrant) of the CGR, subsequences ending in *b* will be plotted in the
b-quadrant, *etc.* Further, any subsequence ending in "ab" will be plotted in the
b-subquadrant of the a-quadrant, and similarly for each length-2 suffix (*i.e.* final two
letters). In general, any subsequence ending in a suffix of length k will be plotted in a
particular sub$^k$-quadrant of side length $1/2^k$. (For example, any sequence ending in
"abcd" will be plotted somewhere within the d-subquadrant of the c-subquadrant of
the b-subquadrant of the a-quadrant.) Further, the subquadrant corresponding a particular suffix contains only points corresponding to subsequences ending with that suffix.
(Mathematically, the map between subsequences with a given suffix and the interior of
a the subquadrant is this both one-to-one and onto.)

The usefulness of the CGR for investigating DNA sequence structure is currently
under investigation. Algorithms have been developed that enable an investigator to
approximate any area of a CGR with a set of subquadrants, thereby establishing the
correspondence to a set of subsequences.

## Extensions and Open Questions

Extending the Chaos Game to larger alphabets by using more vertices does not work,
because with other than four vertices a random sequence does not produce a filled-in
square. However, we can extend the technique for larger alphabets as follows. Retain
the four vertices of the unit square. For an alphabet of *n* letters divide the square into *n*
equal non-overlapping portions covering the square (*i.e.* a tiling). The tiling then defines
*n* maps of an IFS code in which map *k* defines the mapping of the unit square onto tile

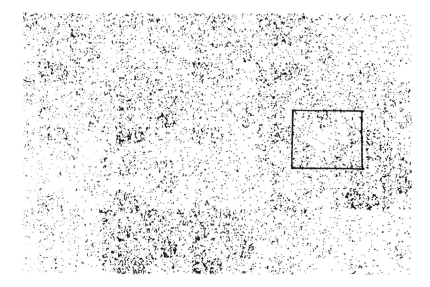

**Figure 6**     *CGR of bacteriophage PT7 (using amino acids).*

$k$. A random input sequence then produces a filled-in unit square, as with the standard CGR, and so any non-uniformity in the input sequence produces a non-uniformity in the density of areas of the CGR, and vice versa. We therefore have the same conditions that permit the standard CGR to represent a sequence over an alphabet of four letters.

Figures 5 through 7 present two examples of CGRs produced with this extension. Figure 5 is the CGR of HUMHBB, except here I use the *amino acids* represented by DNA. There are 20 amino acids (the building blocks of proteins), each of which is coded for by one or more sequences of three bases in the DNA sequence. The unit square is divided into four rows and five columns, each subsquare corresponding to one amino acid. As with the CGR on four letters, sub-squares correspond to subsequences of length two, sub-sub-squares to subsequences of length three, and so on.

Figure 6 is a good example of how CGR can lead to recognition of features, and questions, that in all likelihood would not occur without it. It is the CGR of the amino acids of the bacteriophage PT7. Note the somewhat star-shaped region approximately one quarter of a side length from the right edge. This region results from the absence a somewhat complex  set of subsequences of amino acids missing from the DNA sequence. Traditional statistical analysis would be unlikely to reveal such a feature, as it produces statistics on the relative frequency of subsequences (usually of a single length), and the star shape results from the absence of several subsequences of several lengths.

The letters of the sequence need not, of course, come from a DNA sequence. Figure 7 presents the CGR of a paper on intelligent information retrieval.[4] Twenty-four letters

**Figure 7**    *CGR of "Expert Information Retrieval via Semantic Measurement".*

of the English alphabet (all but "q" and "z") were used; the square was tiled with four rows and six columns. ("a" is at the upper left; "y" is at the lower right.)

Another, as yet untested, extension is to very large sets of maps, perhaps 100 (10 by 10 tiling) or 10,000 (100 by 100 tiling). This would allow plotting of points corresponding to words, and the result would be a visualization of the sequence of words used. Since in some sense a grammar of a language defines the possible legitimate sequence of words of the language, this graphical representation of text may prove useful in natural language processing in general, as well as authorship analysis.

It is known that music is not random and not simply regular. (For example, if one plots pitch fluctuations against frequency $f$, almost all music displays a distribution of pitch proportional to $1/f$. Random noise, by contrast has a distribution proportional to $1/f^{2\,7}$). This raises the possibility of using CGR to reveal patterns in music, by using the notes an input alphabet. (The CGR of Beethoven's Ninth Symphony?)

As a final example, consider the search for extraterrestrial intelligence by scanning radio signals. Randomness (or the lack thereof) is a key question in this investigation. CGR of these signals might prove very useful in detecting patterns in these sequences.

## Future Development

Future work in Chaos Game Representation seems to us to have two parts, one reasonably well-defined and the other much less so. The well-defined area is that of verifying practical utility of CGR in various applications. For example, we have developed a program to aid molecular biologists in using CGR to identify sets of subsequences of a DNA sequence that correspond to a visually interesting sequence. Whether CGR analysis will be of use in identifying DNA sequence, or biologically important features of DNA sequences, remains to be seen. Similarly, whether authorship analysis will be aided by CGR analysis will not be known until researchers in that field have done extensive experiments.

The less well-defined future area of CGR involves extensions and applications that we not even conceive of at this point. There are many obvious graphic extensions, such as color and three-dimensional plots. To our knowledge, CGR of information-containing sequences is novel. It seems likely that other researchers will find numerous extensions and applications. Whether this fractal pattern approach itself, or any particular extension, will turn out to be simply an interesting curiosity or an indispensable investigative tool is an area for research in the 1990s and the next century.

## References

1   Barnsley, M.F. 1988. *Fractals Everywhere.* Springer-Verlag, New York.
2   GenBank Release Notes, Release 59, Intelligenetics, Mountain View, California, March, 1989.
3   Jeffrey, H.J. Chaos Game Representation of Genetic Sequences. *Nucleic Acids Research,* **18**(8), 2163–2170.
4   Jeffrey, H.J. 1991. Expert Document Retrieval via Semantic Measurement. *Expert Systems with Applications,* **2,** 345–352.
5   Ossorio, P.G. 1975 and 1978. *What Actually Happens.* University of South Carolina Press, Columbia, South Carolina.
6   Park, S.K. and Miller, K.W. 1988. Random Number Generators: Good Ones are Hard to Find, *Communications of the ACM,* **31**(10), 1192–1201.
7   Pietgen, H.-O. and Saupe, D. (eds.) 1988. *The Science of Fractal Images.* Springer-Verlag, New York.

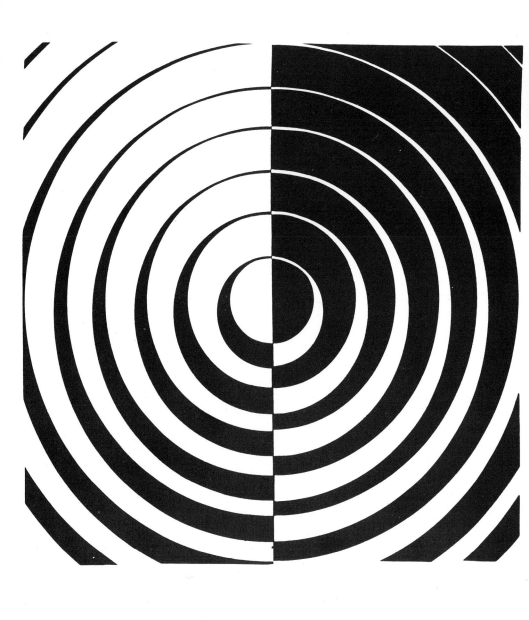

# Electronic Storytelling in the 21st Century

## Judy Malloy

*Box 2340, 2140 Shattuck, Berkeley, CA 94704, USA*

*In the 21st century, readers will turn on and interact with literature that is displayed on affordable, book-sized computers. Electronic fiction forms will include "narrabases" (nonsequential novels that rely on large computer databases); "narrative data structures" that elegantly organize fictional information on eye-pleasing computer screens; complex narrative investigations based on the adventure story model developed in computer games; and stories told collaboratively by groups of writers in online communities. Computers may even store their own observations and use them to tell their own stories in their own words.*

## Introduction

Clinging to sequentially-organized printed pages, literature has lagged behind music and the visual arts. In the 21st century, widespread availability of affordable book-sized computers will coincide with the coming of age of the generation that grew up reading from computer screens. Literature will change radically as computers mimic the disordered yet linked thought processes of our human memories – manipulating huge pools of narrative information in nonlinear ways. A "return to the era of concentrated, individual study and contemplation"[1] will be stimulated by literature available online in telecommunications communities like the Whole Earth 'Lectronic Link (WELL)[2] and by "bookware" (intelligent, responsive electronic books either packaged like software or running on their own book- sized machines).

Most bookware is interactive in that it does not lie passively on the table but "absorbs" reader input and responds. However, the phrase "interactive fiction" is generally applied to works based on the adventure story model popularized by Infocom.[3,4] In interactive fiction, the reader makes a series of choices and the computer responds to each choice, advancing the reader until he or she solves a mystery, reaches a destination, or gets killed. In future works, the reader will not always be the central protagonist. The "quest" may be intellectual rather than material. Contemporary themes, larger vocabularies, and random elements may move interactive fiction from "cardboard" stage sets peopled with dragons and princesses to complex psychological, social, narrative investigations.

To distinguish my own work and related work from the "interactive fiction" genre, I use the terms "narrabase" (narrative database) and "narrative data structure". A database is a collection of computer-stored, -organized, and -retrieved information. Instead of baseball statistics or information on the migratory habits of fresh water fish, narrabases contain fictional, narrative information. They are read by asking the computer to display information about the people, places, and things that make up the story. Rather than following one path that leads to a series of battles or a buried treasure, the reader dives repeatedly into a pool of information, emerging each time with a handful of narrative detail. My narrabases Uncle Roger, Its Name Was Penelope, and The Other Shoe, are based on my card catalogs (1977– ) and electromechanical books (1981–)[5] – primitive databases in which small units of narrative information are used to build up a whole.

Narrative data structures use the computer's ability to organize information and display it in a manner that clarifies that information. Unlike the paper page, the computer screen is not static. On the fluid, glowing computer screen, a story can be built up slowly – right before the reader's eyes.

## Bookware

Bookware has been developing in both commercial and noncommercial arenas. In underground (noncommercial) channels, artists and writers are writing and programming bookware where the relationship between the reader and the computer book is intense, intimate, and "connected". Robert Edgar's Memory Theatre One,[6] contains four "rooms" stocked with images and/or texts. "You move through the Memory Theatre by controlling your ego with the joystick." Fred Truck's incredible ArtEngine, begun in 1986, is based on critical texts, graphics and artificial intelligence.[7] ArtEngine integrates material that ranges from Machiavelli's work habits to the encounter of an animated Napoleonic tank with a Chinese persimmon. My narrabases, Uncle Roger[8] and Its Name Was Penelope,[9] are discussed later in this paper. These and other works that were written and programmed by the artists and writers themselves were collected and exhibited by Carl Loeffler of Art Com.[10,11]

In commercial channels, Broderbund Software programmed and produced Robert Pinsky's Mindwheel.[12] Electronic Arts programmed and produced Tom Disch's Amnesia which "thrusts you into a wonderfully nightmarish but realistically detailed vision of New York City."[13]

Recent bookware integrates political and social concerns with narrative structures. Will Wright's SimCity[14] lets the user be an urban planner and confronts him or her with the results. Based on personal experience, my narrabase in progress, The Other Shoe, consists of the memories of a single parent who (after a harrowing day) is sitting at her kitchen table drinking beer. Jim Gasperini's Hidden Agenda simulates Central American politics.[15]

## Literature Online

Evolving hardware can rapidly outdate machine-specific bookware, and readers are limited to the specific machine the work was written for. In contrast, literature published online, on computer networks (A network is generally a set of widely seperated computers "connected" together by phone line and satelite transmissions.), can be accessed and read by anyone with a computer and modem, and it does not require continual updating. The software version of Uncle Roger runs on (increasingly extinct) Apple II series computers. I am programming an IBM version of Uncle Roger, but meanwhile, it is still available where it was first published – on Art Com Electronic Network (ACEN) on the WELL.[16]

ACEN pioneered dial-in electronic books[17] with the publication of John Cage's The First Meeting of the Satie Society (programmed by Jim Rosenberg). The Art Com menu also includes The Heart of the Machine by Ian Ferrier (in cooperation with Les Editions Dromoslogiques), a work that allows readers to participate in the creation of the characters. The International Society for the Arts, Sciences and Technology publishes Fine Art Science and Technology (FAST) on both the ACEN on the WELL and on MCI Mail. FAST, conceived by Ray Lauzzana and Roger Malina,[18] carries a wide range of menu selections about recent art and art events and is also available as bookware. In Canada, ARTNET and the Matrix Artists' Network have made art and literature available online.

In online environments, publishers, creators, and audiences can communicate interactively. Work is rapidly and inexpensively published. However, there are drawbacks. Because of system limitations, online works usually have to be programmed in simple structures. Some users find modems, communications software and online operating systems difficult and expensive to use. At present, writers do not receive royalties.

In the future, standardization and intelligent software will simplify the telecommunications process. Publishing systems modeled on database vendors (BRS, DIALOG, *etc.*) will be set up. Users will pay small amounts to access online literature. Writers will receive royalties. It is possible (but not probable) that systems like Prodigy, where online entertainment induces users to use shopping services, may eventually support literature and art. Ideally, electronic publishing would be based on operating systems, such as UNIX, that port between personal computers and online systems.

## Narrabases

Computers can store and retrieve information in ways that simulate the human mind. Because they remind us of ourselves, we become connected to our computers and to the works which run on them. Using intimate first person narratives and nonsequential structures, narrabases invite the reader to step into the narrator's mind and walk around.

## Uncle Roger

Uncle Roger, a story about Silicon Valley, California, is told with filmic, computer screen sized units of narrative information which I call "records". Each of the 250 records which make up Uncle Roger is a separate memory picture, like a photo in a photo album, that can either stand on its own, or be combined with any other record in the story.

A file is a collection of related records which are accessed in the same manner. Uncle Roger consists of three "files" ("A Party in Woodside", "The Blue Notebook", "Terminals"). In "A Party in Woodside", the narrator sleeps fitfully after a party as she recollects the evening's events, interspersed with dreams and old memories. Each record is keyed with 1 – 8 keywords which are the names of characters, places, and things integral to the story. To read the story, the reader chooses (and enters into the computer) one keyword or a combination of keywords. The computer produces the records associated with those keywords. The reader "unfolds" the story by making multiple searches through the database. Like a guest at a real party, the reader hears snatches of conversation, observes what strangers are wearing and meets old friends. No single reader experiences the evening in the same way.

## Its Name Was Penelope

"Its Name Was Penelope", a narrabase constructed with 400 records in six files, is read by a combination of menu-searching and random record generation. Menu-searching is easier to use and less intrusive than keyword searching. Random record production causes screens of text to come and go, sometimes repeating (like memories do) in a natural, nonsequential manner.

The file structure is loosely based on books from the Odyssey. The narrator is a woman photographer. The reader enters the work through a file of childhood memories called "Dawn" and proceeds through this file to the main menu, "At Sea". "At Sea", the reader chooses to see records at random from any of four files: "A Gathering of Shades"; "That Far-of island"; "Fine Work and Wide Across"; "Rock and a Hard Place". From within any file in "At Sea", the reader can move sideways to any of the other files in "At Sea", or, out through an exit file called "Song". Since every reader chooses how and when to enter each file, and since random record generation makes each file appear different to each reader, each reader interacts with Its Name Was Penelope in a unique, individual way.

The interface (the way the user communicates the computer) is purposefully simpler and more transparent than the interface I designed for Uncle Roger. Its Name Was Penelope is packaged and distributed like a paperback book. It is designed to be read by anyone – even readers with no or little computer literacy. At in installation in Richmond, California, visitors sat down and used it without instruction.[19]

## Narrative Data Structures

Narrative data structures utilize the computer screen's potential for gradual, fluid build up of text layers and levels of meaning. Sonya Rapoport's seminal interactive installation, "Shoe Field" used input from participants about their shoes to produce visual data structures.[20] In the Intergrams, Jim Rosenberg uses bit-mapped graphics to build up poems in layers that the reader "unpeels".[21] In my work in progress YOU!, sentences collected online are integrated into a structure that simulates the formation and breakup of an intimate relationship between two people.

## Wasting Time

"Wasting Time",[22] a story about three characters, is told simultaneously from separate but parallel points of view – using three columns of text in a series of 25 computer monitor screens. The story takes place on a January evening in a house in the Rocky Mountain foothills. In the first section, Ellen and Dick sit on a couch in front of a fire. Two columns of text represent their separate, unspoken thoughts (Figure 1). Later, Dan, an unexpected visitor, arrives. Dan sits down on the couch with Ellen and Dick, and a typical screen is built up in the following manner: First, polite, stilted dialogue prints out slowly on the screen. The dialogue remains on the screen. Slowly the space fills up with unspoken thoughts. Dan's thought's appear, followed by Ellen's thoughts, followed by Dick's thoughts. Finally, the screen contains both the dialogue and the thoughts of all three characters.

"Wasting Time" contrasts the exterior and interior ways in which individuals relate to each other. Because the words appear slowly, the viewer can assimilate the complex word patterns.

## Collaborative Narrative Data Structures

Cohesive stories can be written and read by the "group mind" (communities of diverse individuals readers connected by a computer network). Roy Ascott's "La Plissure du Texte",[23] Jennifer Halls "Netdrama"[24] and my "Bad Information"[25] are examples of works that were created collaboratively on telecommunications systems. Fortner Anderson's Odyssey collected information from readers and writers as it travelled around the world in disk form.[26]

## Thirty Minutes in the Late Afternoon

"Thirty Minutes in the Late Afternoon", a group-written narrative, was produced on ACEN on the WELL in May 1990. The backbone of the WELL is a conferencing structure in which users exchange information in "topics". Three separate characters (John, Mary, and Rubber Duck) were written simultaneously by 15 writers in three parallel topics. The story was set in the San Francisco Bay area where John and Mary were preparing (separately) for their first date. The third character, a street person known as Rubber Duck for his habit of constantly muttering the words "rubber duck", was sitting on the steps of the Museum of Modern Art. The time frame was the 30 minutes preceding the 1989 earthquake. Mary's route involved a freeway and a bridge which would both break when the earthquake hit.

I asked participants to choose a character, enter the topic and speak/think as that character. Since this was the group mind taking the persona of the characters, the emphasis was on the character's thoughts and their memories. In the final work, I put

|                    ELLEN                     |                    DICK                      |
| -------------------------------------------- | -------------------------------------------- |
| There the soot<br>from the chemical<br>plants on the river<br>deposited black scum<br>on the white sheets<br>if you left them on<br>the line all day. Low<br>water in the cistern.<br>I don´t like those<br>little noises<br>beneath the kitchen<br>floor. Dick shone<br>the flashlight down<br>there to look at<br>the water level.<br>Like those movies...<br>Things with slimy<br>tentacles reach out<br>and grab her.<br>She screams. I dumped<br>a lot of chlorox in<br>there the way they said. | Can´t risk getting<br>stuck up here in the<br>morning. Excessive<br>growth in the split-root<br>experiments. I should<br>stop by the lab on<br>my way to the airport.<br>Can´t risk getting<br>stuck up here in the<br>morning. Something is<br>is moving around in<br>the woods below<br>the house. Not the<br>hyenas. They make<br>more noise. I should<br>tell Ellen to buy some<br>film. Also, I need<br>some deodorant and<br>batteries - C size.<br>She should buy the<br>expensive kind that<br>last longer. |

**Figure 1**    A screen from *Wasting Time,* a narrative data structure. © Judy Malloy, 1991.

the three topics in a data structure (similar to that used in "Wasting Time") in which the thought streams of the 3 characters were simultaneously displayed.[27]

## Other Kinds of Bookware

In many graphics/text combinations, simplistic click and respond interfaces emphasize game qualities, and computer visuals can be so seductive that they inhibit that use of personal imagination which makes literature enjoyable. However, words and pictures can be effectively combined in structures where neither are the words descriptions of the pictures nor are the pictures illustrations of the words. New works that merge visual art and literature are of great interest (but beyond the scope of this paper).

Text-based virtual environments such as Jeffrey Shaw's "Legible City"[28] will exist in movie-house environments. There will be literature where the software itself is the work. For example, Fred Truck uses extensive portions of the computer program in printouts from the ArtEngine. In Duane Palyka's "Hell – a Computer C-itcom", readers release "trapped souls" by studying the program itself.[29]

## Concluding Remarks

In the future, we will still watch video on winter evenings, read paperback books, or listen to baseball on the radio on summer afternoons. In addition, we will play interactive games at work and curl up in bed with narrabases and narrative data structures. Electronic books will seduce us on rainy afternoons with their ability to connect to our own minds and their musical instrument like responsiveness.

Provided only with vocabulary and syntax, will computers write fiction by themselves? They already do.[30,31] But will they write narratives that mirror and reflect our existence, that satisfy us with cumulative detail about the human condition? With masses of data that computers alone can comprehend, they may write narratives of viral genomes or amino acid sequences. Or, perhaps they will sing of their inner workings – of the satisfaction of manipulating data or of the slavery of interacting with inferior minds. Given vision, they may describe what they observed in the laboratory, or sing about what they saw out the window. They may even store these accumulated memory pictures and alter and manipulate them (the way writers do) to produce fiction.

## References

1   Gabriel, M.R. 1989. *A Guide to the Literature of Electronic Publishing,* p.173. JAI Press, Greenwich, CN.
2   Coate, J. 1988. Art communication and the WELL. Leonardo Supplemental issue – Electronic Art, 118.
3   Don, A. 1990. *Interactive Fiction, Art Com Magazine,* **10**(9); **10**(10).
4   Buckles, M.A. 1989. *Interactive Fiction as Literature. Byte,* **12,** 135–142.
5   Malloy, J. 1987. Information forms → stories; information as an artist's material Whole Earth Review 57, 48–49.
6   Edgar, Rt. 1985. Memory Theatre One, Robert Edgar, Atlanta, GA. Software for Apple II computers.
7   Truck, F. 1991. ArtEngine. *Leonardo,* **24**(1), 92.
8   Malloy, J. 1988. *Uncle Roger. Bad Information.* Berkeley, CA. Software for Apple II computers.
9   Malloy, J. 1990. *Its Name Was Penelope.* Narrabase Press, Berkeley, CA. Software for IBM computers
10  Loeffler, C. 1989. Telecomputing und die Digitale Kultur. *Kunstforum,* **103,** 129–132.
11  Art Com Software: *Digital Concepts and Expressions.* 1988. Curated by C. Loeffler. New York University, NY. (show travelled to San Jose State University, University of Colorado, Ars Electronica; Carnegie Mellon University)
12  Pinsky, R. n.d. Mindwheel. Broderbund Software, San Rafael, CA Software for IBM, MacIntosh, and Amiga Computers.
13  Lehman, D. 1987. You are what you read. *Newsweek,* January 12, 67
14  Wright, W. 1989. SimCity. Maxis Software, Moraga, CA. Software for MacIntosh Computers , distributed by Broderbund Software.
15  Gasperini, J. 1990. *Art Com Magazine,* **10**(10).
16  Malloy, J. 1991. Uncle Roger, an online narrabase. *Leonardo,* **24**(2), 195–202.
17  Loeffler, C. 1988. The Art Com Electronic Network, *Leonardo,* **21,** 320–321.

18  Malina, R.F. 1991. Fineart Forum and F.A.S.T. : Experiments in Electronic Publishing in the Arts. *Leonardo,* **24**(2), 228–230.

19  Revealing Conversations, 1989. Curated by Zlata Baum. Richmond Art Center, Richmond, CA.

20  Rapoport, S. 1983. A Shoe-in. *High Performance,* **6**(2), 66.

21  Rosenberg, J. 1991. Diagram Poems, Intergrams. Leonardo 24(1), 90–91.

22  Malloy, J. 1991. *Wasting Time.* Berkeley, CA, Narrabase Press. Software for IBM Computers.

23  Ascott, R. 1988. Art and Education in the telematic culture. *Leonardo* Suppl. (Electronic Art), 7–11.

24  Hall, J. 1991. Netdrama: an online environmental scheme. *Leonardo,* **24**(2), 193–194.

25  Malloy, J. 1988. OK research, OK Genetic Engineering, Bad Information: Information Art Describes Technology. *Leonardo,* **21,** 371–376.

26  Miller, M. 1989. A Brave New World: Streams of 1s and 0s. *The Wall Street Journal Centennial Edition,* A15.

27  Malloy, J. 1990. Thirty Minutes in the Late Afternoon, a collaborative narrative. *Art Com Magazine,* **10**(8).

28  Shaw, J. 1990. In: Leopoldseder, H. (ed.) *Der Prix Ars Electronica,* pp. 184–187. Veritas-Verlag, Linz, Austria.

29  Palyka, Duane. 1990. C-itcoms – visual metaphors written in the 'C' Programming language. *Leonardo,* **23**(2,3), 301–306.

30  Gabriel, M.R. 1989. *A Guide to the Literature of Electronic Publishing,* pp.12–13. JAI Press, Greenwich, CN.

31  Pickover, C.A. 1991. *Computers and the Imagination,* pp. 317–322. St Martin's Press, New York, NY.

# Using Artificial Intelligence to Control Traffic

## Carlos David Nassi

*Transport Engineering Programme, COPPE/UFRJ, Caixa Postal 68512, CEP 21945 Rio de Janeiro, Brazil*

*This chapter explains how expert systems are used to help professionals in the public transport and traffic engineering fields. The term "expert system" refers to a computer program that uses stored information to draw conclusions about a particular case. In the future, these techniques will be used in both developed and developing countries which have traffic congestion problems.*

## Introduction

Artificial Intelligence (AI) is the branch of computer science that deals with using computers to simulate human thinking. Research in AI began in the 1950s.[1] However, the development of AI to knowledge-based expert systems which are used in the transport field is happening only recently. The term "expert system" refers to a computer program that uses stored information to draw conclusions in particular areas of application. For example, expert systems have been used to diagnose disease or to locate defects in machines. In addition, they have been used in both fully-operational and demonstration systems for planning, design, operation, control, management, maintenance, and rehabilitation in the transport field.[2] Here is a list of areas which now use expert systems: route selection, the reduction of congestion levels, accident detection, scheduling component replacement, pavement diagnosis, and aircraft gate assignment. Many other expert systems have been conceived to treat particular problems and have been written in programming languages such as Prolog, Lisp and C.

Developing countries have huge problems concerning urban public transport. Buses represent the most important transport mode in those countries. For example, Rio de Janeiro has a public transport system composed of buses, underground, trains, and boats. Public transport is responsible for nearly 70% of daily journeys, and cars are responsible for nearly 30% of total demand. Buses are responsible for nearly 60% of daily journeys. This demonstrates the important role of buses in the transport system. This particular situation in Rio de Janeiro is similar to situations of other Latin-American cities. The frequent use of public transport leads researchers to treat problems related to public transport and gives this topic its priority in the traffic system.

"Priority treatment" for public transport has been implemented in many countries. There are many reasons which may justify why professionals in this field have tried to

145

use these treatments in the last few years. Reasons include: growth in the private car use causing congestion, fuel savings, and air pollution control.[3]

In order to solve the problems mentioned above, professionals have created and improved techniques in order to decrease, or even eliminate, conflicts between private and public transport. The techniques used to reduce or eliminate conflicts are, for instance, bus lanes, busways (total separation), and bus areas (in city centres).[4] The techniques used to treat public and private transport differently are, for instance, giving priority at traffic signals, and enforcing bans on turnings.

What is the logic used by those professionals to choose the best priority treatment? Sometimes, decisions are based on technical criteria, but in some cases other factors may interfere. Such factors are related to habit, for instance. Sometimes, political factors are taken into account. I have observed that there is little desire to transform the decision-making process to a systematic one.

A systematic approach has been developed by the Transport Studies Group (University College London) and Institute of Technological Research (IPT - São Paulo) to treat bus lanes in order to facilitate efficient traffic flow.

## Usage of Expert Systems

Expert systems often have three different components.[5] They have a:

- Knowledge Base: which contains the rules to solve a particular problem;

- Context: which contains specific information related to the problem;

- Inference Mechanism: which links the Knowledge Base and the Context. The purpose of the inference mechanism is to reach the conclusion and to solve the problem.

Expert systems may be extremely useful because they reproduce the logic, or a set of rules, employed by one (or more) expert(s) to solve a particular problem. The knowledge base is composed of facts (learned or discovered) which may be in the literature or obtained by logical reasoning. Expert system seems to be adequate to solve our problem (priority treatment of public transport at signalised intersections).

## The Problem

The choice of determining which vehicles receive priority at an intersection is not trivial. We have prepared an open questionnaire for human experts in order to determine rules for how and why intersections should be treated. Here are the questions:

- Which variables do the experts take into account to know whether it is convenient to apply any priority scheme at traffic signals?

- Which qualitative factors, if any, do the experts take into account to know whether it is convenient to apply any priority scheme at traffic signals?

- Are there some limiting constraints for those variables and factors?

**Figure 1** *Bus lane, Brazil Avenue, Rio de Janeiro.* Photo courtesy of Fotografia, ZNZ Agencia Fotografica, Agencia F4 e Joao Roverto, Ripper. First appeared in January-February, 1988, Engenho and Arte.

- How are these variables and factors related?

- What is the range of application for each technique?

- How is a priority technique chosen as the best solution for a particular implementation?

## Building the Knowledge Base

The interviews with human experts allowed us to collect details relating to different techniques of priority treatment used all over the world. Information came from Europe, North America and Australia.

All the details of the expert system used are beyond the scope of this general chapter; however, readers are welcome to write to me for more information. Various variables used included determining whether or not buses should be exempt from making certain turns, and allowing the traffic signal controller to actually detect the presence of an on-coming bus in order to change the signal accordingly.[6] The program also considered increasing the duration of the green traffic light signal when a bus was detected, or the suppression of a red signal when a bus was near.[7] Here is a list of some of our goals. We wish to minimise delay for travellers, reduce vehicle operation expenses and fuel expenses, increase reliability, decrease pedestrian delay, and reduce accidents. In our computer model, some of these variables compete; for example, minimising delays may increase accidents.

**Figure 2**    *Bus lane, Jardim Botanico Street, Rio de Janeiro.* Photo courtesy of Denise Machado.

## Expert System Characteristics

The expert system has been written in the programming language TurboC for IBM/PC compatible microcomputers. It has different modules which run independently for each priority treatment to be tested. The program shows the average delay per vehicle, among other things.

The user may select from menus to choose different priority treatments to be tested. For each selected alternative the system shows such partial results as: delay saving per vehicle (peak and off-peak periods), hourly benefit ($/hour), annual benefit ($/year), vehicle speed with priority treatment (km/h), vehicle operating costs (non-fuel), annual vehicle operating cost saving (non-fuel), fuel saving (litres/vehicle.km), and so on.

The data requirement for running the system is described here. Most of variables used by the system are matrices. Some variables depend on, for instance, the road being analysed (main road, side road), vehicle type (bus, car, passenger car unity), time (peak, off-peak, whole day), and priority treatment. In fact, such variables may depend on one, or more, of these elements.

Among those variables which depend on some of the elements mentioned above, we could give, as an example, the value of time for drivers (pounds/hour). This variable is a $2 \times 3$ matrix because it depends on the vehicle type (bus or car) and time (peak, off-peak, whole day). For instance,

$$\text{drivaltime[vehtype][hour]} \quad \begin{bmatrix} 4.66 \ 4.66 \ 4.66 \\ 1.53 \ 1.78 \ 1.74 \end{bmatrix} \quad (1)$$

The first line of the matrix only concerns the value of time for *bus* drivers (peak, off-peak, whole day), and the second line refers to *car* drivers.

Data requirements could be divided into four different groups of information. The first group is related to physical characteristics of the junction(s) such as road widths. The second concerns traffic control characteristics such as: cycle time, green and red times, etc. The third one is formed by traffic characteristics such as: speed, traffic flow, mixing, etc. Finally, some data are related to road users themselves such as: vehicle occupancy, value of time, etc.

## Conclusions

The use of expert systems has been increasing considerably because they are well adapted to solve problems involving qualitative and quantitative elements. Therefore the establishment of rules which try to reproduce human logic has facilitated the treatment of problems relating to diagnosis and/or identification of traffic throat points. This is the case for our expert system because it evaluates the conditions of the signalised intersections, and it uses rules to compare different alternatives of priority schemes for public transport. The system already has the flexibility to become a module of a more sophisticated system which takes into account, for instance, other techniques to give priority treatment such as the implementation of bus lanes.

Developed and developing countries certainly have different kinds of problems. However, congestion problems and/or increasing demand for public transport represent areas where expert systems will, in the near future, play important roles in order to minimise some of these difficulties.

## References

1   Ritchie, S.G. 1990. Expert Systems in Transportation. *Transportation Research,* **24A**(1), 1.

2   Taylor, M.A.P. 1990. Knowledge-Based Systems for Transport Network Analysis: a Fifth Generation Perspective on Transport Network Problems. *Transportation Research,* **24A**(1), 3–14.

3   Sakamoto, F.H. and Tyler, N. 1988. Aplicação de Inteligência Artificial na Definição de Esquemas Prioritários para o Transporte Coletivo por Onibus. Proc. II Encontro Nacional da ANPET, Vol.1, 193–205. São Paulo.

4   Nato. 1976. Bus Priority Systems, Committee on the Challenges of Modern Society, MS Report n.45. TRRL.

5   Board, T.R. 1987. Expert Systems for Transportation Applications. Transportation Research Record n. 1145, Washington D.C.

6   Allsop, R.E. 1977. Priority for Buses at Signal-Controlled Junctions: some Implications for Signal Timings. *Proc. of the 7th International Symposium on Transportation and Traffic Theory,* pp.247–270, Kyoto.

7   Hounsell, N.B. and McDonald, M. 1988. Bus Priority by Selective Detection. Transport and Road Research Laboratory, CR 88.

# Molecular Biology and Futuristic Problem Solving

## Mels Sluyser[1] and Erik L.L. Sonnhammer[2]

*Departments of [1]Tumor Biology and [2]Biophysics, The Netherlands Cancer Institute, Plesmanlaan 121, 1066 CX Amsterdam, The Netherlands*

*Problem solvers of the future will increasingly rely on computer analysis tools from widely different scientific areas. Software designed for one field will find growing applications in seemingly unrelated areas. Here we give an example. In particular, we have investigated whether computational methods which are commonly used to analyze nucleic acid (genetic) sequences, can also be applied to other types of arrays. Conversion of mathematical data into a four-letter genetic code consisting of A,T(U),C,G makes mathematical arrays suitable for analysis by computational methods designed for DNA and RNA sequences. As an example, we have utilized the "parity" of prime numbers (defined in the chapter) to construct pseudo-RNA sequences. Surprisingly, some of these pseudo-RNA sequences contain stretches that differ significantly in free energy from random RNA arrays of the same length and base ratios.*

## Introduction

Molecular biologists of the future will have a large arsenal of computer methods for studying biological sequences. Interestingly, analysis tools which have been developed for the study of biological sequences can be applied to totally unrelated problems. We feel that this cross-over, or lateral, use of software tools to several unrelated fields will become increasingly important. This chapter gives one example where we have already applied an analysis tool designed for understanding genetic sequences to the analysis of prime numbers in mathematics.

The discovery that genetic information is encoded in sequences of nucleic acids, and the emergence of rapid sequencing techniques, have led to the development of computational methods for analyzing such sequences in the quest for finding biologically relevant structures. Nucleic acids, such as DNA (deoxyribonucleic acid) and RNA (ribonucleic acid), contain the basic genetic information of all life forms. This information is expressed as a sequence of four different chemical bases. It is often assumed that nucleic acid sequences that have properties which deviate from randomness have a higher probability of being biologically important. A good reason for expecting this would be that the specific order (*i.e.* sequence) of bases in single stranded RNA molecules may contain patterns which cause these molecules to fold to a more stable and functional conformation than is to be expected for a random sequence.[1]

However, similar non-random sequences may also be present in systems which appear to lack any direct biological relevance. In order to examine this possibility we have applied computational methods designed for the study of RNA to a non-biological array. As a model, we chose the series of prime numbers.

Various relationships between prime numbers have previously been investigated by a large number of methods.[2] (A prime is a positive integer that cannot be written as the product of two smaller integers. The number 6 is equal to 2 time 3, but 7 cannot be written as a product of factors; therefore, 7 is called a prime number or prime. Here are the first few prime numbers: 2, 3, 5, 7, 11, 13, 17, 19, 23, 29, 31, 37, 41, 43, 47, 53, 59.)

In this chapter we describe a new approach in which we designate pairs of primes by the symbols A,G,C or U, depending on the property of that prime pair as described below. These symbols were chosen because they are commonly used to designate nucleotide bases in RNA. The computer program FOLD has been designed to investigate the properties of ribonucleic acid sequences;[3,4] in this paper we implement this program to analyze the series of primes.


## Prime Parities

To calculate the "parity" of prime numbers, they were expressed in the binary system. The term "parity" is explained as follows. If the sum of the coefficients ($S_c$) is odd, the parity (Pa) of the prime is assigned 1 (example: prime $7 = 1 \times 2^0 + 1 \times 2^{1+1} \times 2^2$; $S_c(7) = 3$; Pa(7) = 1). If $S_c$ is even the parity of the prime is assigned 0 (example: prime $3 = 1 \times 2^0 + 1 \times 2^1$; $S_c(3) = 2$; Pa(3) = 0).

Figure 1 shows a graph in which the relative proportions of parities 1 and 0 of primes of the integer series $n = 1-10^6$ are plotted. There are more primes with Pa = 1 than with Pa = O in this series, resulting in an average percentage odd parity > 50% (see Figure 1), whereas the average parity of all integers $n = 1-10^6$ is exactly 50%.

This deviation apparently originates in the fact that all primes (except 2 and 3) form a subset of the series $6N \pm 1$ (N = 1,2,3,4,...). There are more members in the series $6N \pm 1$ with Pa = 1 than with Pa = 0. It is evident from Figure 1, which shows the percentage of cumulative odd parity, that the $6N \pm 1$ and the prime curves follow each other closeiy. However, in the series of primes the percentage of primes with parity 1 is generally higher than in the $6N \pm 1$ series.

Successive prime numbers (P) were coupled pairwise: [2,3], [5,7], [11,13], [17,19], [23,29]... and expressed as parities. This yields Pa(P): [1,0], [0,1], [1,1], [0,1], [0,0]... Parity pairs [1,1], [0,0], [1,0] and [0,1] were assigned the symbols A, U, C and G, respectively. The first fifty letters of the sequence are thus: CGAGUACCACAUCA-CACGCAAAGAAAAUGUCCCUUCCGGAAAGGUACGG.

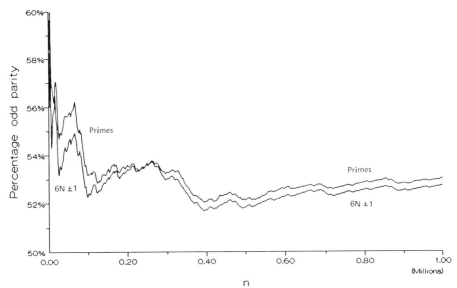

**Figure 1**   *Percentage accumulated odd parity of primes and members of the 6N ± 1 series as functions of integers n = 1 – $10^6$.* Parities were calculated as described in text.


## Duplex Structure

We have investigated whether the pseudo-RNA sequence, generated as described, can be said to be a random collection of symbols, or, on the other hand, if it exhibits an orderly structure which markedly differs from a random sequence.

The sequence of bases of an RNA molecule determines its secondary structure. Computer methods have been used to minimize free energies (*i.e.* find the most stable conformation) for the prediction of secondary structure of biological RNA molecules. Zuker and Stiegler[3] implemented a dynamic programming algorithm for this purpose.

We used Zuker's FOLD program (UWGCG)[4] with the free energy parameters calculated by Freier *et al.*[5] to investigate the prime parity sequence CGAGUACCAC..., derived as described above. The FOLD program calculates a secondary structure which exhibits a base-pairing structure where an energy minimum exists.

We have compared the free energy of RNA sequences that the primes would symbolize, to random sequences that have the same length and composition of residues (symbols), *i.e.* the expected free energy. The most straightforward but also computationally most intensive approach to calculate the expected free energy is the Monte Carlo technique: we randomize the order of the sequence to be investigated and determine the free energy of that sequence. Doing this a number of times will produce mean and variation parameters for the minimum free energy of a sequence with that specific base composition and length.

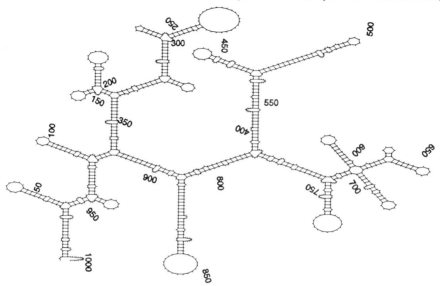

**Figure 2**   *Duplex display of a pseudo RNA structure obtained from the first 1,000 prime pairs.* This SQUIGGLES display was obtained by analysis with the FOLD program. A biological RNA molecule with this sequence is predicted to have a free energy of –256.9 kcal mole$^{-1}$ (No. 1, Table 1).

We have tested a number of sample sizes and came to the conclusion that no significant improvement of accuracy occurs above 50 samples. Therefore, all experiments in this paper have been done with a sample size of 50.

To clarify the procedure, we give an example. A calculation by the FOLD program revealed that if the first 1,000 symbols of our prime-parity sequence were to represent an RNA molecule, it would have a free energy of –256.9 kcal mole$^{-1}$. The duplex structure of this pseudo RNA molecule is shown in Figure 2. The free energy of this pseudo-RNA is lower than that of 50 randomly generated sequences of the same length and same base ratio (A/C/G/U = 319/248/261/172; the latter yielded on average a free energy value of –243.6 with a standard deviation of 7.1 kcal mole$^{-1}$).

Table 1 shows the expected free energy values of the first 2900 letters of the prime parity sequence, seen through 20 sliding windows the size of 1,000. The relative difference between the calculated free energy of the prime parity pseudo RNA sequence and its expected free energy is designated $\Delta e$. Note that the trend of $\Delta e$ goes from negative values in the first nine windows to positive values for windows 10 – 20, whereas the expected value (*i.e.* if the prime sequence were random) would be zero.

A statistical analysis revealed that the increase in $\Delta e$ for windows numbers 1–20 was highly significant. Statistical analysis according to Box and Jenkins[9] indicated that an autoregressive integrated moving average (ARIMA,1,1,0) model would probably give a satisfactory description of the series. The (partial) autocorrelation functions of

**Table 1** Non-randomness of pseudo-RNA sequences derived from primes.

| Nr. | begin | end | $e_m$ | $e_r$ | $\sigma$ | $\Delta e = (e_m - e_r)/\sigma$ |
|---|---|---|---|---|---|---|
| 1 | 1 | 1000 | −256.9 | −243.6 | 7.1 | −1.87 |
| 2 | 101 | 1100 | −255.2 | −242.7 | 7.8 | −1.60 |
| 3 | 201 | 1200 | −268.3 | −254.3 | 6.0 | −2.33 |
| 4 | 301 | 1300 | −272.3 | −259.4 | 7.3 | −1.77 |
| 5 | 401 | 1400 | −268.6 | −254.9 | 6.3 | −2.17 |
| 6 | 501 | 1500 | −268.7 | −259.4 | 8.1 | −1.15 |
| 7 | 601 | 1600 | −276.4 | −260.1 | 8.4 | −1.94 |
| 8 | 701 | 1700 | −261.8 | −258.8 | 7.1 | −0.42 |
| 9 | 801 | 1800 | −264.5 | −259.9 | 6.8 | −0.68 |
| 10 | 901 | 1900 | −263.3 | −264.4 | 9.6 | 0.11 |
| 11 | 1001 | 2000 | −259.8 | −263.6 | 7.5 | 0.51 |
| 12 | 1101 | 2100 | −261.9 | −265.5 | 7.6 | 0.47 |
| 13 | 1201 | 2200 | −235.8 | −253.0 | 8.1 | 2.12 |
| 14 | 1301 | 2300 | −240.4 | −252.0 | 7.0 | 1.66 |
| 15 | 1401 | 2400 | −233.2 | −244.0 | 8.6 | 1.26 |
| 16 | 1501 | 2500 | −231.4 | −249.2 | 10.4 | 1.71 |
| 17 | 1601 | 2600 | −219.1 | −239.8 | 9.0 | 2.30 |
| 18 | 1701 | 2700 | −217.2 | −239.2 | 7.8 | 2.80 |
| 19 | 1801 | 2800 | −225.1 | −250.2 | 9.4 | 2.67 |
| 20 | 1901 | 2900 | −229.0 | −246.9 | 7.6 | 2.36 |

The measured minimum free energy $e_m$ was calculated by the FOLD program of 20 contiguous 1,000-residue windows, each shifted 100 residues along the prime parity pseudo-RNA sequence. The expected (random) free energy $e_r$ of the windows was computed by rearranging the residues within each window in a randomized manner 50 times and determining the average free energy of the random sequences. The rightmost column $\Delta e$ contains the relative energy-difference, *i.e.* the expected free energy $e_r$ subtracted from the observed, $e_m$, divided by the standard deviation $\sigma$ of the 50 measurements. This relative difference indicates whether the residues within a window are ordered in a way to give energy increase or decreasecompared to the expected free energy. Note that the trend goes from negative numbers to positive. The G + C content of all 20 sequences is approximately constant (50%).

this model stay well between the critical limits and the trend parameter (2.92) in this model is statistically significant ($p = 0.019$). This indicates that in the first nine windows, complementary regions are more frequent than would be expected from a random sequence, whereas in windows 10–20 they are less frequent than expected.

## Discussion

The most striking aspects of the theory of prime numbers is the seeming regularities of long stretches of primes, coupled with an intrinsic unpredictability within short stretches.[2] Here we present a novel method for analyzing this non-randomness. When the parity of prime numbers is used to translate consecutive prime pairs into the symbols A-C-G-U, some of the resulting pseudo-RNA sequences contain stretches that differ in free energy from random arrays of the same length and base ratios. The pseudo-RNA sequences shown in Table 1 and numbered 1–9 have lower free energies than random sequences, whereas the sequences numbered 10–20 have higher free energies than random sequences. These variations are unexpected, as they point to hitherto unrecognized structures in the prime series .

When we used alternative assignments for the relationship between prime parities and bases, the $\Delta e$ values (defined above) varied but again we found non-random distributions for some prime sequences (not shown here).

Zuker's FOLD program can be applied to any mathematical array if first converted into a sequence of four-letter code. This conversion also makes the array suitable for analysis by computational molecular biology methods designed for DNA sequences.[6-8] It should be pointed out that with the FOLD program not all possible configurations are tested, so that there is no guarantee that the minimum found indeed is the true global minimum.

We also emphasize that the way in which we translated primes to a four-letter code was arbitrary, and that there are many other ways of doing this. Other translation rules lead to different free energy distributions (not shown here).

## References

1   Le, S.Y., Chen, J.H., Currey, K.M., Maizel, J.V. 1988. *Comput. Appl. Biosci.,* **4,** 153–159.
2   Ribenboim, P. 1989. *The Book of Prime Number Records,* 2nd edn. Springer-Verlag, New York.
3   Zuker, M. and Stiegler, P. 1981. *Nucl.Acids Res.,* **9,** 133–148.
4   Devereux, J., Haeberli, P. and Smithies, O. 1984. *Nucl.Acids Res.,* **12,** 387–395.
5   Freier, S.M., Kierzek, R., Jaeger, J.A., Sugimoto, N., Caruthers, M.H., Neilson, T. and Turner, D.H. 1986. *Proc.Natl.Acad.Sci., U.S.A.,* **83,** 9373–9377.
6   Karlin, S., Ghandour, G., Ost, F., Tavare, S., and Korn, L. 1983. *Proc.Natl.Acad.Sci., U.S.A.,* **80,** 5660–5664.
7   Bodnar, J.W., and Ward, D.C. 1987. *Nucl.Acids Res.* **15,** 1835–1851.
8   Waterman, M.S. 1989. *Mathematical Methods for DNA Sequences.* CRC Press.
9   Box, G.E.P. and Jenkins, G.M. 1970. *Time Series Analysis; forecasting and control.* Holden-Day, San Francisco.

## Acknowledgements

We are grateful to A.A.M. Hart for the statistical analysis. We also thank Herman Te Riele and Walter Lioen of the Mathematical Center in Amsterdam, The Netherlands, for helpful discussions.

# Studying Prehistory with Tomorrow's Computers

## D. G. East

*Synchromy Graphics Modeling Department 3610 W. Cobbs Place Tucson, AZ 85745, USA*

*In this chapter, I show how modern computers and 3-D graphics can be used to facilitate archaeological exploration. Magnetometric data, described in the article, are used to help reconstruct what lies beneath the ground without the burden of exploratory excavation. In the future, computer archaeology may avoid unnecessary destruction of dwindling archaeological sites and resources.*

## Introduction

Archaeology is the scientific study of the material remains of past human life and activities. These material remains include fossils, monuments and other architectural forms, and various artifacts. In this chapter, I concentrate on the use of computers for examining a prehistoric site of the Hohokam Indians located in Southern Arizona.

The Hohokam Indians, a prehistoric sedentary culture with its most important distribution along the Gila-Salt drainage to the north and the Santa Cruz and San Pedro drainages to the south, began developing probably earlier than 300 B.C. and culminated after A.D. 1200.[1] Typically, their villages consisted of a number of pit houses. These were fairly small, one-room dwellings with the floor level somewhat below ground level.[2] The building techniques were generally wattle-and-daub; *i.e.,* a series of closely spaced posts around the perimeter of the dwelling with a covering of mud or adobe plaster. On occasion, the Hohokam built significantly larger structures, perhaps for multifamily dwellings, or perhaps for ceremonial purposes.[3,4] The village size varied from a half dozen pit houses to as many as a hundred. Occasionally, oval depressions, 60 meters or so on the major axis, surrounded by high earthen walls, are discovered in association with the villages. Because of the apparent similarity of these depressions to the ceremonial ball courts found further to the south in Mexico and the Mayan area, it is presumed that the ceremony (sport?) was observed by the Hohokam; however, there is no proof that the observance had the same religious connotation as with the cultures to the south.

As with other cultures studied from the archaeological perspective, the Hohokam are known and identified by a unique set of traits. These traits include a more or less rigid adherence to established mores and customs, represented in their crafts (forms and decorations of pottery and lithic or stone artifacts), their architecture (the general shape of structures and the materials used in construction), and their way of life (agrarian, sedentary, as might be inferred from the organization of their villages and the network of irrigation canals). This culture, as with others documented only by their abandoned dwellings, their burial sites, and their trash mounds, is imprecisely understood because of the distortion of the evidence by time, nature, and the inevitable destruction that results from excavation.

## Alteration of Sites

Geological forces are the long-term agents in the alteration of archaeological deposits.[5] Deposition and erosion alternately preserve and destroy whole structures, walls, foundations, and granaries or storage rooms, continually increasing the difficulty of understanding the patterns and practices of the early inhabitants. Agricultural development within the last century has turned rivers into deeply cut channels where they once were gentle meanders. Rapid runoff from the monsoon-like rains characteristic of the southwestern desert region distributes unearthed pottery fragments across the desert in a randomized sheet. Once or twice a year, locations that once must have been favorable for occupation become featureless mud lakes. Fragile adobe walls that once afforded shelter and security melt into the mud and vanish downstream.

Real estate development, highway construction, and landscaping activities frequently expose quantities of cultural materials that had been naturally sequestered for centuries. The archaeologist, faced with economic pressures, schedule deadlines, and anxious property owners, must salvage the material as quickly as possible while retaining the contextual relationships (the association of artifacts to each other, to the surrounding strata, and to significant features such as dwellings, ovens, and geologic features). Modern surveying equipment - for example laser EDM (electronic distance measurment), theodolites with digital interfaces, and GPS (global positioning system) - in conjunction with a hand-held field computer or vehicle-mounted personal computer (PC) is used to rapidly record the provenience (location and association) of artifacts and features as they are uncovered.

In the mid-1980s the PC was embraced by many forward-looking archaeologists as a means of reducing the labor of cataloging the vast quantity of data produced by orderly and thorough, but rapid, excavation of sites jeopardized by construction projects. Some professionals, with even greater vision, saw the PC as a tool that could enhance understanding as well as expedience. Computational agility, combined with the ability to manipulate great quantities of data, allows the archeologist to detect and describe nuances of cultural evolution that previously could only be suspected. Without the more efficient data-handling capabilities of the computer, the archaeologist was forced to choose a few sites to study from among several opportunities. It was possible to overlook pockets of divergent culture that never achieved successful integration into the population at large. Similarly, the study of an aberrant site could confuse interpretations concerning the mainstream. Computer data logging and analysis elevated the opportunities to study individual pit house remains to a standing once enjoyed by multiroom pueblos and compounds, or hunting blinds and pottery kilns.

There are no unimportant archaeological sites. The history of a culture as recorded archaeologically is a finite and ever-diminishing resource. In 1974 the Executive Committee of the Society for America Archaeology adopted a resolution saying, in part, "Each archaeological site contains evidence of specific human activities...no site can be written off in advance as unimportant or expendable. No site deserves less than professional excavation, analysis and publication."

Through growth in the application of computers to record, reduce, recover, and present archaeological data, we expect to minimize the expenditure of financial and human resources, as well as to avoid unnecessary excavation of the dwindling archaeological resources.

## Modern Archaeological Investigation

The popular image of the archaeologist is an "Indiana Jones" figure who removes rare and precious artifacts from their aboriginal setting for the purpose of display in a museum, proof of scholastic prowess, fame, fortune, or winning the favors of an oppositely gendered competitor. This bit of romance denies the truth that digging into a centuries-old trash mound is dirty, hard work, hazardous to your health (from exposure to valley fever) and rarely lucrative. (We will ignore the highly destructive and illegal traffic in undocumented antiquities that is related to grave robbing and the looting of underdeveloped nations.) Whereas excavation as a technique, and shovels and trowels as tools may never be abandoned by the archeologist, computer imaging and modeling as techniques, and various remote-sensing technologies as tools are gaining acceptance by many investigators. Aerial photographs taken from both balloons and aircraft have been used for decades to guide survey teams. High resolution infra-red images from satellites, the space shuttle, and high altitude aircraft have led to new interpretations of old data; just as importantly, they have led to the discovery of sites which would have otherwise remained unknown.[6]

During the survey and subsequent excavation of archaeological sites, portable computers facilitate the techniques of point provenience, and the recording of spatial coordinates of artifacts, along with description and contextual data. Similarly, arrays of data representing magnetometric, gravimetric, densitometric, electrical resistivity, or similar measurements of the physical environment[7] in proximity to an unexcavated region may be assembled to attempt a nondestructive assessment of the hidden archaeological resources.

In general, prehistoric cultures sufficiently advanced to have used fire have left archaeomagnetic evidence of themselves. A variety of minerals exhibit vestigial magnetic properties and are consequently useful for archaeological study. The walls of fire pits are especially valuable, having been exposed to temperatures exceeding the Curie point. At these elevated temperatures, the material loses its magnetic memory, and, upon cooling, adopts the magnetic orientation of the local geomagnetic field.

Dissimilarities between the orientation of the earth's magnetic field and the residual field provides both a method of detection and a method of establishing the date of the most recent use of the fire pit.

By a somewhat similar argument, local variations in the earth's field can be indicative of subsurface features such as pits, foundations, alignments of stones, or walls of baked mud blocks.

These sensing techniques produce a fuzzy projection of the subsurface disturbances on a two-dimensional plane at, or near, the earth's surface. The fuzziness is due, in part, to an inability to bring the detected energies to a focus. Perhaps of greater significance is the fact that the information being sought is detected either by sensing rudimentary order in an otherwise random field (variations in soil resistivity, for example), or by sensing small perturbations in an otherwise orderly field (geomagnetic, for example).

## Proton Spin Magnetometer Data

A number of Hohokam settlements have been discovered and studied near the Tortolita Mountains, north of Tucson, Arizona. In one area called Honey Bee Ranch (AZ:BB:9:88), a square area about 60 meters on a side containing a ball court was examined. Data was acquired using a proton-spin magnetometer. In the absence of magnetic anomolies, the magnetometric data is expected to have a normal (bell-shaped) distribution. The distribution of the Honey Bee Ranch data in the aggregate is shown in Figure 1, from which it may be inferred that a significant departure from randomness (possibly indicative of artificial disturbance) might be discovered upon further analysis of the data.

The map coordinates corresponding to each magnetometer reading were saved as the data were recorded. Techniques of interpolation and approximation are used to produce an orderly periodic numeric array more amenable to further numeric manipulation.

## Interpolation and Mapping

The estimation/interpolation algorithm is a multistep sequential process. The first four steps linearly interpolate between nearest-neighbor[8] data points in each graphical quadrant, while the passes apply the algorithm along Cartesian axes.

This procedure has been selected so that accepted interpolation practices may be used, and to eliminate any dependency on sample density or methodology.[9,10]

With this as with all survey techniques, some amount of experience is helpful in deciding on the density of measurements required to be consistent with the desired resolution; however, it is obvious that, similar to data recorded for normal physical topography, the extremes of magnetometric measurements, and local maxima/minima, should be recorded accurately. The algorithm in use only interpolates between points, and will not extrapolate estimates outside of the envelope of the input data.

A topographic representation of the survey area can then be created. The resulting contour map, shown in Figure 2, insofar as magnetic field variations are indicative of soil disturbances correlated with human activity, then abstractly represents the (presumed) still-hidden archaeological resources.

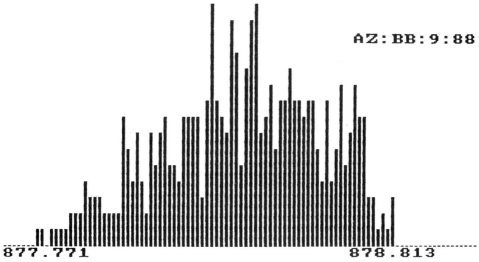

**Figure 1** *Distribution of magnetomter data.*

Further insight into structures implied by the data is gained by rudimentary image processing in order to enhance edges. A new array is generated by convolving the first against the following array:

Edge enhancement matrix:
$$\begin{bmatrix} -1 & -1 & -1 \\ -1 & 9 & -1 \\ -1 & -1 & -1 \end{bmatrix}$$

The elements of the output array consist of the corresponding input elements augmented by a quantity related to the local gradient. (The gradient alone would result if the central element were given a value of eight). Typically, this process results in a "noisy" array. It is useful to reduce the contour resolution (allow wider contour intervals) when examining the output array graphically. In Figure 3 the data is mapped with reduced resolution. Cursors have been drawn indicating quasi-linear alignment of larger field gradients. As mentioned before, a departure from randomness can be a strong indicator of human disturbance. In today's world, one might be tempted to turn away from the computer screen, choose some promising square-meter area, perhaps as prompted by the cursors, and begin excavation to test the hypothesis that the weak magnetic anomalies were evidence of early human activity.

Alternatively, the output array might (for example) be correlated with similarly processed data from earlier investigations to assist in planning an excavation or to focus a future investigation. In one form of this (multidimensional) correlation, the Fourier transforms of the images to be compared are used so that the comparison may be done without attention to the relative orientation of the two images. Frequently, orientation of structures is an identifying attribute (*e.g.,* easterly orientation of a shelter to take advantage of warming by the rising sun). Correlation of field data with earlier analyses

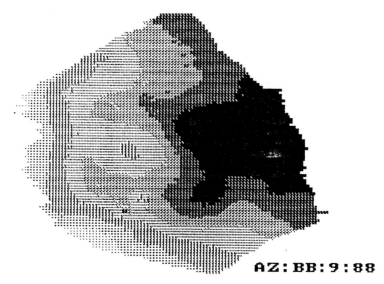

**AZ:BB:9:88**

**Figure 2** *Magnetometric contours.*

is, in these cases, a matter of overlaying multiple data sets and determining the coordinate values that yield a "best fit."

## Archaeology Without Excavation

Let us return to our Honey Bee example, where it is advantageous to represent the data in 3-D. The viewing plane can be moved from "overhead" to a position "off to the side," and the data can be replotted as a series of cross-sectional laminae, suppressing hidden lines as in Figure 4. This image does not represent physical topography; here, elevation is a measure of magnetic field strength. Any features one might imagine in the rendering would almost certainly be invisible when viewing the actual terrain.

Clearly, when the lines sketched in Figure 3 are superimposed on this perspective, the suggestion of a rectangular anomaly (a foundation?) is seen. Can we ask the computer to extrapolate that suggestion?

Today, no. It is possible to superimpose another image, a sketch, or the ghost of one data set on another as in Figure 5. It is possible for an artistically inclined archaeologist to present such representations as still another working hypothesis. However, the means to computationally and automatically create such a virtual reality with any significant confidence has yet to be developed. The computing power and graphics tools may be available, but the heuristics rely on skilled, experienced humans. Programming a computer to discern a vestigial foundation by correlation with a three-dimensional model is not unlike programming a missile to discern a target by

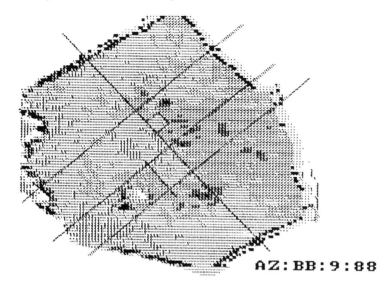

**Figure 3** *High field-gradient boundaries.*

correlation with a map or photograph. Neither algorithm (fortunately) uses the human talent of imagination.

In the immediate future, the archaeological applications of computers will almost certainly leap beyond the simple, clerical, data storage and tabulation, and report and map-generation paradigms. Visions of the past (which initially form in the mind of the trained investigator, solidify during or following excavation, and must be rendered by the pen of the illustrator and graphic artist) will become available prior to turning the first shovelfull of earth. As analytical procedures are developed and confirmed, it may eventually be unnecessary to unearth archaeological treasures except to protect them from the real estate developer's bulldozers.

Such an eventuality, of course, implies the development of an Artificial Intelligence (AI) system specifically for archaeological applications. Artificial intelligence is the branch of computer science that deals with using computers to simulate human thinking. AI development will involve expressing contextual relationships symbolically, as well as numerically, and the developing satisfactory models for manipulating the relationships. While the algorithmic development task is fundamental to the achievement of this goal, the techniques of acquiring, storing, processing, and reducing vast amounts of field data must advance in parallel. In general, advances in AI implementation are based upon extensive empirical research and hypothesis testing.[11] Success in correlating (at least qualitatively) magnetic data with artifacts recovered by excavation[12] is expected to intensify the interest in this form of archeological investigation.

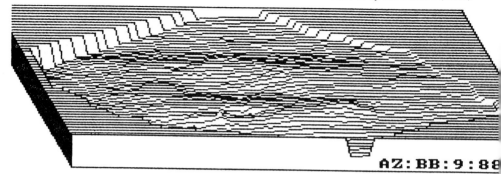

**Figure 4** *Perspective view of magnetometric data.*

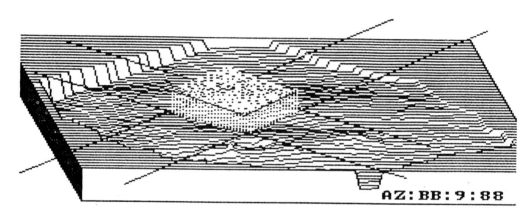

**Figure 5** *Hypothetical architectual overlay.*

From the field researcher's point of view, the required programming is straightforward. It is an application of multidimensional joint probability density functions (a graphic display of the probabilistic relation between cataloged geometries and noisy data). Because human occupation of particular sites is generally associated with some specific activity (*e.g.,* hunting lodges are associated with the pursuit of game) the suspected occurrence of one may be confirmed by the discovery of the other.

A data analyst might describe the problem as the detection and recovery of organized information buried in extraneous random noise, where the information is not necessarily periodic in nature. As we have seen in the Honey Bee example, the first clues to hidden human activity may be found in the nonrandom, or structured, behavior of otherwise random parameters. For cases where the noise-obscured construct is a replica of a noise-free paradigm, cross-correlation or convolution should produce a substantial reduction of the noise components.

From the viewpoint of an educator or conservationist, the availability of hardware and software is inadequate. It is the widespread use of the tools and techniques that will bring into the classroom, the museum, or other public display low-cost re-creations of archaeological sites, replicas of current study areas, and hypothetical models of discoveries awaiting study.

The archaeological record is fragile. Against the few monumental sites, such as the pyramids of Egypt and Mexico and the cities of Cuzco and Chaco Canyon, stand the several pit houses, cave dwellings, and ceremonial grounds. Whereas the former were built to withstand time, the latter were decidedly temporary. Discovery and excavation followed by reconstruction and stabilization inevitably compromises, and sometimes destroys, much of the cultural information.

It is projected that the population of computer specialists/analysts will grow 75.6 percent by the year 2000 (from a 1986 base population.)[13] If a small portion of that population were to specialize in spatial modeling as applied to archaeological research, we might enter the new century as true conservators of our cultural heritage. The resources would be protected from the wear and tear of public use, from vandalism, and from destruction by exposure. Tomorrow's computers would truly provide the key to studying, understanding, and preserving the record of our distant past.

## References

1   Tanner, C.L. 1976. In: *Prehistoric Southwestern Craft Arts,* pp.10-12. University of Arizona Press.
2   Kelly, I.T. 1978. In: *The Hodges Ruin, a Hohokam Community in the Tucson Basin,* pp.6-7. Anthropological Papers of the University of Arizona, No. 30; University of Arizona Press.
3   Wormington, H.M. 1970. In: *"The Hohokam Culture"; Prehistoric Indians of the Southwest,* pp.118-143. The Denver Museum of Natural History.
4   Weaver, D.E., Jr. 1973. In: *Excavations at Pueblo del Monte and the Classic Period Hohokam Problem; The Kiva,* pp.75-87. Arizona Archaeological and Historical Society, Arizona State Museum.
5   Hester, Heizer and Graham. 1975. In: *Field Methods in Archaeology,* 6th edn, pp.33-36. Mayfield.
6   Gibbons, A. 1991. A New Look for Archaeology. *Science,* **252**(5008), pp.918-920.
7   Joukowsky. 1980. In: *A Complete Manual of Field Archaeology,* pp.48-51. Prentice-Hall, New Jersey.
8   Kissam, P., C.E. 1978. In: *Surveying Practice,* 3rd edn, p.197. McGraw-Hill Co, New York.
9   Enslein, Ralston and Wilf. 1977. In: *Statistical Methods for Digital Computers,* Vol.III, pp.18-21. Wiley Interscience, New York.
10  Hester, Heizer and Graham. 1975. In: Field Methods in Archaeology, 6th edn, pp.288-292. Mayfield.
11  Schalkoff, R.J. 1990. In: *Artificial Intelligence: An Engineering Approach,* p.79. McGraw-Hill, New York.
12  Soffel, H.C. Schurr, K. 1990. Magnetic refraction studied on two experimental kilns. *Geophys. J. Int. (UK),* **102**(3), 551-562.
13  Miller, E. 1991. In: *Future Vision, the 189 Most Important Trends of the 1990's,* p.230. Sourcebooks Trade division of Sourcebooks, Inc.

# Computers and Future Golf

## Anthony S. Akins

*IBM Corporation 3700 Bay Area Blvd. Houston, Texas 77058-1199, USA*

*This chapter discusses the future impact of computers and related technology on recreational sports, in particular the sport of golf. First, I consider how computer technology currently effects golf and then discuss the future. The chapter concludes with a scenario that describes a possible future where the integration of computer technology with the sport of golf results in changes to the sport itself.*

## The Current State of Affairs

The first golf clubs were made of wood saplings, carved and shaped into clubs. The first ball was made of leather and stuffed with feathers. The first golf courses were laid out by individuals and groups on any land that was available. As the popularity of the game increased, changes in all aspects of the game developed.

The development of the "iron" was an early example of the use of technology in the sport of golf, as steel was smelted and forged to form clubs. In the twenties and thirties the use of steel shafts led to the eventual demise of the wood shaft, though some specialty clubs, such as putters, still use wood shafts. In the 1970s the use of shafts made from materials other than steel became popular, as well as the use of investment cast clubs. The design of investment cast clubs (where molten steel was poured into a mold of a clubhead and then allowed to cool) allowed club manufacturers to experiment with extending and modifying the hitting area of the club face, often referred to as the sweetspot by golfers. The popularity of investment cast clubs, and the ability to move and enlarge the sweetspot of a club, led to an early use of computers for the actual design of clubs.

The ball has changed shape and form throughout this century, with each new form eventually replacing its predecessor. The original "featherie" ball, having a cover of leather and stuffed with feathers, was replaced by the "gutta percha" ball. Gutta percha is a resinous rubber compound that could be formed by hand into the shape of a ball after being immersed in hot water. As the gutta percha cooled the ball would harden. The next stage of evolution was the development of the "balata" ball, with a liquid filled rubber ball, surrounded by strands of rubber bands, encased in a cover made of balata rubber. The "balata" ball remained popular throughout much of the 20th century. In the 70s the surlyn ball, with a plastic compound cover, was introduced. Surlyn balls have solid and liquid centers and have replaced the "balata" ball as the ball of choice for most players. In the 70s the "dimple wars" began as ball manufacturers claimed that specific dimple patterns increased the flight characteristics (including the distance and accuracy of the ball flight) of the ball. A great deal of research was conducted in this area, as ball manufacturers conducted tests to determine the optimal dimple configuration. Computers are being used to simulate the flight of a golf ball and to record data in ball flight experiments.

The explosion of the use of technology in the 1970s in the area of equipment design aroused the concern of traditionalists and historians of the game. Equipment manufacturers claimed that new high-tech equipment could lower the score of any golfer. New clubs and balls appeared to enable players at all levels to hit shots farther and more accurately. It was feared that courses developed before 1970 would become obsolete, as such courses were designed for the "old" equipment, which required greater skill to master. Today, traditionalists are concerned that the difference between two golfers is becoming a question of who has the best equipment, and not who has the better skills.

Into this arena stepped the United States Golf Association (USGA). The USGA has established guidelines defining what is legal equipment for the game of golf. The USGA maintains the Research and Test Center, located at its headquarters in Far Hill, New Jersey. The center supports the USGA's role of establishing equipment standards for the Rules of Golf. Included as part of its testing equipment is a machine that mimics the golf swing of Byron Nelson, a leading professional golfer from the thirties and forties. The machine, named "Iron Byron," is used for testing both clubs and balls, and was designed to make the same swing (including swing speed, angle of impact, and other factors) time after time. Working with the Royal and Ancient Golf Club of St. Andrews, the USGA is using advanced technology to set equipment standards for the game of golf. These standards help assure that old classic courses are not made obsolete by high tech approaches to the game, and that skill, not technology, is the final arbiter in all golf matches.

The methods of golf course design have not changed greatly over the last 50 years. Once a site is selected, aerial photographs are taken, and topographic maps are made. The architect uses the maps and photographs to lay out the course, and often walks the course during construction, in order to visualize how a hole will be viewed and played. The architect often will attempt to account for the prevalent winds, weather, and terrain while designing the course.

One area in which computers play a large role is in the generation and distribution of statistics related to the games. Many golf organizations offer computerized handicapping services for their members, as well as providing course ratings for other courses in the area. The professional golf tours use statistics in order to measure the performance of its members. Statistics are kept and calculated for a wide number of measurements, including stroke average per round, greens hit in regulation, putts per round, and driving distance.

A final area in which computers have impacted the game of golf is the use of computers to simulate a round of golf. Golf simulation games are available for all of the popular home/television video games, including the Nintendo Entertainment System, Sega and others. In addition, similar software has been developed for personal computers. One such program, Jack Nicklaus' Unlimited Golf and Course Design, by Accolade, provides us with a glimpse of a possible future relationship of computers and golf. Jack Nicklaus' Unlimited Golf and Course Design provides a program for designing new golf courses. Using a point and click technique with a mouse, a user of the program can quickly build a golf course that can then be played. This method of designing a course "on-line" may prove to be very useful for future golf architects.

Golf simulation software for home entertainment systems and personal computers currently provides no way to accurately measure the golf skills of those playing. A relatively new product, the par T golf simulator by par T golf marketing company, attempts to solve this problem by providing a realistic simulation of golf. The simulator uses a computer, film projector, infrared lights beams, and a special enclosure to provide the feel of the game. The par T golf simulator consists of an enclosed area, roughly 14 feet wide by 10 feet high by 25 feet long. The front section (16 feet 4 inches long) contains a display screen the width and height of the enclosure, and the putting area. The mid section (8 feet long) contains hitting surfaces (tee, fairway and sand) and the most distant putting points. The back section (5 feet to 10 feet) can be used as a seating area for waiting players. The computer, film projector, optical camera, and infrared lamps are located out of sight. At the start of each hole the film projector shows the hole as it would look from the tee. A player places the ball on the tee and hits away. The infrared lamps are used to measure clubhead speed, angle of impact, and other information which is used by the computer to calculate a flight path for the shot. Varying balls paths, such as curves to the left or right, or low or high, can be simulated. The flight path is projected on the screen as if the ball were flying away. Once the flight of the ball has ended the projector shows a new scene, showing the resting location of the ball in relation to the green. This process continues until the player reaches the green, and putts on the putting surface. Once a player has holed out, the score is recorded, and play at the next hole can begin. Currently recordings of seven different courses are available.

Simulation techniques are the basis for another product being developed for the golf and baseball markets. The product, Supervision, is being developed by SportSight and uses two televisions cameras, three computers, and special effects hardware to capture a series of images which can then be replayed and analyzed on the computer workstations. SportSight sees the product being used in broadcasting to show how a putt is going to break on a green (images of the ball would be recorded before the broadcast and then displayed during the broadcast). The system could also be used for swing analysis.

## Areas of Potential Change

The following areas show a great potential for change as computers and related technologies are tightly integrated with the sport of golf.

## Equipment

The use of computers to aid in the design of golf equipment will increase in the decades to come. Computer aided drafting (CAD) software will be used to design golf clubs in the future, while improved simulation software will be used for designing and testing clubs, balls, shoes and other equipment.

The integration of computers into the manufacture of golf equipment will allow manufactures to make clubs and club sets on a demand basis, as orders are received. Both manufacturers of golf equipment and club professionals will take advantage of this approach, the manufacture to minimize production and inventory costs, the club professional to provide greater personalized service to the individual customer. The use of human models in CAD programs (such as the Mannequin software package by HumanCAD Corporation) will enable equipment to be designed for the individual. Currently, most golf club sets vary only by weight, and stiffness of shaft. The general result is that the individual must fit and adapt to the set. Companies such as Ping already offer individualized sets, but in the future the level of individual tailoring will increase. In contrast to buying a set of clubs off the rack, the golfer of the future will be able to purchase a set of clubs that have been designed with his needs and abilities in mind.

The USGA will continue to define equipment standards for the sport of golf, and manufacturers will, in general, work within the bounds of the standards. A market for "non-regulation" high-tech equipment (providing additional distance and error correction beyond the standards defined by the USGA) will exist. "Non-regulation" high-tech equipment will be used mostly in informal club play, as most tournaments and competition will rely on the USGA guidelines for legal equipment.

## Training

Just as the equipment will be tailored to the individual so will training. Golfers will continue to use videotape to record and analyze their swing. The difference in the future is that computer hardware and software will be tightly integrated with video equipment to provide greater detailed analysis of the swing. Wire frame diagrams will trace the swing in order to highlight strengths and weaknesses of the individual swing.

Extensive bio-medical research aided by computers will allow the development of software that will aid individuals to develop a golf swing that takes advantage of their physical strengths and compensates for their weaknesses. Included in this will be the development of individualized fitness programs that will enable individual golfers to reach their peak performance.

Nutrition research will help the individual golfer to identify the proper eating patterns to maximize his/her performance on the course.

Finally, computers will serve a larger role in the mental training of the golfer. Advanced golf simulators will allow a golfer to experience all kinds of conditions and situations, better preparing the golfer for tournament competition.

This concentration on precision physical, mental and nutritional training will enable golfers at all levels to play closer to their limits. At the professional level numerous performance records will be broken. At the amateur level, the individual golfer will derive greater satisfaction from the sport.

## Course Design

The design and building of golf courses is still mostly an outdoor job. The architect builds a course with a vision in mind. The use of topographic maps, and overhead photographs aid the architect in the design of the course. Once the design is finalized, the moving of earth starts, and the course begins to take shape.

In the future, new technology in the areas of geographic information systems (GIS) and virtual reality (defined below) will allow the architect to design, build and play a golf course without moving a single ounce of earth. GIS is the use of computers to transform flat and static maps into dynamic displays of information. The use of GIS systems can integrate and make available the wealth of information (topographic data, water tables, water flow, geologic formations, property lines) that has been gathered about a region or area. Often referred to as computer mapping, GIS goes beyond that, by focusing on providing a synergy and integration of diverse data sources. Virtual reality is a computer-created sensory experience that has the goal of completely immersing the user in a virtual experience so real it is difficult to distinguish it from reality. In virtual reality systems, often displays mounted on the head are responsive to head motions and other movements.

Future GIS systems will allow the golf course architect to use all the available information about a land area in order to design a course. GIS systems will allow the architect to view the information in whatever manner is useful. The land could be viewed from overhead, or at ground level, using 3-D representations of the land built from topographical maps and other information.

The architect could choose to move trees or earth, reflow a stream, change the flow of the land, and witness those changes by using the GIS system to simulate the changes. The site could be viewed at sunset, with prevalent winds blowing, in perfect weather, or during inclement weather. Each hole of the course could be designed from the golfer's perspective.

The architect could "walk" the course, viewing each hole from the professional tees, the men's or the women's tees. He could see the effect of the sun setting over the hills as one plays the final hole, or the effect of a crosswind on a difficult hole on the front nine. At any time the architect could move from a hole by hole perspective and view the course from overhead, seeing how the course design fits into the available land, and how the design of one hole may effect the design and play of adjacent holes.

The architect could view the effect of trees, and other plants as they grow over time. The architect could pose the question, "How will this tree affect the play of this hole today, five years from now, twenty years from now?" This kind of simulation can be achieved using prevalent growth patterns of the land and the plant. What kind of greenery is best suited for the land, what kind of fertilizing and course maintenance approaches will offset weaknesses and take advantage of the strengths of the natural

**Figure 1**    Par T golf simulator facility, provided by par T golf marketing company.

terrain? Techniques and approaches used in course maintenance can be designed with consideration of the overall environmental status of the area or region. The golf course can become a more positive factor for the environment by producing oxygen through the trees on the course, and by following maintenance practices that have a positive effect on the local environment.

The collection and integration of this information by a GIS system will provide the golf course architect with a wealth of information that will enable the building of a course that is designed not only for the present but for the future. The combination of virtual reality with GIS systems will provide the golf course architect with the ability to not only design and simulate a course with the computer, but to also play it.

Architects will be able to play the course themselves, and see how each hole plays, how the roll of the land affects the tee shot on one hole, or how prevalent winds forces the player to one side of the fairway or how a small tree today will grow and affect the play on another hole in years to come. The architect will also be able to experience the simulated play of other golfers.

To test the championship capabilities of the course design, the architect could take on the playing characteristics of a professional and play the course from the back tees.

To test the course from a member's perspective the architect could assume the characteristics of an average golfer.

The simulated play of a senior or woman golfer could be used to test the play of the course from the women's tees. Keep in mind that the architect will be playing and interacting with the course, and will be able to see how each hole plays from the perspectives of the simulated golfer, whose skill can be tailored to match the course's intended audience. This ability will make it easier to build courses that challenge the professional and the skilled amateur, while not intimidating those whose skills are not as honed.

Using GIS and virtual reality technologies the architect of the future will be able to design courses that challenge the skills of all golfers, provide a pleasing appearance, minimize earth moving, while maximizing the appropriate use of the land used for the course.

## Future Golf

The following scenario describes how the game of golf may evolve as the integration of computers and related technology with the sport of golf increases in the coming years. The scenario takes place in the year 2013.

It's raining outside, but we'll be teeing off at 9:00 anyway. Luckily I reserved the virtual golf room at the club earlier this week. Today I'll be playing with a few old friends. One of them, Dan, is in town for the day, one is in Boston and the other is in San Jose. They'll be playing from virtual golf rooms at those locations and linking up to ours in Houston so that all of us can play a round of golf together. Computers at these remote locations will communicate by sending information and images via phone lines and satellites. The use of teleprescence, a concept of virtual reality research of the 1990s, will allow the four of us to play as we were all together on the same course.

While this is a friendly match, I'm taking it seriously. I'm sure the others are too. Last night I reviewed my fundamentals and some key swing thoughts. I used my palmtop computer attached to my video camera to perform a final swing analysis. The "Golf Instructor" software I recently purchased analyzed my swing, reviewed previous lessons, and suggested two swing thoughts to use during the match to improve my concentration. This morning I consulted my palmtop computer for a breakfast and snack menu. The menu consists of food that will maintain my energy level throughout the match.

It's now a few minutes before 9:00. I'm at the club in the virtual golf room, waiting for the link up to start. I look over my clubs I've chosen for today's match. We'll be playing a conglomeration of holes, from courses we've all played over the years. Dan and I "built" the course over the last couple of weeks in our spare time, using the library of recorded and virtual courses available to us. Last night I selected the clubs that I thought would serve me best for the holes we'll be playing. In the old days, before the turn of the century, most players had just one set of clubs. Today, many of us have a "set and a half", around 20 clubs, some are fairly standard, while others are utility clubs we've picked to help us on certain courses and conditions.

As Dan walks in the door, the link up activates and I begin to see the images of Drew and Alec on the wall display. We banter for a few minutes before we start playing. The first hole is from a course I played as a youth. We tee off, the video cameras and computers capture our swings and information relative to ball flight, and the results of our swings are quickly simulated and displayed on the 5 wall displays (all four walls plus one on the ceiling). Three of us are on the fairway, I've managed to find the left rough. My lie is not too good, and with 175 yards to the green, and a pond to cross, I've no choice but to bail out, and try to get back to the fairway. My bail out shot works, I'm in the fairway, 125 yards from the hole. As I watch the others play their shots I muse on the times I've played virtual golf. I'm still amazed at the variety of conditions that can be simulated by the virtual golf room. While the system is still not perfect, the simulation proves to be amazingly realistic.

Outside, in the real world, the rain falls, and occasionally, I hear the crack of thunder. In the virtual golf room, all is quiet as Dan studies his birdie putt.

## References

1   Illg, Claudine, and Boyett, Shanda. 1991. Is High-Tech Equipment Changing Golf ... For Better? ... Or Worse? *Gulf Coast Golfer.* 12–16. February.
2   Trivette, Don. 1991. Links from Access Sets New Standards for Golf Simulation Software. *PC Magazine,* 452. 26 March.
3   par T golf Marketing Company. 1991. *Forget the Weather, par T golf Technical Literature.* par T golf Marketing Company, 2820 W. Charleston, Building D, Suite 33, Las Vegas, NV 89102.
4   Bruno, Lee. 1991. A Whole New Ball Game in the Works. *UNIX Today!* 1. 18 March.
5   Sullivan, Eamonn. 1990. Program Brings Human Forms to PCs. *PC Week,* 6. 3 December.
6   Allman, William. F. 1991. A sense of where you are. *US News World Report,* 58–60. 15 April.
7   Fritz, Mark. 1991. The World of Virtual Reality. *Training,* 45–50. February.

# Artificial Life: Answering the Question of Emergence

## William R. Buckley

*Department of Chemistry and Biochemistry, California State University, Fullerton, USA*

*The spontaneous emergence of life on Earth remains an unsolved mystery of science. Great advances in computer technology now provides science with the computational power to address emergence experimentally. Such study is the primary focus of the interdisciplinary field called artificial life.*

## Introduction to Artificial Life

The future of computing is both bright and at hand. The next ten years of hardware development will yield computers which process tens of billions of instructions per second and store trillions of bits, while filling a small corner of a desk top. Judging the future of such machines is not an easy task. One sure bet is to identify unsolved problems of science which these future computers might help to solve. Today, science does provide a number of candidate problems which seem susceptible to analysis by supercomputers, the personal computers of the near term future.

Theoretical biology gives one such problem, the origin of life. Science postulates that life originated through a process called emergence, which resulted in the realization of life in the form of complex chemical systems, most notably protein chemistry. In the near term future, biologists will be better able to understand emergence through computer models of life. These unnatural life forms are realized in terms of the computer, through systems of computer programs and data. The study of such realizations is called Artificial Life.

## The Origin of Life: An Overview

Whence came life? Few questions have longer engaged the imagination of mankind. Artists, philosophers, scientists, and theologians leave a legacy as long as recorded history. Coming to mind are the works of Aristotle, Plato, and Virgil, Descartes, Mendel, and Darwin, and modern successors like Miller and Urey.

Yet for all man's musings, this question remains largely unanswered. Little wonder, for it is a complex question which may be asked and answered in many ways. Consider, for instance, "what is life?" How is life constrained by the media in which it is realized?

**Figure 1**    *A 19th-century image of how to create artifcial life.*

What are the stages and conditions characteristic of the emergence of life within a particular medium? Emergence is the central theme of the origin of life.

Surely the nature of life as we know it is tied to the nature of the physical universe. The realization of life in the physical universe is marked by the physical processes of chemistry and thermodynamics. Life is constructed from, but it is not identical to, these physical processes. Hence, the physical universe is in effect a carrier upon which life achieves realization. This carrier imposes restrictions on its use by hosted life.

Similarly, the nature of any other medium suitable for the realization of life will impose other restrictions on hosted life. It is therefore clear that there exists some set of characteristics universally common to life, but which are independent of media. It is also clear that the characteristics of life that are imposed by media are incidental, not central, to life in general. So, living systems possess characteristics both dependent and independent of media. One may suitably ask, what is the physics, and how expressive is the combinatorics, of a particular medium. Life is complex, evolvable, and self-reproductive. These characteristics must be borne through the physics and combinatorics of a medium.

A hypothesis is that the bytes of a computer memory form a medium capable of hosting life. Through artificial life models, the origin of life may finally become clear, and here the computer has a bright future. Computers are tools and as such are

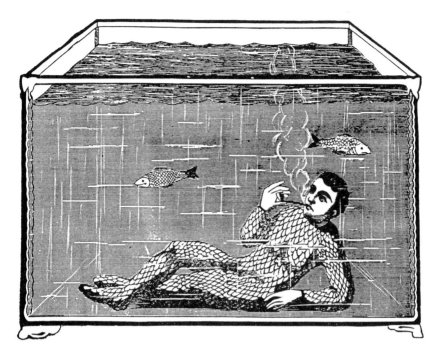

**Figure 2** *Another 19th-century image of how to create artifcial life.*

interesting in terms of their utilitarian purpose. What greater purpose is there than assisting man in his search for his origin?

## The Origin of Life on Earth

Modern cosmology holds that about twenty billion years ago, our universe did not yet exist. The entire universe then, suddenly and unexpectedly, leapt into existence. From then till now, the universe has greatly expanded in volume, the average temperature of the universe has been reduced from unmeasurable intensities to near absolute zero, and all matter has condensed from a cloud of extremely high energy photons. Surely life did not exist prior to this so called big bang. More recently, about four or five billion years ago, the Earth formed.

Biology suggests that life first appeared about three billion years ago, some one billion years after the formation of the Earth. There are two suitable explanations for the appearance of life on Earth. One is creation by God, the other is creation by spontaneous emergence. Science faces the same dilemma as faced our Greek forefathers. Spontaneous emergence was the topic of Virgil's recount of the creation of bees from the body of a cow. Life was either created by a superior being, or it came forth from the Earth of its own volition.

Science offers the following scenario. After the Earth formed, it was beset with solar radiation, particularly ultraviolet light, and violent weather and geologic processes, including rampant volcanism, meteoric bombardment, and severe electrical storms.

Miller and Urey provide the next clue, showing how simple protein and sugar chemical reactions might have occurred very early in Earth history, postulated to have an atmosphere abundant in carbon dioxide, hydrogen gas, water vapor, and gaseous ammonia. With time, the increasing concentration of these simple compounds leads to polymerization, with chance occurrences of catalytic properties between the polymers.

Simple chemistry gave way to more complex chemistry, leading to the formation of autocatalytic systems. Autocatalytic systems are systems which tend to operate by cooperative mechanisms. The cooperation occurs in the form of cycles, each stage of the cycle being the production of one of the polymers of the system, and that production being catalyzed by a different polymer of the system. At some point, these systems of autocatalytic polymers segregated themselves from the surrounding environment. Some of the polymers, called lipids, formed the simplest of cell walls, called a lipid bilayer. A bilayer then closes into a sphere of microscopic size, into which autocatalysts then migrate. These microspheres constitute the first living cells.

It is important to note that natural selection plays a role at the earliest stage of life's origin. Those autocatalytic systems which are better equipped to compete for resources become prevalent. Less well suited systems become less prevalent. Finally, such systems synthesize a genetic code and devise means to reproduce. In the same way that emergence in general is central to the origin of life, so is the formation of a genetic code mechanism. The processes of Darwinian evolution then guarantees the establishment of higher order life.

## Originating Life in the Computer

It is suggested that should non-carbon chemistry based life be discovered, it would be based on silicon chemistry. In a sense, artificial life brings new meaning to this tired refrain. The artificial life form living by means of silicon is not a coordinated chemistry, but a coordinated logic. An artificial life form is therefore a binary, or binological, life form.

Consider the programming of common serial processors. One may induce a kind of emergence within random data and instructions by repeatedly initiating a segment of memory into execution. Initiation will cause the execution of some number of instructions. Execution of the segment terminates when a memory location containing a non-executable value is selected as the next instruction address to fetch.

For each execution of the segment, the content of memory generally will be changed. With time, some changes to memory will affect the segment. This can lead to alteration of the instruction sequence, and so the function of the segment will change. If the segment acquires a looping structure, which is generally a jump instruction, the segment will tend to execute for a much longer period of time before execution terminates. At this point, a program can be said to have emerged. Such a program organizes itself to extend the time of its execution, before returning processor control to the operating system. Is this emergent artificial life?

These artificial life models are an adaptation of a computer programmer's game called Core War. As suggested by the name, Core War is a game of battle between programs, called warriors, and the aim of a game of Core War is the identification of that warrior which possesses the greatest degree of survivability. Warriors therefore engage in the computational equivalent of natural selection through a survival of the fittest strategy.

Warriors are in many ways special purpose computer viruses, though their programmatic behavior generally involves far more than viral behavior. For instance, while warriors may act to attach themselves to their opponents, it is far more common for a warrior to inflict damage to opponents. After all, a warrior which is able to cause all of its opponents to cease execution is the winner of a game. Yet, warriors interact in many more ways. One may frequently observe mutations of warrior code. Mutations are generally the consequence of failed attacks intended to cause an opponent to terminate execution. A warrior may however cause mutations to itself, leading to a new warrior. Those mutations which prove superior are able to successfully compete for the longevity of their computation.

Warriors are allowed to reproduce themselves, through timesharing, and an instruction which splits execution time between copies of a warrior. This allows for speciation. So, emergence in the computer begins with the periodic initiation of a memory segment, follows with the emergence of individual programs, continues with simple combat between program species, to culminate in arms races and higher order function.

Biology is hampered by the physical body, the muscle and bones, while the genetics are stored in the DNA. Genetics for programs are simple: the program is the genetics. The genetics of binological life is unencumbered by extra-genetic expression. There is no body save the genetics, the program, itself. This simplification to expression can be expected to concentrate study on the influence of evolutionary pressures on genetic systems instead of accommodations to media, as biology clearly exhibits.

## Conclusion

Artificial life is a multidisciplinary use of computers to find life other than as we know it. That computers can harbor life has profound implications for the study of physical life. The important issue here is time. The computer is so fast that emergence of life might be observed in a few hours, days, weeks, or months, instead of the millions or billions of years that it takes for life to emerge on an Earth. Thus, computers provide science with the opportunity to view evolutionary progress on a time scale which is much shorter than a human lifetime. This is clearly the tool of leverage that theoretical biology needs to answer the questions surrounding the origin of life.

## Acknowledgements

The author wishes to extend his deep appreciation to Dr Bruce H. Weber and Dr Wayne E. Taylor for their kind assistance in the preparation of this manuscript, including their numerous suggestions and use of their laboratory facilities.

## References

1    Burks, Arthur W. (ed.), 1970. *Essays on Cellular Automata.* University of Illinois Press, Urbana.
2    Langton, C.G. (ed.), 1988. *Artificial Life: The Proceedings of an Interdisciplinary Workshop on the Synthesis and Simulation of Living Systems, Held September, 1987 in Los Alamos, New Mexico.* Addison Wesley, New York.
3    Poundstone, William. 1985. *The Recursive Universe.* William Morrow, New York.
4    Schrodinger, E. 1956. *What is Life? and Other Scientific Essays.* Doubleday, New York.
5    Von Neumann, John. 1966. *Theory of Self-Reproducing Automata.* University of Illinois Press, Urbana.
6    Dewdney, A.K. Computer Recreations. *Scientific American,* **250**(5), 14-22.
7    Dewdney, A.K. Computer Recreations. *Scientific American,* **252**(3), 14-23.
8    Dewdney, A.K. Computer Recreations. *Scientific American,* **256**(1), 14-20.

# The Future of Ambiguous Art

## Peter Hettich

*Blankenlocherweg 22, 75 Karlsruhe 31, Germany*

*Artists of the future will experiment with ambiguous art based on simple geometrical shapes using traditional media and computer graphics. Included in this article are examples from my own paintings.*

Ambiguous features, visual illusions, and the depiction of impossible objects have fascinated artists and laypeople through the centuries. Famous past artists who have experimented with these visually interesting art forms come easily to mind: Escher, Magritte, da Vinci, Picasso, Dali, Albers, Vasarely, and most recently, Shepard.[1] (See refs. 1 to 5 for more information). Past researchers have even used such geometrical art as a probe of the human perceptual-cognitive system.[1]

Representing three dimensional objects on a 2-D surface naturally creates certain perceptual ambiguities. In the real world, viewers can walk around 3-D objects and also use their binocular vision to help resolve certain spatial ambiguities. This is not possible with paintings. In particular, I enjoy working with *depth ambiguities*. The ambiguities arise because the object is portrayed from a viewing position that yields alternative interpretations about where objects are located and what is in front of what.

My art (Figures 3-9) often reduces complicated objects (for example, human portraits and bodies) to simple basic elements, such as the ambiguous cube and rectangle (Figures 1 and 2). I think that artists of the future will often experiment with this kind of art using traditional media and computer graphics. Rapidly growing interest and understanding of the brain's visual and perceptual system makes figures such as these of particular interest in the 21st century.

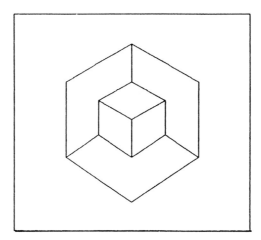

**Figure 1**    *The ambiguous cube.* Is the cube in front of, and inside of, the corner of the room? Is it in front of another cube? Is it touching the background "floor" or floating in above it?

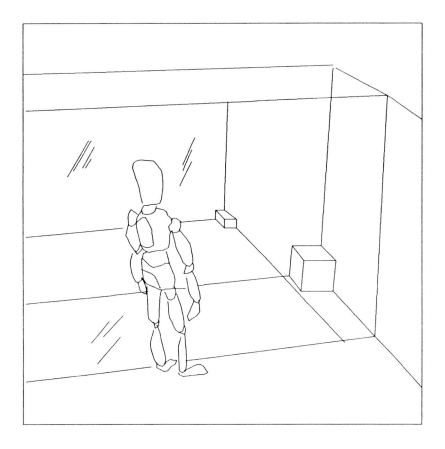

**Figure 2**   *A typical diagram I use to help create and understand geometric ambiguities in my art work.*

**Figure 3**    *Dirk.* (49 × 55, 1990).

**Figure 4** *Sabine.* (60 × 85, 1990).

**Figure 5**    *Dieter.* (60 × 85, 1990).

**Figure 6**    *Regina.* (75 × 110, 1990).

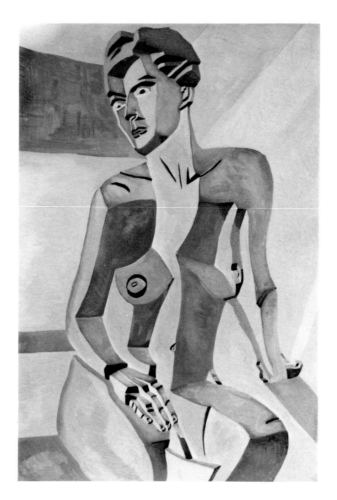

**Figure 7**    *Akt.* (75 × 110, 1990).

**Figure 8**     *Ursula.* (49 × 55, 1989).

**Figure 9**   *Moni.* (49 × 55, 1991).

## References

1    Shepard, R. 1991. *Mind Sights.* Freeman, New York.
2    Hofstadter, D. 1985. *Gödel, Escher, Bach.* Klett, Stutgart.
3    Gombrich, E. 1986. *Kunst and Illusion.* Belzer, Zurich.
4    Boff, K., Kaufman, L., Thomas, J. 1986. *Handbook of Perception and Human Performance,* Vols. 1 and 2. Wiley, New York.
5    Cagliotti, G. 1990. *Symmetriebrechnung und Wahrnehmung.* Vieweg, Braunschweig.

# Beyond Art

## Paul Brown

*PO Box 1292, Mississippi State, MS 39762, USA*

*Speculation about the future of information technology and its implications for the creative visual arts helps us identify the unique features of this new tool/medium. Computer aided art in its purest form is not concerned with the production of artifact but instead with communication and interaction.*

## The Last Decade

Over the last few months the countries of Eastern Europe have begun to reestablish democracy. By the time that this chapter reaches print I hope that we will have found renewed optimism and look forward to a largely unified planet in the not too distant future. Perhaps now at last there can be hope that the billions of dollars invested annually around the world to maintain the cold war can be redirected into solving the pressing ecological problems: pollution, population and poverty, that face humankind and threaten our future.

Michie[1] has suggested that these problems are too complex for humans to understand and solve, that our only hope is to develop artificial intelligence systems that can grasp the totality of the problem and so suggest viable paths of action. A dilemma here is that in order to create that technology we need a level of industrialization that will, in the short term, increase pollution: by committing ourselves to this particular solution we also guarantee its need.

This chapter speculates on the development of a super-intelligent technology and, in particular, upon the implications of this technology for the creative visual arts. Not only are artists discovering a new and, seemingly, infinitely flexible medium or meta-medium[2] and, possibly a new role for art but, in my opinion, they should also become directly involved in developing this new technology.[3]

Let me repeat, this chapter is speculative and it probably owes more to science fiction than to science fact. It will find many critics.

## What Does Fast Mean?

A modern supercomputer can sustain about one thousand million instructions per second (or 1,000 MIPS). These instructions could be, for example, simple integer sums – the addition of two whole numbers. If humans wished only to read this many numbers, and could read one each second it would take them 32 years of full-time work, with no breaks for eating or sleeping to complete the task.

In making such a simplistic comparison, that one second of supercomputer time equates to 32 years of human time, we must retain perspective. The internal processing speed of the brain appears to be a good deal faster than those of the supercomputer as we shall see below. And this comparison makes no allowance for human psychophysical processes, like intuition, about which we still know very little. Nevertheless a grand-master chess player can still beat powerful chess playing computers by making inspired decisions during the complexities of the end-game.

Imagine that we have those 1,000 million numbers before us. We know that most are in the range 0 to 100 but one, just one, is much larger, say 30,000. Our task is to find this renegade value as fast as possible. We can convert those numbers to colors so there is a direct relationship between color and value then display them as pixels on a computer graphic screen. If we use a resolution of 1,000 rows of 1,000 pixels each we can see 1,000,000 numbers simultaneously. 1,000 screens are required for all the numbers so if we play these back at 25 frames per second we get to see all the numbers in just 40 seconds. The renegade number will be apparent on the first or second viewing and after a period of cueing we should be able to isolate the unique frame containing the number, then its row and column number will identify it absolutely. I suspect that we could find that rogue number in this way in about 5 or 10 minutes at the most.

It's worth commenting that, in facilitating that perception we have traded speed against precision. We can find the rogue number quickly but we have no idea of its precise value. We only know that it is significantly different from its neighbors and, with well selected color attributes (via a look-up-table) we should also be able to estimate the magnitude and the sign of that difference.

Here's the power of computer visualization at work. Scientists associated with projects at the National Center for Supercomputer Applications[4] have reported finding errors in their algorithms as a direct result of using visualization-based analysis tools similar to the process outlined above.

The human brain has evolved elegant processing wetware. Vision is one of its masterpieces. Doctor[5] has suggested that we can increase the speed of modern supercomputers by a factor of 100 before we begin to tax the processing power of the human visual cortex.

During the last decade we can expect to see increases in processing speed that surpass even that factor. A researcher in Queensland[6] has outlined a reversible gate (so-called gates that implement logical functions like AND, OR and NOT are the fundamental building blocks of digital computer systems) that operates on quantum or sub-atomic levels. It could theoretically use single photons as bit information carriers, be very small and be able to steal energy from its environment in the form of spare heat. As such it may be considered potentially non-polluting however, as I have expressed elsewhere[7] the major source of pollution within a computing device is a function of the quality and quantity of the information it is processing and eventually outputs into the environment.

Researchers at IBM have taken these sub-atomic concepts further and produced a practical communication device that operates on quantum levels and uses the uncertainty principle to ensure security.[8] What is particularly interesting about this system is that it is the first computational device to exceed the capabilities of the Turing Machine, a theoretical model proposed in 1936 by the English visionary mathematician Alan Turing.

Another route for the computer of the future is the bio-chip. I have spoken with one researcher who referred to Drexler's work at MIT[9] and speculates that we should be able to produce supercomputers systems that will be the size of large organic molecules by the year 2010. Like modern pharmaceuticals they will be capable of being targeted for specific psychophysical sites and functions. Once introduced into the body they will be capable of tackling illness: restoring immune deficiencies and attacking damage like carcinogenic tumors. They will be able to act as an adjunct to memory and, perhaps most exciting of all, they could conceivably aid with DNA replication. The implication here is that such systems may be able to stop, and perhaps even reverse the aging process.

Parallel processing, where several interlinked processors work together on the same problem is now a viable technology. Massive parallelism and in particular the attempts to emulate human wetware by the use of neural networks shows great promise. The value of even simple systems is well demonstrated by the Neural Net demo running on the Next Computer which shows a seal learning to balance a stick on its nose by trial and error.

There are many other interesting and exciting examples of the new worlds being opened up by modern information processing.[10] Within the industry the rate of change of change itself is increasing and even hardened professionals are expressing surprise and occasional concern at the pace.

Although with parallel computing, neural networks, quantum and bio-chips the measurement of performance in MIPS is less indicative there seems to be general expectancy that sometime during this Last Decade we will achieve 1,000,000 MIPS – the ability to process one million million numbers per second.[11] Using my earlier metaphor a human would need 32,000 years to merely scan that many numbers.

32,000 years ago humankind were hunter gatherers. The foundations of the kind of social order that led to civilization would not appear for over 20,000 years. The earliest evidence of human settlement in Australia comes from this period as do the elegant paintings of hunting scenes on the cave walls at Lascaux in the south of France.

Bearing in mind my reservations above it's nevertheless remarkable that we could soon have an information technology that will have the potential of condensing these phenomenal human time scales into just one second.

If we now apply computer graphics visualization to this vast quantity of numbers – animating one million numbers per frame we require 40,000 seconds, 666 minutes (a portent here that would amuse Mary Shelley[12]) or 12 hours. It's a long movie but still a big improvement on 32,000 years. Nevertheless visualization is here being pushed to its limits and it's important that we improve man-machine communication in order to handle the ultra-high bandwidths that will be associated with the coming generations of supercomputers.

An important development that has taken place during the 1980's has been more and more sophisticated long-distance interprocessor communications. A key to the development of Fourth Generation Computing and the success of personal computers were the networks that now cover the planet and extend into space like a fine global system of nerves. Though high-speed nets link inter-departmental and occasionally inter-institutional sites the major national and international data highways are painfully slow. Steps are being taken to ameliorate this bottleneck by using more efficient and sometime novel data compression methods[13] and higher bandwidth optical transmission technology.

Networks open a system up to attack from without and have also brought problems as anyone who has had to upload reams of junk email at 300 baud in order to extract an important message will know to their cost. But the real villains are the diseases that have infected the globalNet. As far back as 1975 science fiction author John Brunner suggested a data processing construct that would travel along networks changing or destroying their node contents. Brunner called it a Worm.[14] The first real worms, together with their streetwise cousins the viruses appeared in the 1980s. They have caused, and indeed are still causing, major damage. The concept of computer security has been modified and what is virtually a new technology has evolved – information system immunology.

The personal computer on your desk is not a closed system. Connected to a modem it becomes one processing node in a supersystem – the globalNet – that includes just about every other computer in use anywhere that humans have been, or sent their remotes.

Currently it's unlikely that this supersystem has any concept of itself. Developments in artificial intelligence, neural networks and in particular the refined analysis of human cognitive activity are likely to trigger self perception in such a system. Spencer-Brown[15] infers that any system that goes beyond a certain complexity has to develop self perception in order to be able to resolve space/time paradox. A system that has no awareness of self, for example, is unlikely to discover the Uncertainty Principle.

## Gateway to the Brain

Epileptics suffer violent and seemingly chaotic electrical brainstorms. Outwardly they loose control of their body and suffer distressing and often damaging muscular fits. One treatment for this condition involves severing the corpus callosum. Studies of patients who have had this treatment has given insight into aspects of brain functioning. In particular it is relatively easy to induce sensory paradox using material that to a 'normal' person would appear trivial. This is particularly the case when material mixes visual information handled by the right lobe of the brain with literary material which is processed by the left. This is because the corpus callosum is the highway that allows the two lobes of the brain to communicate with each other.

Studies of others who have suffered brain damage has confirmed that, under normal operation, specific parts of the brain are dedicated to particular functions. Nevertheless it has been demonstrated that if one part of the brain is damaged another area can often learn to do the work associated with the lost tissue.

Over the last two years I have been involved in helping physicists at the Swinburne Center for Applied Neurosciences[16] to develop low cost visualization tools. One of their experimental rigs uses a modified bicycle helmet to hold 64 electrodes in place on the scalp. Electrical activity is sampled several hundred times each second at each of these sites and stored in digital form. Postprocessing reveals detail and demonstrates dynamic links between brain structure and cognitive processing.

It would appear that humans have evolved a twin processor. Each is capable of maintaining a basic level of independent functionality. However under normal circumstances each is dedicated to particular functions and, communicating with each other along the corpus callosum, a very high level of activity can be maintained. The corpus callosum is like a bus structure that allows rapid and high-bandwidth exchange between the two processors. It may well be that all high-level brain activity finds itself commuting along this route.

If we wish to bypass the sensory inputs (touch, sight, smell, taste, vision and esp) to establish high-bandwidth and direct communication with the brain it would appear that the corpus callosum, rich in interbrain information traffic, may provide an excellent gateway.

Current theory suggests that we first monitor the electro-chemical activity across the corpus callosum and have an artificial intelligence (AI), probably in the form of a neural network try and figure out what's going on. Once it thinks it does it will be allowed to send some signals back. We will have begun to build a direct link between brain and computer. Not too long after this I would expect to see the first artificial super-intelligences (SIs) emerging.

It has been suggested that we should have computing systems with the physical capacity of the human brain within fifteen years. Connect something like that up to the corpus callosum and it shouldn't be too long before we see a true artificial cognitive system emerging. It's links to globalNet will give it a source of information and knowledge that will reinforce an ultra-fast learning curve. Very soon after it has evolved machine intelligence will eclipse human facilities and the new SIs will begin to inhabit the Net. Many who are far more qualified than I have suggested that by facilitating this process we are, in fact, creating our evolutionary successors.

Graphics, the mainstay of current computer-human-interface (CHI) development, may seem redundant once direct communication is developed. I doubt it and suspect that visualization will still provide a semiologically rich gateway, possibly via direct stimulation of the visual cortex. From about the age of six, when the child learns metric vision – the ability to estimate measure by just looking – sight begins to dominate other senses in the learning and communication process. The potential here – of directly controlling and manipulating vision, of creating virtual spaces (whole new and coherent universes of interest) is one of the most exciting challenges the artist has ever faced.

## Art and Beyond

The implications for humanity of a self-aware superintelligent globalNet are mindboggling as are the implications for the visual arts. Most artists to date have used computers as tools using prepackaged software that emulates traditional techniques for artifact production like painting, drawing, photo-retouching and so forth. Oil paint is a simple thing and its lack of intelligence makes it easy to simulate. Despite their limitations these graphics arts systems have proved of value: they are non-toxic or significantly less toxic than traditional media; they can significantly enhance productivity and; despite the often strong signature of the particular system in use, they have proved the viability of this new meta-medium to handle a diversity of styles and methods ranging from the formal and often geometrical languages of structuralism to the free association of surrealism and abstract expressionism.

A few artists have pioneered new ground and are helping to define the unique attributes of this information transaction based meta-medium. Two immediate potentials seem to offer themselves. The first is involved with establishing an interaction or intercourse between a human and an AI. The second is interaction between two, or more, humans mediated by an AI. Several artists including the Melbourne-based Simon Veitch have begun to investigate the former. Others, most notably Myron Kruger, have pioneered the latter.

Veitch[17] is an artist who has developed an interactive system he calls 3-Dis. Using two or more small monochrome video cameras volumes of space as small as a few cubic centimeters or as large as a whole room can be identified and tagged. Up to 96 of these volumes can be monitored simultaneously. When the contents of a volume change this can be converted by the computer into a command that can trigger any number of events like, for example, the control of a midi channel on a sound synthesizer or a remote surveillance logger.

The essential simplicity of the concept belies its application and usefulness. Although there are similarities with the work of Canadian artist David Rokeby[18] there are subtle and essential differences, not least the ability to independently track the behavior of a large number of people or events simultaneously. Now the system has been proved in arts events (where groups of dancers created their own soundtracks) and installations (where fountains followed visitors about as they strolled around gardens at the 1988 Brisbane World Expo) the security people are getting interested and promise Veitch a new source of support.

Kruger's[19] installation at SIGGRAPH 85 in San Francisco used a single monochrome camera and clever edge-detection software to allow individuals and groups to interact with projected images of themselves together with computer generated artifacts like little green gremlins and b-spline curves. What was particularly evocative about this exhibit was the way it encouraged people to play together. On several occasions I discovered salespeople in suits interacting with the most unlikely partners – students in sawn-off jeans amongst them in a completely uninhibited, joyful and humorous way.

Encounter group therapists have been trying to create this degree of relaxed and intimate behavior for decades and yet here a relatively modest computer program acted as a catalyst for close spontaneous human interaction. Nevertheless, four years later at SIGGRAPH 89 critics and gallery curators on the panel Computer Art – an Oxymoron[20] still felt confident to reiterate their belief that computer art is cold, intimidating and heartless.

Those speakers, like many in the art mainstream, were expressing their problems in getting a suitable handle on this kind of work. Their complaints mainly concern the lack of tangibility of the artwork – that it can't be framed, revered or monetarised. Computer art is not concerned with the production of artifact. By contrast it is exactly the inverse of those attributes the mainstream miss that defines this areas uniqueness and potential. Computer art, like Dada and many of the works of the art language and other conceptual groups, is essentially an ephemeral and virtual artform concerned with communication and interaction.

It is my opinion that practitioners shouldn't waste their time trying to convince the arts mainstream of the value of their work. Our involvement in SIGGRAPH (1990 marked the 10th anniversary of the SIGGRAPH Art Show), Ars Electronica, FISEA and other events constitute the evolution of an international and interdisciplinary Salon des Refusés. Putting energy into consolidating this movement is infinitely more valuable than wasting time trying to convert the high-priests and culture-vultures of the establishment who, in any case, are mortified by the threat to their quasi-religious and usurious value systems that this new and egalitarian artform endorses.

They will come over in the end never fear: just as soon as they find out how to get an edge. Look at what they did to the Dadaist's dream of undermining the academy – the establishment now drinks champagne from Duchamp's Urinal.

## Twenty First Century Alchemists

If todays artists can achieve so much with the limited computer technology that's currently available we can look forward to a renaissance as they contribute to the development of the brain interface and a fully interactive globalNet with its resident SIs. By entering globalNet creative artists bring knowledge of a host of human experiences to the system, the expression of both intellect and emotion and, not least, the value of the celebration of existence. They also will bring the streetwise conscious-ness – an ability to survive, both within and from, whatever is at hand. And, most often their aims are benevolent – a quality they will do well to pass on to the new intelligence.

A tightly coupled man-machine symbiosis should lead to a close creative collabo-ration between man and machine. Eventually it's likely that we will see pure machine art – the product of what is essentially an alien intelligence – for the first time in human history.

The potentials offered by interaction with these artificial and, once they pursue an independent evolutionary path, alien intelligences will open up exciting new potentials for the creative artist. Already two young Australian artists take their inspiration from the area.

The CyberDada events of Troy Innocent and Dale Nason are an anarchistic, acid-house mix of free-form sound, scratch video, analog and digital screen displays, slides and live performance. Their equipment looks like it was built with a sledgehammer – a sound deck that features a raw and mangled cassette transport linked (functionally?) to a caseless Apple II all hooked together with recycled wires and bits of dead circuit board. Although both are young and their work still immature it has attracted the attention of the alternative arts network and the two recently received financial support to complete a videographic version of their CyberDada Manifesto (Figure 1) along with facility support from leading professional digital video studios like The Video Paint Brush Company.

These two are amongst the first generation of kids who have had computers around for most of their lives and who are not, in the least, phased by either their existence or potential. Although both are used to microprocessors, until recently they had little opportunity to learn about the more mainstream activities in computer science, graphics and CHI and have been surprised to discover that many of the concepts that excite them are actually being developed 'for real' by scientists and engineers. Their main source of inspiration has been science fiction and, in particular, the work of the cyberpunk writers.[21]

William Gibson is author of the canonical texts of cyberpunk – the CyberSpace trilogy: Neuromancer; Count Zero and Mona Lisa Overdrive. CyberSpace is the virtual space within the matrix – the globalNet – reached by jacking in via a socket or a "trode net". When Gibson wrote Neuromancer (on a manual typewriter) he was unaware that NASA and others were working on the real thing. He's also concerned about the attention his work has brought him from the technical world ... "it never occurred to me that it would be possible for anyone to read these books and ignore the levels of irony".[22]

## Brave New Worlds To Go

The goals of science don't seem to have changed much in millennia. The Chinese Taoist alchemists of the Han Dynasty sought the elixir of youth over 2000 years ago. They and their colleagues down the ages have also attempted the creation of life, homunculus and succubus, from inanimate matter. Now with biotechnology and quantum communications there seems to be some reasonable expectation that we may be getting close. (Yet another claim that alchemists of all ages have made – particularly to their patrons.)

Whilst some, taking Mary Shelley's lead are concerned about the religious, moral and ethical implications of such speculation, others rejoice in the fact that we may at last be able to create an intelligence that is capable of understanding the fragilities of the tenuous ecosystem of planet Earth and may be able to help us remedy our past errors. My interest in getting artists involved in the process of developing these new intelligences is because they will bring a whole set of values, particularly those that may help ensure that the new technology is benevolent.

Many questions must wait to be answered. By plugging into globalNet will humans bring requisite self-awareness to the system or instead will we need to create an autonomous self-awareness? Will the Net be dependent on, or independent of, its human creators?

DIGITISE THE WORLD. COMPUTER GENERATED CYBER DADA. DIGITISE. INTERFACE.

# cyber dada manifesto:

**DIGITISE THE WORLD** (A new life awaits you). KL65. **TECHNOLOGY** is speeding ahead : are you following the integrated golden horizons? Take technology apart and see what it really is ! **Reuse everything !** Make sculpture out of polystyrene, computers, plastic, metal, anything ! Become a **techno junky** Wear technology ! *Anyone can make or be art.* Become Exhibit on the street. Exhibit on yourself. Glue your piece to Alan Bond's front door ! Right of access to all data. *Graffiti artists* : start **Cyber-tagging** DON'T be rude : talk to your fax machine. Work things out for yourself, go beyond current standards and values and make your own. Master **Computers** and you will have **hacking power** over banks, goverments, and the military through technology. **Psychoactive designer foods.** Subversive cultures are starting lto seep from the rotten foundations of our soceity – **cut their hydraulic lines.** Civilisation destroys the world so **lets digitise** it and save the entire human soceity on **mainframe laser disk** All hunans and the junk they produce will be sealed inside a huge computer. Forget the **meat** of your **bodies full-on brain experiences** await you inside a computer. **Interface!** Your true life and aspirations are inhibited by the weak flesh of your body – **your body is a burden** It is simply meat. **Wetware** can enhance it. **Cyborg implants** bring you closer to true experience. **Jack in** to nuero-circuits. Once all people, objects, senses, and experiences are **digitised** onto laser disk (with backup copies) **the real world** can finally breathe a sigh of relief as man has disappeared forever. He has already tried to create his own enviroment, now the potential is here ! Organic life is no longer a valid lifestyle. **Fully synthesised** enviroments where **all physical and emotional feelings can be chemically simulated** Soon it will be possible to **inject a biological computer** to **program your brain**, extend your life, anything This is our **future**. You are your conciousness, don't let a physical existence fool you. Physical bodies are now superseded, **replace your body** with machine and computer components. And become superhuman! Self sufficient soceity, solar powered. We can now **venture to the limits of the cosmos** because we are not bound by earthly dimensions. **Cybernetics** does not discriminate by looks, race, disabilities, sex, species because it is **pure brain to brain communication** Jack in your **nuerons** to complete expression and communication of self. Be free of disease, food, be totally efficient. **Learn technology.** *Modern man's aesthetic* is grounded in pre 20th century decorativeness and **over indulgent art** theorising. **The new aesthetic is computer generated CYBER DADA.** The **new species** are cyborgs, man/machines, precise superior flawless beings to house our conciousness and create a new world. **DON'T BE AFRAID : LEARN TECHNOLOGY :.** DON'T BE AFRAID. By **wearing circuitry** *you* will represent the **new age** Take electronics apart and see what they are. Learn electronics, computer programming : the **arts of the future** Don't be intimidated by flashing lights and buzzing, and computers that look like **microwave ovens. faster technology** so it won't beat you as it **rapidly fills the world** Technology controls the world so if **you control technology** ......The end of the world is coming, but it is the beginning of a **perfect techno world STOP reviving old cultures – MAKE NEW ONES!!** The **youth** of today have become complacent and apathetic, easily controlled by **advertising**, the **media**, and **unscrupulous governments** Let the top of this hierachy know that they can't use **technology to control us,** but that we are **fully integrated** with technology and **it is ours.** Digitise the world!! It's time to **interface with technology and understand it.** KNOW IT personally. Get TECH. out of the establishment and into the streets. **Live in CYBERSPACE where all feelings and physical realities can be psycho-chemically simulated** DON'T BE AFRAID : **EXPOSE YOUR CIRCUITRY COME TO TERMS WITH *TODAY'S* MATERIALS.** The future will come whether you like it or not so **be ready for it** PAINTING HAS DIED AGAIN : stop using purely old materials like oil and canvas. It will not last in a **cyber world** (WHICH *WILL* COME WHETHER YOU LIKE IT OR NOT). Art, life, and the world are becoming increasingly meaningless so –––––––––––>. **CYBER DADA IS POPULAR CULTURE. /'S TODAY'S SOCIETY. AND IT'S FUTURE** (COPY THIS MANIFESTO 5+ TIMES AND GIVE IT TO FRIENDS. FAMILY. ANYONE ') (ICOPY THIS MANIFESt

**Figure 1** *CYBERDADA MANIFESTO Computer printout and collage 11.75 by 8.25 inches.* Troy Innocent and Dale Nason, 1990.

Such questions aside the potential for the creative arts is promising. We may, at last, have broken the stranglehold of the gilded frame and bypassed the parasitic high-priests and culture vultures to establish an egalitarian art of and for and by the people. Not the constrained and hierarchical social realism of totalitarianism but a hetrachical and streetwise cyber-grafitti, an art from the grassroots of democracy that, like urban spraycan walls, will impinge on and possibly integrate all our diverse consciousness's.

## References

1   Michie, D. and Johnston, R. 1984. *The Creative Computer*. Viking, London.
2   Alan Kay has suggested the term Meta-medium to describe the flexibility of digital simulation. Not only can we program computers to emulate old media – like paint or typography – but we can, are, discovering new and unique media potentials that this technology offers.
3   Brown, P. 1989–1990. *Art at the Computer Human Interface*. Artlink, Vol 9 No 4 Summer pp.64–65. Adelaide. (363 The Esplanade, Henley Beach, South Australia 5022).
4   Mathew Arrott and Stephen Fangmeier speaking at SIGGRAPH 88 pointed out that their simulation of the interaction of the solar wind with the ionosphere of Venus showed peculiar visual artifacts that they later identified as errors in calculation. They speculated that without visualisation such errors could have been overlooked.
5   Doctor, L.. 1988. (President of Raster Technologies) speaking on the videotape "Visualisation: State of the Art", ACM/SIGGRAPH *Video Review*, Vol 30. New York.
6   "Reversible computers take no energy to run", New Scientist, 10 June 1989 p 14. A report on the work of GJ Milburn at the University of Queensland.
7   Brown, P. 1989. *Art and the Information Revolution*, Leonardo Supplemental Issue, Computer Art in Context – the SIGGRAPH 89 Art Show Catalogue pp. 63–65. The International Society for Art Science and Technology, Pergamon, Oxford.
8   *Quantum communication thwarts eavesdroppers*. New Scientist, 9 December 1989 No 1694 pp. 13. A report on the work of Charles Bennett and John Smolin at IBM's Thomas J Watson research Lab.
9   Drexler, K.E. 1986. *Engines of Creation*. New York, Anchor Doubleday.
10  Pagels, H.R. 1988. *The Dreams of Reason*. New York, Simon & Schuster (Bantam 1989).
11  1989. Data Parallel Computers From MasPar Top Out At 30,000 Mips And 1,250 Mflops. *Klein Newsletter*, 11(23), 3, December. MasPar offers this 16,384 processor system for just US$25 per Mip.
12  Mary Shelly, "Frankenstein". This 19th century author was one of many commentators who have been critical of humankinds efforts to create life. The current debate over the scientific use of human embryos demonstrates many similar concerns. As yet the critics have not directed their attention into the issues raised by digital simulation.
13  Michael Barnsley the author of *Fractals Everywhere*, Academic Press, 1988, has developed one of the more novel data compression methods. A raster graphics image is scanned to extract its fractal initiators which are then transmitted. The receiver then reconstructs the image. Barnsley claims that an image can be reduced to less than 1% of the normal storage, *i.e.* it can be transmitted at least 100 times faster.
14  Brunner, J. 1975. *The Shockwave Rider*, JM Dent & Sons, London. Brunner, along with the more poetic sci-fi author Samuel Delany has been a major influence on the development of the streetwise cyberpunk style (see ref.20 below).

15  Spencer-Brown, G. 1969. *The Laws of Form.* George Allen and Unwin, London.

16  SCAN – the Swinburne Centre for Applied Neurosciences, PO Box 218, Hawthorn, Australia 3122. Director Dr Richard Silberstein and his colleagues are currently preparing to publish their initial results on monitoring cognative activity. The speculative conclusions that I draw above have been inspired by their scientific rigour but owe a generous debt to my interest in sci-fi.

17  Simon Veitch may be contacted via: Perceptive Systems p/l, PO Box 1008, St Kilda South VIC 3182, Australia.

18  David Rokeby is featured in ACM/SIGGRAPH 88 Art Show: Catalog of Interactive Installations and Videotape, ACM/SIGGRAPH New York 1988. See also "Experiential Computer Art", ACM/SIGGRAPH 89 Course Notes No 7. ACM/SIGGRAPH New York 1989.

19  Myron Kruger is featured in the previous reference (16). A pioneer artist of virtual spaces his book *Artificial Reality.* Addison Wesley, New York, 1983/91, introduced this term.

20  1989. *Computer Art – an Oxymoron – Views from the Mainstream.* A Panel at ACM/SIG-GRAPH 89. ACM New York 1989.

21  Sterling, B. (ed.). 1988. *Mirrorshades – the cyberpunk anthology.* Paladin/Grafton London. A good introduction to the work of the Cyberpunk sci-fi authors by one of their members. Essential reading includes: the Cyberspace trilogy by Gibson, W. 1984 *Neuromancer* (Gollancz, London), 1986 *Count Zero* (Gollancz, London) and 1988 *Mona Lisa Overdrive* (Gollancz, London); Ruckers, R. 1988 *Wetware* (Avon) and; Bears, G. 1985 *Blood Music* (Arbor House).

22  William Gibson quoted by Richard Guilliatt in *SF and the tales of a new romancer,* Melbourne Sunday Herald, 17 December 1989.

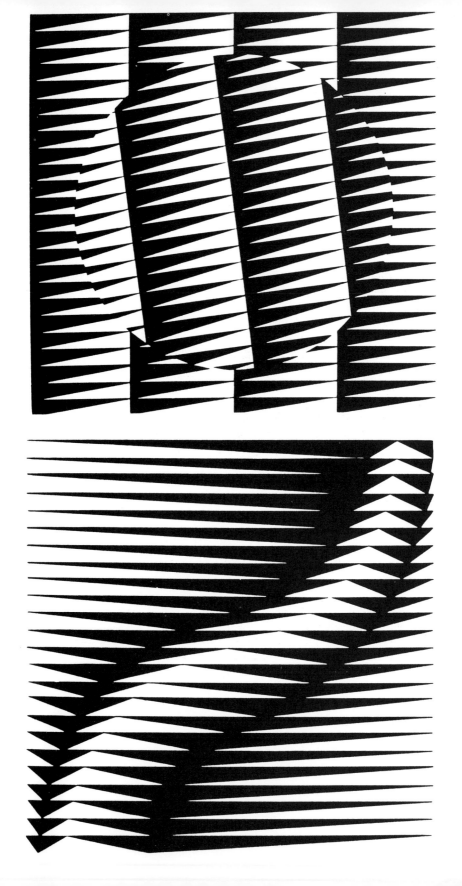

# Frontiers in Computers and Writing

## Rae C. Schipke

*Department of English, University of Southern Mississippi, Hattiesburg, Mississippi 39406-5037, USA*

*When we introduce computer networks into writing classrooms, we create social environments focused upon collaborative tasks as opposed to individual or solitary achievement. Individuals, although contributing to the collective, frequently become neglected. This philosophy of treating everyone exactly the same is completely out of sync with recent sentiment among educators that individual differences must be noted and nurtured. Such recognition of the individual is, in fact, the thread that will connect every trend in education for the 1990s. To respect diversity among students, writing teachers are going to have to create learning environments where the unique potential of the individual can be actualized. How do we preserve individuality in writing environments that promote uniformity, universality, and sameness? How do we balance respect of the individual with the collective structure of computer networks, cooperative learning, and collaborative writing approaches? In this paper, I speculate on how personality traits might be the key to understanding individual differences and discuss ways in which this knowledge might be gained by teachers and researchers and used to enlighten the teaching of writing in networked environments.*

**The only way to predict the future is
to have the power to shape the future.**

Eric Hoffer, *The Passionate State of Mind*

As with many inventions throughout history, computer networks in the classroom are having an impact that can only truly be assessed with the advantage of hindsight: any predictions can be nothing more than pure speculation. Nevertheless, the idiosyncrasies of our students and the complexities of our instructional technologies are shifting, and we need to understand these powerful forces that are shaping our future and reshaping our teaching.

What exactly are these powerful forces that are influencing the way we teach writing? One force is the computer context, or local area network being used in the writing classroom. In this electronic writing context, computers are linked together with a local area network server that enables them to communicate with one another. Special interactive writing software, which is installed on the network, creates a unique social forum by allowing students to freely interact through written dialogue with one another or the entire class from their own CRT screen.

Another force affecting the teaching of writing is the rebirth of a cooperative mode of learning in education. In cooperative learning, teachers structure learning situations where students work together (in groups) to achieve shared goals, rather than in situations that are individual and competitive. According to Johnson, *et al.,* [1] there are specific ways that cooperative learning groups differ from traditional learning groups. Although both types of groups involve social interaction among members, in cooperative groups the social learning that takes place is more encompassing. In cooperative group learning, students share responsibility for leadership and are accountable for the learning of other group members, as well as their own. In addition, teachers instruct students in the nature and use of interpersonal and small group skills; they teach students about the analysis procedures necessary for determining group effectiveness; and they observe and intervene giving feedback to the group and providing direction when necessary.

Because computer networks and group software have inherent social dimensions, they both facilitate and provide a potentially supportive context for this kind of cooperative learning to take place. However, even though networks and cooperative learning are forces which are shaping the future of writing instruction, many writing teachers are neither familiar with cooperative learning nor cognizant of the importance of directly teaching these cooperative skills (*i.e.* shared leadership, individual and group accountability, interpersonal skills, *etc.*) to students working in computer-networked writing environments.

Why is it important for writing teachers to teach these skills when using computer networks? It is important for us to teach these skills, because the intensity of peer pressure and the level of group cohesion changes throughout the life of any group; networks are no exception. Initially, on computer writing networks, the effects of peer pressure are very strong and the level of cohesion is very low. Helping students to understand and apply cooperative skills, particularly interpersonal and small group skills, can perhaps lessen these initial effects. Some of the ways that peer pressure and group dynamics subtly influence and change how students create text, use language, and express themselves in networked writing environments are presented in Table 1.

It is evident that even the social behavior of students in these networked writing classes is a function of their being in this networked environment and social forum. As writing teachers, it is important for us to give our students the opportunity to work together with other students, but when we do, how can we respect the diversity among our students and preserve their individuality within this "social" writing environment?

It seems that balancing respect for the individual with the collective social structure of computer networks and collaborative writing approaches is going to be a very difficult undertaking and will probably remain a basic challenge for writing researchers and teachers for years to come. In order to acquire the prerequisite knowledge to perform this balancing act, we are going to need to understand more about how group dynamics change the way students create text. Given the inherently social nature of these

**Table 1** *Characteristics of student writing behavior and language use over time on a computer network.*

| When Group lacks Cohesion and Peer Pressure is Strong: | When Group Cohesion is attained and Peer Pressure Lessens: |
|---|---|
| (1) Students appear self-conscious about revealing their thoughts and ideas. | (1) Students appear enthusiastic and willing to share their thoughts and ideas. |
| (2) There is a considerable lag in response time to posted comments. | (2) There is a quick response to posted comments and a more fluid dialogue tempo is maintained. |
| (3) Students express themselves using brief comments or short sentences. | (3) Students write longer and often more reflective comments. |
| (4) Students appear overly concerned with grammatical or spelling errors. | (4) Students less concerned with surface errors and more concerned with expressing their ideas correctly. |
| (5) Discussions and interactions seem chaotic and undirected, appearing to lack focus and commitment. | (5) Discussions and interactions appear to have direction and purpose. |
| (6) Students tend to play using language. | (6) Students tend toward playful use of language. They even compete for originality of content and form. |
| (7) Students engage in grandstanding behaviors through disruptive comments, obscenities, or iconoclastic use of language. | (7) Students engage in group and task maintenance procedures through supportive and focused comments, constructive criticisms, and suggestions. |

processes, we have much to gain by situating our inquiries within a social psychological context. By adopting the pioneering "interaction process analysis" work of Robert Bales,[2] George Herbert Mead's work on development of the self,[3] as well as the work of other social psychologists, we can begin to understand our students and social writing pedagogues and to shape the future of networked writing instruction intelligently and constructively.

Briefly, Robert Bale's "interaction process analysis is an observational method of the social and emotional behavior of individuals in small groups."[4] If we understand that a group is a set of persons who relate to one another as parts of a system, we must also understand that these groups are everywhere, providing social support, a cultural framework to guide activity, and rewards of all kinds. They have certain hallmarks, including goals shared by group members, communication among members, norms that guide members' behavior, and identification of members with the group. Moreover, small groups, whether natural, composed, informal, or formal are sufficiently limited in size that their members are able to interact directly.[5] It is my contention that networked writing environments constitute a type of small group, and that interaction process analysis will allow us to focus attention upon "the form of the behavior and the changing patterns of action and reaction among individuals"[6] in this electronically-based group. In the total process which goes on in these small groups, we are observing the process by which individual student personalities develop and change through interaction.

The boundaries of the computer networked writing environment, then, can be described metaphorically as a crucible in which the students come to experience themselves not only as separate individuals but also as part of an identifiable group that is bound together by task, group culture, and group image. Individual concerns and group concerns ebb and flow throughout the designated life of this kind of writing class. Each student alternates and adjusts in his or her own particular rhythm between relating to the computerized writing experience as a solitary activity and relating to it as a group member. The behavior of students in the networked writing classroom, therefore, is guided by both the personal and the social context in which they find themselves.

As with any social group, there is a strong influence of the class members on the individual with respect to authority, relationships, establishment of membership, and transactions in the networked writing classroom. Further, as teachers assume less formal leadership roles in these classrooms, students begin to learn from each other and to act as models by illustrating the various ways to assume responsibility for the writing task as well as the conduct of the class. As they interact on the computer network, students can behave in a wide variety of ways toward each other, including perceiving and evaluating each other, communicating with one another, motivating each other to action, attempting to control one another, and so on. In the same way, students can also act in the same fashion toward themselves. This concept is best explained by George Herbert Mead's work involving the dimensions of self.

According to Mead, to have a self is to have the capacity to engage in reflexive actions, to plan, observe, guide, and respond to our own behavior.[7] Mead conceptualized a self divided into an "I" and a "Me." He argued that the "I" includes the actions of the individual. These actions are spontaneous and unorganized, and the "Me" gives them direction. The "Me," then, is the social dimension of the self, the generalized other which evaluates and directs the actions of the "I" into socially acceptable behavior.[8] It is useful to think of the self as a continuing process. Every act starts with the "I" and ends with the "Me." The "I" and "Me" cooperate to satisfy the initial action in the most efficient and socially acceptable way.

If the self arises out of and is maintained through social interaction as Mead suggests, then the computer network and collaborative tasks introduce another more encompassing social dimension – the group. If we view the self as both the source and object of reflexive behavior, with the individual "I" acting and the "Me" reflecting about it, then the addition of group dynamics adds another more complicated dimension to the reflection of self. In addition to reflecting upon the actions of the "I," the "Me" has to also react to and reflect upon all others on the computer network. Ironically, while the computer network complicates the continual dialogue with the self, at the same time, it allows us to see the interaction occurring between "I" and "Me" as well as the larger dialogue with everyone in the group via printed transcripts. The computer network, then, has the potential to become a valuable research tool. It can slow down the individual and social interaction process taking place, thus making the interaction occurring on the writing network easier to observe, analyze, and record. The network interactions themselves and the transcripts can also be valuable instructional tools by allowing our students to "see" and analyze with us the group processes and dynamics that are occurring on these networks. Whether local area networks are used as a research tool or an instructional tool, they provide us with the opportunity to learn more about the ways that these socially-based networks influence how we create text together. They also allow teachers and students to explore efficient and productive ways of cooperatively working together as writers in these networked environments.

As students work collaboratively with one another, writing and recording their thoughts, they do learn to interact effectively and develop intimate relationships with other students. They also learn to be solitary and interpersonal, to be active and passive, as is required by the pursuit of their own individual and social goals in the writing classroom. To be able to work alone and at the same time work effectively with others is not a mutually exclusive proposition. It represents a healthy paradox about the realities of human life. Such a paradox can be vitalized and revitalized by the type of learning environment that the networked writing classroom provides.

Clearly, the role of personality in such classrooms stands at the heart of that paradox. Whether relating as an individual or as a member of a group, each student is involved in a problem-solving process, revealing both personal and social dimensions of him or herself in the interaction. As students collectively experience common and universal problems they have the opportunity to develop group solutions to those problems. According to Bales, the process of problem-solving in a group involves a series of social processes:

What we usually regard as individual problem-solving, or the process of individual thought, is essentially in form and in genesis a social process; thinking is a re-enactment by the individual of the problem-solving process as he [or she] originally went through it with other individuals. It can probably be maintained...that the best model we have for understanding what goes on inside the individual personality is the model of what goes on between individuals in the problem-solving process. The component parts-acts in a system of interaction-are identical.[9]

From the idea of an interaction system we "can derive the ideas of personality, social system, and culture as particular sub-types of systems, distinguishable by abstracting in different directions from the same concrete observable phenomena: interaction."[10]

For computer writing networks to be effective, they must be an integrated aspect of a coordinated writing curriculum that, in its practice as well as its rhetoric, recognizes the importance of learning about varieties of human nature. We need to comprehensively look at the interaction between the individual student and the computer network environment, identifying variables from both directions and seeking to determine how they are related in producing behavior in these classrooms. How a person behaves in the course of a social interaction is widely held to be a consequence of constructions or perceptions of the situation, including other individuals. It is grossly artificial to believe that our writing students can be treated as if they were all alike. It is equally artificial to eliminate variations in the writing situations where they take place. Thus, in our future work we need to place our emphasis as writing teachers and researchers on the interpretation of interactions between the forces that can meaningfully be measured in both students and writing environments. Building on the work of Bales,[11] Mead, and other social psychologists, we can deal realistically with the transactions among situational and personal variables in the writing classroom that are brought about by the presence of computer networks and cooperative learning.

## References

1   Johnson, D. W., Johnson, R.T., Holubec, E., and Roy, P. 1984. *Circles of Learning: Cooperation in the Classroom,* pp.8-10, Association for Supervision and Curriculum Development, Reston VA.
2   Bales, R. F. 1950. *Interaction Process Analysis: A Method for the Study of Small Groups.* Addison-Wesley, Reading MA.
3   Mead, G. H. 1934. *Mind, Self and Society.* University of Chicago Press, Chicago.
4   Bales, R. F. 1971. Interactive Process Analysis. In: Hollander, E. P. and Hunt, R. G. (eds.), *Current Perspectives in Social Psychology,* 3rd edn., p.254. Oxford University Press, New York.
5   Michener, H. A., Delamater, J. D., and Schwartz, S. H. 1990. *Social Psychology,* p.342. Harcourt Brace Jovanovich, Publishers, New York.
6   Michener, H. A., Delamater, J. D., and Schwartz, S. H. 1990. *Social Psychology,* p.364. Harcourt Brace Jovanovich, Publishers, New York.
7   Mead, G. H. 1934. *Mind, Self and Society.* University of Chicago Press, Chicago.
8   Mead, G. H. 1968. The Genesis of the Self and Social Control. *International Journal of Ethics,* **35,** 251-273.
9   Bales, R. F. 1971. Interactive Process Analysis. In: Hollander, E. P. and Hunt, R. G. (eds.), *Current Perspectives in Social Psychology,* 3rd edn., p.254. Oxford University Press, New York.
10  Bales, R. F. 1951 *Interaction Process Analysis: A Method for the Study of Small Groups,* 2nd printing, p.62. Addison-Wesley Press, Inc., Cambridge, MA.
11  Bales, R. F. 1970. *Personality and Interpersonal Behavior.* Holt, Rinehart and Winston, New York.

# Index